PRAISE FOR *RIVER OF LOST SOULS* BY JONATHAN P. THOMPSON

"An important work of investigative journalism, especially relevant for those living in the Mountain West."

—*ALBUQUERQUE JOURNAL*

"Thompson documents the sacrifice of the entire area with unusual detail, vibrancy, and no small amount of passion, and with a keen eye for the effects on people and other living things. Highly recommended."

—*CHOICE*

"Thompson knowledgeably and sensitively addresses ethical questions at the heart of his inquiry, including what it would mean to restore the water system to its pre-colonial state."

—*PUBLISHERS WEEKLY*

"Aficionados of Western history, environmentalists, and even general readers will enjoy this cautionary tale that takes an intimate look at the side effects of human industry."

—*LIBRARY JOURNAL*

"An elegy of sorts for a beloved natural area with a long history of human exploitation."

—*FOREWORD REVIEWS*

"The reader will revel in the beauty of the Colorado landscape while recoiling from descriptions of cruelty towards the Native Americans and the horrors of acid mine drainage."

—*BOOKLIST*

T0151772

SAGEBRUSH
EMPIRE

SAGEBRUSH
EMPIRE

How a remote Utah county became
the battlefront of American Public Lands

Jonathan P. Thompson

TORREY HOUSE PRESS

Salt Lake City • Torrey

First Torrey House Press Edition, August 2021
Copyright © 2021 by Jonathan P. Thompson

Published by Torrey House Press
Salt Lake City, Utah
www.torreyhouse.org

International Standard Book Number: 978-1-948814-44-7
E-book ISBN: 978-1-948814-45-4
Library of Congress Control Number: 2020946734

Cover photo by Kirsten Johanna Allen
Cover design by Kathleen Metcalf
Interior design by Rachel Leigh Buck-Cockayne
Distributed to the trade by Consortium Book Sales and Distribution

Torrey House Press offices in Salt Lake City sit on the homelands of Ute, Goshute, Shoshone, and Paiute nations. Offices in Torrey are on the homelands of Southern Paiute, Ute, and Navajo nations.

This book is dedicated to Wendy, Lydia, and Elena;

to my parents, who introduced me to the marvels of the canyon country;

and to all of the people who have accompanied me on zany adventures among the sagebrush and sandstone.

TABLE OF CONTENTS

CHAPTER ONE

GATEGATE

A LITTLE HAND-PAINTED SIGN IN THE STYLE OF THOSE clichés that you can pick up for a buck or two in the sale bin at TJ Maxx hangs slightly crooked on the wall of Mark Franklin and Rose Chilcoat's living room above a window that looks out at their Durango, Colorado, neighborhood. It reads: "Live like someone left the gate open." Without context, it makes zero sense. And once you know the story behind it, about how a seemingly insignificant act would throw the couple into an interminable legal quagmire that still hadn't ended three years later, you might wonder why the hell these people have the sign up at all.

The geographical context in which the act took place is the Valley of the Gods. Like the sign, the name of this place doesn't equate without context. The landscape in this part of southeastern Utah appears mostly flat, broken only by a few landforms sticking up in the distance and bounded on one side by a band of cliffs made up of various hues of pink and beige. From the valley the cliffs look unnaturally small, as do the landforms, perhaps an optical illusion resulting from the vastness of the flats and the sky. It is only when you are atop that band of cliffs, otherwise known as the south edge of Cedar Mesa, that you can really see the Valley of the Gods. The illusion from below is shattered and the sheer scale of the valley becomes clear, particularly on stormy days, when clouds rush across the sky like galleons atop a sea the color of dried blood and light plays upon the Kodachrome serpent of earth and stone known as the Raplee Anticline.

Chilcoat and Franklin were in the Valley of the Gods in April 2017 when their lives took a surreal turn, the consequences of which were still playing out three years later, when I sat down with them in their home in Durango to talk about it. Or, rather, we would talk around that fateful day, since they had yet to give depositions in the most recent phase of the legal tussle and therefore couldn't talk about the case itself (details about the case itself come from court documents and exhibits, including depositions from all parties involved, and post-deposition interviews with Chilcoat and Franklin).

Our interview took place in the early days of the coronavirus, when toilet paper and hand sanitizer were hard to find, but businesses were still open, no one was wearing a mask, and some folks still shook hands in greeting. We had no clue what was coming, or that had we waited another week, the in-person interview would have been relegated to our computer screens. As it was, when I entered their house they immediately scooted some hand sanitizer in my direction and we awkwardly elbow-bumped rather than shake hands or hug. Chilcoat was in a wheelchair, a crocheted blanket over her legs, thanks to a brutal ski accident, but her powerful presence was undimmed. Franklin is shorter than Chilcoat, with a white goatee and lively eyes behind square-rimmed glasses.

Franklin's family goes back a few generations in the region. His great-grandparents landed in Leadville, Colorado, during that city's mining heyday, and then, during the Dust Bowl, his family moved from the small burg of Bethune, Colorado, to Gallup, New Mexico. Franklin was born in Albuquerque and spent a lot of time hiking and camping and river running in Utah. "I've been going to [San Juan County] since there was only one paved road into Bluff and the San Juan River didn't require permits," he said. After graduating from the University of New Mexico with a degree in biology, Franklin started fighting wildfires before segueing into a variety of other government work, mostly with land management agencies.

Although Chilcoat grew up in the Maryland suburbs, her parents were adamant about getting her out into the natural world as often as possible, hiking and camping up and down the East Coast. "You're imprinted at an early age," she said. She worked for the Youth Conservation Corps and went to college at Virginia Tech, where she majored in horticulture and minored in environmental studies. In the early 1980s she moved to Durango to take a summer job with the San Juan National Forest doing cadastral surveys and first saw southeastern Utah's canyon country during that time when she went on a rafting trip on the San Juan River.

Soon thereafter, Franklin met Chilcoat at Lee's Ferry on the Colorado River as they embarked on a Grand Canyon rafting trip. Together, in Franklin's telling, they were nomads "following jobs and experiencing diverse public lands." Chilcoat worked as a biological science technician in forest planning and in various park ranger positions at Mesa Verde National Park, Rocky Mountain National Park, Bryce Canyon National Park, and at Lake Roosevelt National Recreation Area, before heading to Anchorage, Alaska, to work for the Park Service there. Franklin fought fires, managed a visitor center, and worked on the Exxon oil spill in Valdez, Alaska. The two worked side by side as raft guides in Big Bend National Park in Texas.

When Chilcoat had their first child, the Park Service would not give her any flexibility in her job, so she resigned. She and Franklin moved back to Durango in 1993, where Franklin started his own business doing interpretive graphic design, mostly for public lands agencies.

Once her kids reached school age, Chilcoat answered a want ad for an assistant to the executive director of Great Old Broads for Wilderness, a Durango-based environmental group founded by Susan Tixier in 1989, on the twenty-fifth anniversary of the Wilderness Act, in order to refute Sen. Orrin Hatch's claim that wilderness areas were inaccessible to the elderly. Since then the organization has grown tremendously and includes members of all genders and ages across the nation. When Chilcoat joined, the director was M. B. McAfee, who was later succeeded by Veronica "Ronni" Egan. Egan owned property in San Juan County, Utah, and residents there would sometimes call on her for help when they witnessed environmental destruction or what they saw as negligence on the part of public lands agencies. The Great Old Broads would step in and bring the matter to the attention of the Bureau of Land Management, which has jurisdiction over much of the public land in the area, and push them to enforce the laws. "Our role with the agency has always been as friends and supporting them, but also holding our friends accountable," Chilcoat said.

This didn't always go over so well in San Juan County, where many of the white locals hold deep animosity for the federal land management agencies and environmentalists. The Sagebrush Rebellion—which will get a lot of attention in the coming pages—rose up across the rural West after Congress passed a host of environmental laws in the 1970s, and it has never completely subsided, flaring up over and over again in reaction to national and regional political swings. Egan retired in 2012 and Shelley Silbert took over as executive director. But Chilcoat, the associate director, moved into the role of bête noire to the San Juan County right-wing crowd—she and her colleagues were even the target of death threats. She held on to that status after she retired in 2016, and was still a focus of animosity in April 2017, when she and Franklin decided to go hiking and camping for a few days in San Juan County, Utah, as they had done so many times in the past.

Franklin had never been drawn to the Valley of the Gods, at least not as a place to go camping. He preferred to ply the deep and winding canyons nearby. But they had friends who were staying in the bed-and-breakfast on the edge of the valley and they wanted to spend time with them. Besides, the valley had been included in the Bears Ears National Monument, designated by President Barack Obama just four months earlier. So just before noon on a cool spring morning, Franklin and Chilcoat left their Durango home and drove west in their red Toyota RAV4, towing a teardrop camper trailer behind it. They continued through the small town of Mancos, past the newish visitor center at Mesa Verde National Park, through Cortez, and down McElmo Canyon, where the fruit trees were in bloom, and into Utah. They stopped for gas in Bluff, which was established by the Hole-in-the-Rock party in 1880 before being virtually abandoned, but that has now become the most progressive—and overpriced—town in the county. They continued westward, crossing the sandstone gorge of Butler Wash and passing over the dramatic landform known as Comb Ridge, before heading up the Technicolor slope of Lime Ridge. It was April 1, 2017.

Franklin, who was driving, needed to relieve himself, so he pulled onto a dirt county road and off of that onto a smaller road that had a turnaround loop next to a circular corral with cows in it. Franklin pulled the trailer around, got out of the car, did his business next to a large opening in the corral fence, and then got back in the car. As he was pulling away, he noticed that some of the cows were sticking their heads into a big tire inside the corral. Being a curious sort, Franklin stopped and tried to figure out what the cows were doing. And then, much to Chilcoat's dismay, Franklin got back out of the car and walked into the corral to check out the situation. He was amazed to find that the tire held water for the cows to drink and marveled at the ingenuity of the ranchers who had managed to convert a tractor tire into a water trough.

His curiosity sated, Franklin began to walk back to the car, noticing as he did one of the cows giving him the stink eye. Like the other cattle in the corral, this one was most likely a Corriente, or what Franklin described as a "scrawny rodeo cow." Corrientes are smaller and rangier than most beef cattle, and therefore do better in arid environments, and have sharp, curved horns. But ol' stink eye, white with black stripes, was bigger than its companions and made Franklin a bit nervous. In order to prevent the cattle from getting between him and his car, Franklin walked to the green gate to the corral and pushed it shut. He could see the cows plodding through the gap in the fence on the other side of the enclosure. Without even thinking about it, he latched the gate and got back in the car.

As he pulled away, Chilcoat asked, "What did you do that for?"

"What?"

"Close the gate? Why can't you just leave things alone?"

"I just…I don't know. I just closed it. Habit, I guess."

Over the years, in his work as a firefighter and interpreter with land agencies, Franklin had interacted with ranchers and their charges on a number of occasions. Once, he broke up a bullfight that would have otherwise resulted in the death of one or both of the animals. While working in the area that is now El Malpais National Monument in New Mexico, he came across a calf with its head stuck between two posts. He and the rancher he called for help did everything they could to save it, but failed. He was heartbroken. Although his wife worked with an organization that has pushed back on unsustainable public lands grazing, Franklin has never felt very strongly about it, except when he saw lines of coyote carcasses hanging from a fence, a ritual some ranchers perform for reasons unknown. "I've always helped ranchers when I can," he said. "I've always closed gates as a courtesy."

Franklin piloted the car and camper back onto Highway 163

and after a few minutes turned right onto Highway 261 before finally turning off the pavement onto the dirt road that leads to the Valley of the Gods Bed and Breakfast, which sits right at the foot of Cedar Mesa's towering cliffs, where their friends were staying. They set up camp a few miles down the road from the establishment and stayed there for two nights, joining their friends for daytime excursions and meals, even indulging in a big chunk of meat at the Swingin' Steak in Mexican Hat. They found that just as the majesty of this place is more apparent from a distance, so too does its subtle beauty only become evident when one slows down, gets out of the car, and silently stands close to the ground and observes one's surroundings: a beetle climbing a rock, a seedpod rattling in the spring breeze, the miracle of a trickle of water falling across umber stone.

April 3 dawned cold and blustery and Franklin and Chilcoat made breakfast, broke camp, packed up, and began their journey back home, stopping a couple of times so that Chilcoat could photograph recently bulldozed earthen-berm impoundments, presumably constructed by ranchers to catch rainwater for their cows to drink. As they approached the road that led to the Lime Ridge corral, Chilcoat asked Franklin to turn down it so that she could photograph another impoundment a little ways beyond the corral. He turned off the highway and passed the corral, where a group of men were working, and then continued up to the pond. They took a few photographs then headed back toward the highway.

As they passed the corral again, they saw a strange sight: two cowboys were running across the red earth as if they were racing one another. Then a late-model brownish flatbed pickup truck tore alongside the corral, too, passing the runners and nearly hitting one, kicking up a big cloud of dust, and shedding a shovel and jack as it bounced haphazardly in the direction of the road. It skidded to an abrupt halt across the county road, blocking Franklin and Chilcoat's forward progress. The truck's door swung open and a large man named Zeb Dalton jumped out. Gesturing wildly, Dalton approached Franklin and Chilcoat, who sat stunned in their now-stopped car. "Looks like we got 'em," Dalton yelled, as if auditioning for the part of a vigilante rancher in some tacky Western. The runners, who reached the scene seconds later and were now gasping for breath, nodded in the affirmative.

"What's going on? What's this about?" a baffled Franklin asked.

"You know exactly what it's about," Zane Odell, one of the runners and the owner of the corral, said.

Dalton took a look at the license plate on the rear of the trailer and yelled something about getting a match. Chilcoat, recovering from her initial shock, got out and started taking pictures of the vehicle and the men, so there would be evidence if things took a turn for the worse. That's when Dalton told her that he had plenty of videos of her closing a gate and trying to "choke Zane's cows to death" by cutting off their access to water. Frightened by the hostility of the men, Chilcoat got back into the car. Franklin, truly mystified, continued to ask Dalton and Odell what the problem was. Franklin finally understood what the cowboys were yammering about. "Oh yeah, yeah, I shut the gate," Franklin said. "But that's what I do, I help you guys."

"You just sit tight until the sheriff comes," said Dalton, a third-generation San Juan County rancher whose TY Cattle Company grazes hundreds of head of cattle on BLM and US Forest Service land in the area, including around the Bears Ears buttes.

Because the flatbed truck was blocking the road, Franklin and Chilcoat had no choice but to wait for the law to arrive and, surely, straighten things out. San Juan County Sheriff Deputy J. R. Begay pulled up in his truck within minutes, as he'd already been in the area responding to a call of a gate left *open* on another fence, allowing cows to escape. Franklin and Chilcoat relaxed, somewhat. The sheriff at the time, Rick Eldredge, had publicly expressed disdain for environmentalists and was seen to be in cahoots with local Sagebrush Rebels, but at least the pair wouldn't have to worry about being the victims of vigilante justice.

Begay approached the three cowboys, who were standing together in the road. Franklin got out of the car and joined the men while Chilcoat stayed in the car.

"They're saying it's illegal to close a gate," Franklin said after introducing himself to Begay.

"Uh, well, did you close it intentionally?"

"Yeah, I closed the gate. There were two gates, both open. The cows had plenty of access. I closed the gate."

"Did you close it knowing you were preventing the cows from going to water?"

"No. They had water."

As the group walked to the corral, Franklin, still clearly dumbfounded by the situation, told Odell, again, that the cows had access to water.

"How my cows get access to water is none of your business," said Odell, carrying a shovel in one hand. Odell, a lean man with deep furrows around his eyes and wearing a black cowboy hat and a jean jacket, appeared to be agitated. The group inspected the corral, but as tempers flared Begay guided Franklin back to his car.

"I shouldn't have closed the gate, but I did," Franklin said as they walked under a stormy sky. "It wasn't any malice, I just closed the gate."

Back in his truck, Begay called Rob Wilcox, a sheriff's department sergeant, and filled him in on the situation.

"It's probably just trespassing," Wilcox said. "I don't even think it was criminal trespassing."

Begay went back to Franklin's car and asked for Chilcoat's information as a witness. She spelled out her legal first name: "R-O-S-A-L-I-E."

"Franklin?" Begay asked.

"Yeah," she said.

Then Begay sent the couple on their way, telling them that the county attorney would be in touch.

Franklin and Chilcoat drove down the highway to Bluff—friendly territory in a county of unfriendlies. They were rattled but relieved to be putting some distance between themselves and the angry cowboys. They knew that the incident might not be over, but also couldn't believe that it would come to anything serious. After all, what kind of crime is closing a gate, when there was no way it could harm anyone? Still, Chilcoat was anxious and couldn't shake the feeling that the ranchers knew who she was and what she did for a living. The Great Old Broads had raised flags about grazing practices in the county, and Rose was also involved with Friends of Cedar Mesa, which pushed hard to get Bears Ears National Monument designated. She worried that the ranchers might twist this odd situation into a form of retribution.

BACK AT THE CORRAL, BEGAY RETURNED TO WHERE ODELL, Dalton, and a younger helper were working in order to get their side of the story. Odell lives in Montezuma County, Colorado, but at the time was a major grazing allottee in San Juan County, holding leases on 4,714 acres of state land in the Valley of the Gods and surrounding areas along with the right to graze on tens of thousands of acres of the BLM-managed North Perkins allotment. Both Dalton and Odell had expressed opposition to the designation of Bears Ears National Monument despite the fact that the monument as designated had no effect on existing grazing leases. Dalton had even starred in a video the previous September in which he laments how badly the monument would hurt public land livestock operators like him. The video was produced by the Sutherland Institute, a Utah-based think tank advocating for "faith, family, and free markets," and a leader of the charge to stop Bears Ears National Monument.

Begay asked Odell what charges he wanted beyond trespassing.

"I'm not sure…livestock endangerment?"

"Livestock harassment, too," said Dalton. "Animal cruelty."

Odell: "They're anti-cow. And I could tell that when I asked them the definition of public lands and he says, 'Why sure, it belongs to all of us.' They hate us. They think this is theirs and we should be gone. I know he's anti-cow."

Dalton started asking questions, seemingly fishing for a specific answer. "Where are they from…Colorado, but what town?"

Begay didn't respond.

Odell: "Durango? Yeah, that's their deal. What's their name?"

Dalton: "What was her name? Were they married? That Great Old Broads environmental group is based out of Durango. And I think they might be involved. And they'll go out of their way and do things to them cows."

Odell: "It could be these same folks…"

Begay: "I'm glad we were able to get them."

Dalton: "I didn't want to talk to them. I know me, I know my temper, and I didn't want to lose my temper."

Odell: "I would go as far as absolutely is possible. Because in their little environmental world, in their social media, the rest of them will catch on, maybe, leave the cowboys alone. It is wrong. Socially unacceptable."

TWO DAYS LATER CHILCOAT SENT A LETTER TO THE MONTIcello Field Office of the Bureau of Land Management pointing out that land had been disturbed within a wilderness study area on Lime Ridge, potentially in violation of BLM regulations. She also recounted her experience with Odell and company, writing:

On April 3, after I stopped to photograph the stock reservoir ground disturbance near the corral at the top of Lime Ridge along highway 163, my husband and I were accosted by three cowboys (one of whom I believe was Zane O'Dell [*sic*] and one who I believe was Zeb Dalton and one unknown to me) who physically blocked our vehicle, accused us of criminal activity, threatened us with jail, and prevented our return to the highway. This was a distressing and fearful experience for both of us. My husband was falsely accused of preventing livestock from reaching water. The San Juan County Sheriff was called, responded, spoke with us and cleared us to leave. …this assault and behavior by BLM permittees is unacceptable. I would like to lodge a complaint and ask that this complaint be included in these permittee's files.

On the same day that she sent the letter, the *Petroglyph*, a right-wing blog run by Monte Wells, who was prosecuted with then–San Juan County commissioner Phil Lyman for organizing an ATV protest down Recapture Canyon in May 2014, gleefully posted that "Good old Rose Chilcoat from the Great Old Broads" had been "caught red-handed harassing and endangering live stock….Gotcha Rose! Ha! Who has the final laugh now?" The comments on the Facebook post were bilious, even by Facebook standards, and included (transcribed here as they were posted, wrong spellings and all):

> "Stupid ass tree huggers think they are above the law! Damn Zeb you should of put a 40 Cal right between there eyes before the sheriff showed up…"
> "Should punish her hanging no!"

A week later, San Juan County district attorney Kendall Laws filed charges against Franklin and Chilcoat. That Odell had continued to pursue the matter, and that the county had carried his water for him, was no surprise. The severity of the charges, however, were shocking. Franklin was charged with "attempted wanton destruction of livestock," a second-degree felony, and trespassing on state lands (the corral was on State of Utah School and Institutional Trust Land and leased by Odell). Chilcoat was initially accused of misdemeanor trespassing and giving false identity to a police officer because she hadn't corrected Begay when he assumed Chilcoat's last name was Franklin. Several days later, the prosecutor added two more charges for Chilcoat: attempted destruction of livestock and retaliation against a witness, victim, or informant, a third-degree felony, on the basis of the letter she had written to the BLM regarding the use of road-moving equipment in a wilderness study area. If convicted, they both could spend years in prison. All for closing a gate.

Thus was launched the bizarre and trying legal saga that became known as Gategate.

FOR THOSE OF YOU LOOKING FOR A "TRUE CRIME" INVESTIGA-tion into a vast cow-killing conspiracy, this book isn't it. I'm not going to relitigate the case, or try to dig and dig until I get to the bottom of what *really* happened out in the southeastern Utah desert on April Fools' Day 2017. After all, the facts aren't in dispute. Franklin closed the gate, period. All that remains up for debate is his reason for doing so, and quite frankly it's a waste of time to hash that one out, especially since no cattle could have been harmed by his action.

This book gets at the question of exactly how it came to this, how an action as seemingly inconsequential as closing a gate could potentially lead to prison time for both Chilcoat and Franklin, a mild-mannered retiree whose political activism peaked with his involvement in the Old Spanish Trail

Association, and would inspire such vile comments and even threats of violence against Chilcoat.

Gategate is not an isolated incident, nor merely the product of a zealous prosecutor going too far. Rather, it is yet another escalation in a war that has gripped the western United States for decades. The fight has played out on the nation's public lands and over how best to manage them, but it has many fronts to it, and many aspects, including systemic racism, stolen lands, looted graves, resource colonization, environmental justice, economic inequality, religion, corporate control of our government, and, yes, cows.

San Juan County, Utah, has, more often than not, been the epicenter of this conflict. It flared up here in the late 1800s, the 1930s and '40s, and as the Sagebrush Rebellion in the 1970s. Cal Black, sometimes considered the original Sagebrush Rebel, was from here. It was here that much of the fictional action in Ed Abbey's *The Monkey Wrench Gang* took place. It was here that the battle over Bears Ears National Monument unfolded, and continues to do so, and here where the voting rights of the Indigenous majority were stifled. It was here that President Donald Trump focused his efforts to eviscerate public lands protections implemented by Obama, and it was here that federal courts redrew voting district lines to give the members of the Ute Mountain Ute, Navajo, and Southern San Juan Paiute Tribes the voice they deserve in local politics. And it is here that the nation's uranium mining industry clings to survival, and where it may ultimately perish. Just days after Chilcoat and Franklin were charged, Sen. Orrin Hatch, the staunch Republican from Utah, declared: "San Juan County is now the epicenter of a brutal battle over public lands."

The nearly eight thousand square miles encompassed by the San Juan County lines are some of the most spectacular in the world. From the county's 11,360-foot highpoint the land plummets downward into a mosaic of stone and sage and forests and badlands and utterly bizarre landforms. Thousands of miles of sinuous canyons cut through pale sandstone, with even the most insignificant-seeming ones holding millions of marvels in the cool shadows: thick slick strips of desert varnish, monkey flowers hanging from mossy seeps, tadpole-teeming deep pools leftover from the last rain, intricate cryptogamic soil, psychedelic lichens.

People have lived and loved and died and built and created here for a dozen millennia or more. Some stayed, some moved on, and now just fifteen thousand or so remain, all of them tied, in one way or another, to the extraordinary landscape. And yet they are also a people deeply divided along ideological, racial, political, and cultural lines. In some ways, San Juan County is like a microcosm of the western United States, maybe even the nation as a whole, only taken to the extreme.

CHAPTER TWO

STATE LINE

I AM WALKING ACROSS THE SOUTHEASTERN UTAH DESERT, looking for the Colorado state line on an overcast day in early March.

It is a few days after I spoke with Rose Chilcoat and Mark Franklin about their harrowing experiences here in San Juan County, and I'm trying to understand what it is about this place that made their ordeal possible, maybe even inevitable. I think that maybe if I could just see the state line, experience it, walk along it, I could understand its power.

I lace up my shoes, put on a little pack with water, snacks, my camera, and my lenses, and head out in search of the prey. It will not be difficult to find. After all, it's a straight line, running due north, that's nearly three hundred miles long.

I slither through a narrow, tumbleweed-clogged sliver of space between two huge blocks of rock, rubbing my hand along its cold and grainy surface. The geology around here is the story of ancient transport, fossilized, of vast rivers carrying sand and silt and soil from faraway mountains and hills and depositing it here, where the current slowed as the rivers met up with a shallow, salty inland sea. I drop through the Dakota Sandstone, across a layer of ash, and then encounter a more unusual sedimentary strata, conglomerate. It is gravel filled with colorful and exotic stones—granite, schist, quartz—that were worn smooth during their long trip from another country. They are lithic nomads that made their way slowly from distant mountains before finding a resting place here, in the mud at the edge of this sea. The color of the stones and their hard surfaces, smooth like skin, beg to be touched. I abide. Then I move onward, wondering whether the sagebrush will smell any different on the other side of the line.

THE COLORADO–UTAH STATE LINE EXISTS BECAUSE BACK IN 1859 a bunch of folks in the budding city of Denver didn't want to be in Kansas anymore. At the time, the Kansas Territory stretched all the way to the Continental Divide, encompassing most of the eastern half of what is now Colorado. The Utah Territory sprawled from the Continental Divide all the way to the California border, roughly following the boundaries of what Brigham Young had hoped would be the State of Deseret.

The Denver contingent wanted to carve chunks out of Utah and Kansas and cobble them together as the massive State of Jefferson. Congress shot the idea down. So, in 1861, lawmakers proposed a smaller, square-shaped territory. The House of Representatives recognized the territory and called it Idaho; the Senate changed the name to Colorado, then passed the bill. Statehood would prove elusive, however, as President Andrew Johnson vetoed enabling bills in 1866 and again in 1867, in part because the population—of white people—was deemed too scant for an entire state. Finally, in 1876, after the federal government took the San Juan Mountains from the Ute people to clear the way for mining and industrialization, Colorado was granted statehood.

Lawmakers determined, for reasons that have been lost to history, that the western boundary of the new state would follow the thirty-second meridian, the line of longitude that lies thirty-two degrees west of the center of the Naval Observatory in Washington, DC. They drew the line on a map, paying no heed to the landscape, the sky, the watersheds, the culture, or anything else that has substance or consequence in this world.

In 1878 the federal government hired surveyor and astronomer Rollin Reeves to assemble a team and to mark the state line on the ground, to make the abstract concrete, to manifest the imaginary grid in the world of rock and sky and stone. He set out in August from Fort Garland, Colorado, located on land stolen from the Utes at the western foot of the Sangre de Cristo Mountains, took the brand-new railroad to its terminus at Alamosa, then continued on horseback into New Mexico in order to skirt around the rugged South San Juan Mountains. He stopped at Tierra Amarilla to resupply before following the Spanish Trail through Ute territory to Animas City, now the north end of Durango, Colorado. There he may have encountered my ancestors, perhaps even purchased some butter or apples from them. My great-great-grandmother came to the Animas Valley from Kansas in the 1870s, part of the white wave of settler-colonists who had crashed down on the region at the time, violently displacing the Indigenous peoples there.

The outsiders came with the delusion that the entire region was an empty canvas on which they could start anew and build a society from scratch. "The very fact of the wilderness appealed to men as a fair, blank page on which to write a new chapter in the story of man's struggle for his type of society," wrote Frederick Jackson Turner in 1893. This illusory sense of possibility was fed by the maps of the day, which tended to depict southeastern Utah inaccurately or, more often, as a big blank spot. On an 1856 map, the San Juan River never crosses into Utah, and the Green and Grand (Colorado) Rivers meet up in the Grand Canyon, below the confluence of the San Juan and the Little Colorado. A year later maps show the rivers more or less in the right places, but the label "UNEXPLORED" is emblazoned across the otherwise featureless San Juan County. Shortly after Reeves made his trip, a group of cartographers under the leadership of Clarence E. Dutton drew a meticulously detailed topographical map of the entire Utah Territory. The remote and isolated Henry Mountains show up on it, portrayed fairly accurately, along with the Waterpocket Fold, the Escalante River and its tributaries, and the Colorado River. But everything east and south of the Colorado River, meaning all of what is now San Juan County, is empty. On his 1885 sectional and topographical map of Utah, Joseph West places the legend on San Juan County since, apparently, there's nothing else there to see.

I suspect that the cartographical omissions come mostly from the fact that very few white people had ventured into this country because at the time they saw nothing there worth mining or farming or otherwise exploiting. Mapping something is a way to lay claim to it, and there was nothing here worth claiming: it was a wasteland, a "badlands of grotesquely eroded rock," as the author Frank Waters would describe it in 1946 and, in the reckoning of Capt. John Macomb, who came through the area in 1859, "a worthless and impracticable region." Besides, attempting to depict the landscape here, with its ups and downs and nooks and crannies, with any accuracy would be a difficult task, indeed.

Reeves and his party wandered into the blank spot in early September, setting up camp on the banks of the San Juan River somewhere near current-day Aneth. Thanks to a tropical storm dumping its load on the San Juan Mountains, the river was in one of its moods, "on a rampage, booming high," according to Reeves. The water was so thick with turbidity that it didn't look like water at all and formed an intimidating barrier standing between the surveyors and the corner marker from which they needed to begin their task.

Undaunted, the team crudely lashed together pieces of cottonwood driftwood to construct a raft, but when Reeves and three others tried to "pole and paddle" it across the river, the current had other plans, carrying them two miles downstream only to land on the same bank from which they began. They tried to borrow a boat, but the owner wasn't willing to risk it, so they constructed another, larger raft, which they were able to pilot to the opposite bank. While all of this was unfolding, "several Navajo Indians, who had come from their Reservation on the South Side of the river, to trade with the Ute Indians on the North Side of the river, forded the river on their horses," according to Reeves's field notes. Reeves did not mention whether he felt just a tiny bit of chagrin for not thinking of that crossing method himself.

The surveying party enlisted a Navajo man to take them to the corner monument, placed three years earlier by a surveyor named Chandler Robbins, who had been there to survey the Arizona–New Mexico line. This corner is now the Four Corners Monument, which, bizarrely, has become a destination for people from all over the world, a place where one can entertain the illusion of being in four different places at once. They could begin their work at last.

That first night, two of Reeves's team members, Captain Tuttle and Mr. Gorringe, zeroed in on Polaris, the North Star, at its eastern elongation. The next morning the surveyors, equipped with sextant, chain, aneroid barometer, and theodolite, set out in the direction of true north, marking their path as they went. While they were guided by the stars, their master was the grid that had been imposed upon the public domain west of the Appalachians with the 1875 creation of the Public Land Survey System. The land was cordoned off into thirty-six-square-mile square townships, which were then sliced into 640-acre sections. The idea was to create a system that allowed for the orderly sale of public land to settlers; call it Cartesian colonialism, the futile attempt to bound sinuous earth and boundless sky. I believe that it was also a way for the strangers to this country to make sense of it. Without the grid to restrain it, the land overwhelms. The grid is artifice, something seen only on maps, based on nothing real. Yet it has profoundly influenced the way Americans relate to the landscape and to one another, and is manifested physically on the American landscape in its state and county lines, its streets and avenues, its county roads and property lines, and in GPS coordinates. "The grid, not the eagle or the Stars and Stripes," wrote John Brinckerhoff Jackson in his seminal *A Sense of Place, A Sense of Time*, "is our national symbol. It is imprinted in every child before birth."

As the surveyors progressed, Reeves painstakingly recorded his observations. Of the first segment, Reeves wrote: "The line traverses a rolling elevated, grass-covered table land, mainly free from brush and timber for about thirty miles, ascending Northward and crossing numerous, rocky ridges, hills, valleys and canyons....The surface is badly broken, the walls and bluffs rocky and steep, and the timber, which we gradually enter about the twenty-fifth mile, is mainly piñon, very tough and stunted, and having its bark full of sand grit, dulling the axes and making our progress slow and difficult."

A CENTURY AND A HALF LATER, I WALK PURPOSEFULLY THROUGH the same country as Reeves did. The country remains broken, albeit less grassy, and the trees are still tough and stunted, just the way the desert made them. I pass through an opening in a fence letting me know that I'm leaving Hovenweep National Monument, where grazing is prohibited, and crossing onto Bureau of Land Management land. The differences are subtle but immediately palpable. The vegetation is not as thick on the BLM side, the soil is lighter in color and smoother in texture, and desiccated cow dung is evident in the dry-wash bottom. In satellite images the differences between the two sides of the line are even more distinct.

I decide to follow the wash rather than the trail, and beneath a steep cut bank a smattering of bleached cow bones lies among the smooth stones. Probably the animal fell into the gully, broke a leg, and died of exposure, hunger, or thirst years ago. Or maybe a predator stalked it up the wash, then pounced from atop the bank, ripping out its throat before the slow beast even knew what had hit it. The hair stands up on my neck. Not to brag, but I think I'd make a pretty good breakfast-time snack for a cougar, what with my fat-marbled flesh marinated in a lifetime of ice cream, wine, and olive oil. I skitter away from the bank and scan the surroundings, half expecting to lock eyes with a sleek and hungry mountain lion as it crouches for the attack. But there is nothing save for a pinyon jay in a nearby bush, begging for a crumb.

I grew up on the Colorado side of the line, but I was brought up as a resident of the entire region, state lines be damned. If I could see the Bears Ears, or Hesperus Mountain, or the Sleeping Ute, or the sharp teeth of the Grenadier Range, or Shiprock, or Huerfano Mountain, then I was home. When my father was a teenager living in Dolores, Colorado, his cousin-in-law Don Ripley—the first National Park Service ranger at Hovenweep National Monument—introduced him to this corner of Utah, and he'd been coming here ever since. I was just a toddler when my parents first brought me to the Utah side of the line and into what C. Crampton coined "Standing Up Country" in his 1964 book of the same name. I was too young to have specific memories of that trip, but I'm certain that we camped in Comb Wash at the mouth of Arch Canyon, which was one of our go-to places.

We must have camped there a million times and in other places up and down Comb Wash another thousand times. Or maybe it was a few dozen, but keeping track is difficult. One camping trip runs into another, time gets jumbled, and yet the memories are clear: fire-blackened coffee pot, the heat of the hot cocoa mug through my mittens on a cold morning; the clear waters of Arch Creek, teeming with what my parents called kil-lifish; the cloyingly sweet and cold first drink of an orange pop, a luxury confined to camping trips. I remember waking up in my pathetic little sleeping bag to the smell of breakfast cooking. I remember plopping down on my belly to slurp up cool water from a tadpole-teeming pothole. I remember the distinctive taste of desert water, like liquid stone on the tongue, and the frisson of tapping at the sticky, chaotic web of a black widow in order to coax her, shiny and venomous, from her lair. I remember eve-ning sunlight on the smooth face of Comb Ridge and the tangled branches of cottonwoods against the cobalt blue of dawn.

I have continued my pilgrimages behind the Slickrock Cur-tain—a moniker devised by my college friends and I for a state of mind as much as a defined place—with family, friends, and lov-ers ever since. My wife Wendy and I were married in an alfalfa field along the San Juan River in Bluff, and spent our honey-moon on Muley Point, gazing in awe at the prehistoric-looking creatures plying the cool waters of deep potholes. In my teens and twenties I was drawn to the narrow, deep canyons, to the cliff dwellings tucked beneath hanging ledges, to the illusion of discovery and the thrill of clinging to a high cliff and hanging my ass perilously over the void. As I've grown older, however, I've gradually become more drawn to this side of the county, the eastern side, the broken side, the Great Sage Plain, a land often abused but more often ignored. Usually I come alone, not because I don't like companionship, but because it allows me to move at my own pace, to meander aimlessly, to slow down and gaze at the intricate seedpod of a mariposa lily or lean up against the fuzzy bark of a five-hundred-year-old juniper tree and try to absorb its memories via osmosis.

I veer to the right, off of the path, and up to the canyon rim where I can orient myself. It's not difficult—orientation, that is. The ominously dark form of Ute Mountain, aka the Sleeping Ute, its folded arms frosted white from a recent night's storm, serves as my omnipresent beacon and companion. I'm reminded of that time my friend Ed and I picked up a couple of hitchhikers down toward Bluff. Two big Navajo guys, about our age—early twenties, that is. They had just crossed the San Juan River on the footbridge near the St. Christopher's Episcopal Mission and needed a lift to Cortez. We were returning from a camping trip somewhere, maybe on Comb Ridge, or Muley Point, and were going that direction and had plenty of room in my old Rambler American station wagon, so we pulled over and they scooted into the back seat.

After a few minutes of silence, one of the guys piped up. "Hey, you know what we Navajo call that mountain up there?"

The only mountain around was the Sleeping Ute, and only then did it occur to me that white people probably gave it that name, and that the Indigenous peoples from here probably had entirely different monikers. "What?" I asked, with genuine, anthropological curiosity.

"Dolly Parton laying down!"

Now I can't get the image out of my head.

A slight breeze tousles my hair. I follow the pale sandstone that lines the edge of the canyon until I arrive at a sturdy but rusty barbed-wire fence. The wire is tautly strung between perfectly vertical steel posts. Where it crosses the rimrock of the canyon, the posts are sunk into the stone, which is covered with a thick layer of oxidation, desert varnish.

This is the state line, which means I must be standing just inches inside of Utah, approximately twenty-nine miles north of the Four Corners Monument. This piece of earth is under the jurisdiction of the Bureau of Land Management, the branch of the Interior Department that oversees federal land that was once destined to be mined, or drilled, or grazed, and that is now quite often destined to be mined, drilled, or grazed, still, albeit with a few more rules in place. I am standing on a slab of what I believe is Dakota Sandstone, capped with a thick veneer of desert varnish.

If I manage to squeeze through the fence to the other side, I'll still be on Dakota Sandstone, still on land managed by the BLM. On the Colorado side, however, I'll be in Canyon of the Ancients National Monument, which has another layer of protection on it, and I'll be in Montezuma County. On one side of the fence I can legally smoke marijuana, on the other side, not so much. County leaders from the west side of the fence once begged a company to dump its nuclear waste within their borders; on the other side, even the right-wing commissioners have grudgingly accepted that the old, extraction-economy model is broken, and they need to try new things, like building and marketing mountain biking trails. On one side of the fence a county commissioner once led an ATV protest down a canyon rife with antiquities that was closed to motorized vehicles. On one side of the fence Mark Franklin and Rose Chilcoat were dragged through a grueling court battle for simply closing a rancher's gate. I don't think that would happen on the other side of the fence.

Far too many barbed-wire fences crisscross the western United States, but most of them, at least the ones put up by ranchers years ago, are typically made with juniper posts and they sag and break and you can bend the top wire down enough to step over the top of the fence without getting testicular tetanus. Not with this fence. The posts are rigid, the wire pulled tight. I take off my pack and squeeze through the third and fourth wires, cringing as I do. Halfway through I notice the imprint in the varnish of a millipede-like creature that must have died here some seventy-six-million years ago. Half of it is in Colorado, half in Utah.

SOMETIMES WHEN I'M AGONIZING AT MY COMPUTER KEYBOARD, staring into the electronic screen and struggling to come up with the words, I envy Reeves and those like him, the surveyor-astronomers of the world. Oh to walk a straight line for 276 miles observing, marking, and recording my progress as I go and get paid for it. No pressure to be witty or brilliant, to be creative or smart or even to get the words in just the right order. As long as one doesn't deviate from the grid they'll do just fine.

And yet, it apparently isn't all that easy to walk in a straight line, even with all those instruments of precision. When the surveyors veered from the grid-line, even by a small amount, it could throw everything off. In 1868, for example, a surveyor named E. N. Darling plotted the path of Colorado's southern border, which follows the thirty-seventh parallel. But his star-readings must have been just slightly askew at the start, something he didn't realize until he reached the Kansas border and found himself far from where he should have been. Rather than start over he just let it ride, but a later survey found that between "the sixth and eighth astronomical monuments gross errors in alinement and measurement existed." For the next several decades New Mexico and Colorado battled over the exact location of the line, going all the way to the Supreme Court, which ruled in Colorado's favor. In order to fix the original error, the line had to be redrawn so that it jogs diagonally for about a half-mile near Edith, Colorado. The "square state" isn't really square at all.

Reeves had his own problems with hewing to the straight and narrow. Just after dropping off of the Great Sage Plain and into the Dolores River drainage, the team encountered "one long range of cañon after cañon, and as general rough and wild a view as we have seen since we left the San Juan River." It was, Reeves noted, a "wretched surface to chain accurately." They did not—chain it accurately, that is—and instead veered slightly to the west for a ten-mile stretch that was so rugged Reeves referred to it as Hades. It wasn't until the following year, when the Reeves team reached the Wyoming line, that they realized they had gone off course by about three-fourths of a mile before resuming their true northward path. Reeves effectively gave Colorado a nearly two-hundred-mile strip of land that should have been in Utah. So much for straight lines.

THE LOCATION OF THE BOUNDARIES MATTERS BECAUSE OF HOW powerful they have become, particularly here in San Juan County, where a certain sect of the population has weaponized state and county lines. This sect, call them Sagebrush Rebels for lack of a better term, embraces the ideology of local control, believing that people who live within the lines that define San Juan County should have the loudest voice—the only voice, even—in making decisions about what happens in "their" county, particularly when it comes to land managed by the federal government. The county and state lines thus become instruments of exclusion and disenfranchisement.

An example: during the debate over designating a huge swath of federally managed land as the Bears Ears National Monument, so-called locals, including right-wing Utah politicians who live nowhere near San Juan County, insisted that leaders from Hopi and Zuni and the other Pueblos should have no say in the matter because they are currently based outside of the county. The county lines, in this case, were used to negate the voices of the people whose ancestors had lived on the land in question for dozens of generations before any white people showed up, before any lines were drawn. And the lines were used to try to obscure the fact that the land now is managed by the federal government on behalf of all American people, equally, regardless of where they live. Later, the same group of people attempted to invalidate the election of a Navajo man, Willie Grayeyes, to the San Juan County Board of Commissioners by alleging that he resided outside of the county. The effort failed. The local-control fanatics responded by trying to draw even more lines and divide San Juan County into two or even three new counties. Thus far the effort has gone nowhere.

I WALK ON A LOW MESA, JUST INSIDE COLORADO. THIS SIDE OF
the line is no different from the Utah side, except that the tum-
bleweed is cozied up against the barbed wire more thickly over
here. The sky is overcast and dull, the light flat, the scent of the
sagebrush among which I walk redolent and, yes, the same as
on the Utah side. Off to my left I see a small rise, a deviation. As
I get closer, the contours of the ancient walls reveal themselves
like a body under a thick blanket. It appears as if the structure,
probably built some nine hundred years ago, is circular. It must
have been a tower, like the ones at Hovenweep just a few miles
west of here. But it seems too large for that, so large that later I
will be able to pick it out on a Google Earth satellite photo and
measure its diameter: thirty-six feet. It may have been a great
kiva, perhaps a place for ceremonies, political meetings, dances,
singing. In his notes on this particular stretch of the state line,
Reeves noted: "Numerous ruins of ancient buildings, in various
stages of preservation, were seen and examined."

As is often the case when I stumble upon a site like this,
I step back and take my bearings and ask: Why here? Why
did the Pueblo people—and the Ute and Navajo and even the
Euro-Americans, for that matter—choose this region as the
place to root their communities? There are no simple answers.
Sure, climate, potential crop yields, availability of building materials, fuel, and the presence of game such as deer, elk, bighorn
sheep, and rabbits all played a role, but there has to be more than
that. After all, one of the largest and most architecturally elaborate Puebloan communities in the region was built in Chaco
Canyon, which isn't, and wasn't, any more amenable to human
habitation than, say, Las Vegas is today. Meanwhile, after being
fairly densely populated for centuries, the Durango, Colorado,
area, which has rivers and creeks and fertile soil, was emptied of
people in the ninth century and remained that way even as areas
just dozens of miles away were thriving. There was more to the
decision of where to live than mere pragmatism.

"Here, the human landscape is meaningless outside the natural context—human constructions are not considered out of their relationship to the hills, valleys, and mountains," noted the late Rina Swentzell, a scholar from Santa Clara Pueblo whose ancestors lived in the northern San Juan region, in a 1991 paper she cowrote with my father and a group of archaeologists. "The material village is one of the concentric rings about the symbolic center of the world. It is not given more weight or focus than the area of the fields, hills, or mountains. It constitutes one place within the whole. The web of human existence is interlaced with what happens in the larger natural context and therefore flows into the adjacent spaces, hills, and mountains."

A few years ago Leigh Kuwanwisiwma, a Hopi elder who was the tribe's cultural preservation officer for three decades, explained it like this: after emerging into this world, his ancestors were guided to place their footprints on the earth, with each clan taking its own path, before finally ending up on the mesas where the tribe is based today. "When you look at history and learn about Hopi history and clan migration, you see how vibrant that area was with Hopi clans. It's part of a huge migration tradition—a covenant [with the Holy Ones]," he said. "They were instructed by spiritual leaders: if in fact they'd be earth stewards, they'd have to endure hardships as they placed their footprints."

Perhaps the people who decided to build here were, like Reeves, following a grid. Only rather than a grid that was forced upon the earth, it came from the earth, or perhaps the Holy Ones, or both, and inhabits all of us. For some, the grid is rectilinear, for others it resides in the stars, and still others follow lines that are serpentine, spirals, concentric circles, an undulating web of existence. The ways in which we harmonize with the grid are what we refer to when we talk of Sense of Place. I think of the Hovenweep towers, gathered as they are at the heads of canyons, near the hackberries and the springs. Pragmatic these towers and locations may be, but they are also architecturally audacious, placed in harmony with one another and the landscape near and far. One twin-structure at Hovenweep is perched upon a free-standing stone pedestal that is split down its center. The structures stand back-to-back on the edge of each half of the stone like mirror images, yin and yang, earth and sky, male and female.

CAPTAIN JOHN MACOMB ONCE STOOD ATOP MESA VERDE, looked west, and described the landscape unfurling below him—the same landscape on which I walk on this spring day— as a "region whose dreary monotony is only broken by frightful chasms, where alone the weary traveler finds shelter from the burning heat of a cloudless sun, and where he seeks, too often in vain, a cooling draught that shall slake his thirst."

I am the weary traveler of whom he speaks. I seek shelter but from what I do not know. If "dreary monotony" is a field of mariposa lilies blooming in springtime, fractals of lime-green and neon-orange lichens clinging to ancient stone walls, elderly juniper trees with roots reaching deep into the Underworld, a place where wind, water, and geology tangle in prurient embrace, where the landscape vividly remembers millennia of human history, and where deep time bares itself for all to see in road cuts and arroyos, then yes, he is correct.

I slip back through the fence and continue my meander, doing all I can to deviate from the grid. The maps of San Juan County are no longer blank. Today, they are digitally rendered, high-definition satellite images showing every detail, every broken rock, every tree, even the piles of rubble from ancient structures. I often get lost in these images, traveling across the landscape like some space-age Rollin Reeves, marveling at how wherever my cursor may alight, the landscape is chock-full of something. As I virtually hover over the area a dozen miles north of here, where public land gives way to private, and forested mesas become cultivated bean, wheat, and sunflower fields, I'm baffled by how apparent the grid is from above, and marvel at the subtle kinks that appear in that grid along the state line. But I am also heartened by the way that the grid collapses when faced with the canyons and "frightful chasms" that are so plentiful around here.

I meander back to the fence, find a place to squeeze through, and gladly step back into the blankness, letting the primal grid guide me home.

CHAPTER THREE

POTSHERD PURLOINER

I MUST BEGIN THIS CHAPTER WITH A CRINGEWORTHY CON-
fession. I was once a potsherd purloiner, a cultural thief, and
a looter of the past. It worked like this: while walking through
the sagebrush, all of it taller than me, I would keep my eyes
peeled to the red-beige ground, always searching. Eventually
my vision would alight on something unnatural, something that
wasn't just another stone. I would reach down and gently pick it
up. Usually it would be a potsherd, light gray painted with black
stripes, maybe, or corrugated, or a burnt red-orange. Sometimes
the pieces were bigger than my hand, large enough to really get a
sense of what the whole pot might have looked like. Sometimes
I'd find a rim piece, polished smooth by its owner's hands eight
hundred years prior, or the handle from a mug or a jug. These I'd
pocket without pause. Arrowheads, whether whole or broken,
were also keepers. At home I spread my artifacts out on a shelf
where I could admire my "discoveries."

I was young, just this side of the line where memories gel,
probably six or seven years old. And I certainly wasn't alone. I was
following the customs of the locals, the white ones, that is, who
like to hike on public lands in the Four Corners country. Collecting antiquities was, and still is for some, a sort of hobby, something to do with the family after church on a summer Sunday.

And it was something my family did, too, although, being agnostic, we skipped the church part.

But my hobby was, thankfully, nipped in the bud. My dad was a freelance journalist who mostly wrote about the Four Corners country, where he grew up. That entailed writing about the Indigenous peoples who have inhabited this region for millennia. In the late 1970s, he wrote a piece about pothunting, vandalism of cultural sites, and looting of antiquities in the Southwest. In his conversations with archaeologists and Indigenous people, he came to a sickening realization: the surface-collecting that his young sons engaged in was just as harmful as digging up sites and even graves to get at the antiquities within. To take a piece of pottery or an arrowhead or even a tiny bead is like removing words from the pages of a book. Take one or two and the meaning can still be discerned. But when a young me picks up ten pieces, and another kid like me takes another ten, and then another family fills up a duffel bag with potsherds, it's akin to tearing pages, even whole chapters, out of the book. Meanwhile, the pile of words that have been purloined lose their meaning once they're taken away, piled up on the mantel, or tossed into a closet somewhere to be sold at a garage sale sometime, or donated to some guy and his "museum," which pays homage to the practice of looting more than to the cultures that fashioned the artifacts.

For this reason, stealing artifacts was, technically, against the law. The Antiquities Act of 1906 had mandated the protection of archaeological resources on public land and given the US president the power to establish national monuments to further that protection. But the law was vague when it came to surface-collecting and even "amateur archaeology," or pothunting, so in 1979 Congress passed the Archaeological Resources Protection Act, which explicitly made it illegal to excavate or remove any archaeological resources from federal or Indian land without a permit.

My father was a gentle man, but he was also deeply ethical and very stern when it came to his children adhering to ethics. He exhorted us in no uncertain terms never to pocket a piece of pottery, arrowhead, or even a precious bead ever again. He explained why it was problematic, and I was flooded with guilt and regret and maybe even a little bit of fear of getting caught and hauled away to jail, even though we had quit our bad habit prior to ARPA's passage. I begged my parents to take me back to the sites so I could return the artifacts to their homes, but they patiently explained that it wasn't possible, because I didn't know which pieces came from which places. I hid the artifacts in a bag and put them in a closet and eventually took them up on the hill behind our house in Durango and buried them under a big rock.

I was just a dumb kid with a developed aesthetic sense who picked up pretty things and took a few home with me. I was just another kid following regional cultural norms and engaging in our local hobby. That's the problem. Behind those cultural norms, behind that local hobby, is something darker, a sense of entitlement to the public lands and everything on them.

CALL IT THE PUBLIC LANDS PARADOX. FROM A YOUNG AGE, many Americans, particularly those in the western states with large swaths of public land, are taught that all the lands managed by various agencies under the Department of the Interior and the US Forest Service belong to all Americans. The BLM signs say: "Your Public Lands." There's an old trope of the wealthy father, one arm on his son's shoulders, the other arm beckoning to his empire, saying: "Someday, son, this will all be yours." In the public lands version the parent beckons to a lovely landscape and says to their child: "All of this *is* yours."

This framing is well-intentioned. If the land belongs to everyone rather than to no one, it can ward off what's known as the tragedy of the commons. If I *own* the land I'll be more likely to take care of it, the theory goes. If the Tonka truck is *mine*, I'm less likely to drive it off a cliff or to pour gasoline on it and light it on fire than if it came out of some communal toy box. So the theory goes. At the same time, that sense of ownership, even if my share is just one three-hundred-millionth of the whole, also could give me a sense of entitlement to do what I wish to that land, whether it's camping wherever I please, hiking across sensitive areas, or picking up artifacts.

The sense of entitlement tends to be stronger among those who live nearest to those public lands, particularly white people like myself whose families have been in the area for a couple of generations or more. We feel as though we have a little bit more ownership over those lands, and that, because those lands are in our metaphorical backyards, we are more entitled to the things and beings that inhabit those lands. I use the first person here because I have been, despite knowing better, guilty of this in a knee-jerk kind of way. I wasn't picking up potsherds just because it was the natural thing for a little kid to do, I was doing it because, in some intrinsic way, I felt as if I had the right to do so, as if those artifacts, like the land on which they sat, belonged to me. It's the same current of entitlement that runs through:

- the kid from Blanding who drives his ATV across the living soil at his favorite stomping grounds, tearing up cacti as he goes;
- corporations that tear up public land in order to reap exorbitant profit;
- the cattleman who thinks that because he's been running his livestock up a fragile canyon for decades he's entitled to continue to do it, regardless of the impacts;
- and the extreme athlete who feels that it is his right to climb every rock formation that tempts him, even if it means desecrating a sacred place.

Here in San Juan County, as in many rural, western counties, that sense of entitlement and ownership infuses the dominant culture. In some cases it *is* the dominant culture, and makes up the foundation of the politics and economics of these communities—and is one of the driving factors behind the Gategate fiasco involving Rose Chilcoat and Mark Franklin.

Worst of all, this sense of entitlement ignores the history of that land. It is predicated on the false notion that prior to the Euro-American invasions, the land was empty and America's for the taking. Frederick Jackson Turner called the public domain of the western United States "the richest free gift that was ever spread out before civilized man." He believed that these "vacant lands" offered an "opportunity for a new order of things." Many Americans still treat it this way. Before the land was part of the public domain, however, it was neither vacant nor free nor offered up to anyone as a gift. The government, using violence, the threat of violence, and coercion, stole the land by forcing out the Indigenous peoples who had inhabited that land for thousands upon thousands of years, and who had built communities and cultures and religions and societies on the land and from it. Only after the land was stolen was it declared "public," at which point the federal government began doling it out, often at no cost at all, to white Americans on the condition that they could put it to "productive" use, whether this meant mining or ranching or farming or logging or railroad-building or housing universities or colleges. Via the Homestead Act, the General Mining Law of 1872, the Pacific Railroad Acts, and so on, the government virtually begged individuals and corporations to exploit and privatize the public lands. Every white community in the western United States was built upon these government giveaways of land that was never theirs to give away, be it Denver or Aspen, Boise or Phoenix. National parks, monuments, and forests were carved from the public domain in order to give specific areas extra protection. Quite often the creation of monuments and parks entailed evicting the Indigenous people who were living there on the public land or even on allotments granted by the federal government.

America's public lands now include any land in the public domain that wasn't claimed or patented or otherwise withdrawn and which now falls under the jurisdiction of the Bureau of Land Management. But it also includes lands managed by the Forest Service, National Park Service, and US Fish and Wildlife Service. And I reiterate: all public lands are stolen lands. For all of those who cherish, depend upon, and even fetishize public lands, who see them as the very thing that makes America great, this can be a hard truth to swallow. Yet it's a fact that must be reckoned with, and it must be kept in mind and considered during every discussion and debate about the management of public lands, whether the topic is Bears Ears National Monument or enforcement of the Archaeological Resources Protection Act or drilling for oil and gas in the region surrounding Chaco Canyon. This in no way means that public lands are inherently bad. Quite to the contrary. Only on public lands that have not been privatized does the opportunity still exist to make things right, to find a new pathway towards justice.

I NOT ONLY WAS ENABLED IN MY ARTIFACT-ABSCONDING BY the public lands paradox, but also by a lie that has long been perpetrated in the Southwest regarding the ancient structures that were constructed all over the region. It goes like this: a prehistoric civilization known as the Anasazi built and inhabited these structures before mysteriously vanishing sometime during the thirteenth century. The bumper sticker version of the myth was, "Who were they? Where did they go? Why did they leave?" Even some in the archaeological community perpetuated the lie, despite knowing many of the answers to their own questions.

The myth of the mysteriously vanishing civilization served a number of purposes, but mostly it helped distance the archaeologists and museums and, for that matter, the pothunters and grave robbers, from the people whose ancestral homes they were excavating and whose artifacts they piled in archival storerooms. It was another tool to "other" Indigenous peoples. It's far easier to pocket a piece of pottery or loot an entire village if the creators and inhabitants of that village disappeared, abandoning their goods when they left. If there is no one remaining of that ancient civilization, then there is no one to offend by fragrantly displaying the mummified remains of human beings in a glass case, as was done to "Esther." That was the name given to the desiccated corpse of a woman who had been buried in a rock shelter near Durango over two thousand years ago and dug up in the 1930s by Zeke Flora, an amateur archaeologist. Esther was taken on tour around the region before ending up at the museum at Mesa Verde National Park—and was still on display there when I was a kid. In 1940 park naturalist Don Watson wrote about Esther in a particularly gruesome and offensive way (the article was entitled "Human Prunes"), cheekily describing her condition and the possible consequences around her death and burial. It's hard to imagine that Watson would have done so had he known that Esther's descendants would read his account. But Watson didn't know that because he had fooled himself into believing the myth of a vanished civilization.

Who were they? Not the Anasazi—an anglicization of the Navajo word meaning "Enemy Ancestors"—but the ancestors of today's Pueblo people, who have certainly not vanished. Where did they go? To the pueblos along the Rio Grande, to Acoma, Laguna, and Zuni in New Mexico, and to Hopi in Arizona. Why did they leave? They didn't, not really, they just moved somewhere else not so far away, and they did that simply because collectively they determined that it was time to pull up roots and go in search of the next place, a decision confirmed or prompted by long-term drought, resource depletion, political strife, warfare, or other factors.

Even the term "prehistoric" is not accurate. Each pueblo has a rich history told among itself, its particulars rarely shared with outsiders, that reaches back through the millennia. The sketchy outline of the Hopi history in this world, for example, begins long, long ago, when the people emerged from the Third World into the Fourth World by way of the *sipapuni*, which for some clans was at the bottom of the Grand Canyon near the confluence of the Colorado and Little Colorado Rivers. The deities then commanded the people to "place their footprints," or migrate, in the four cardinal directions, each circle symbolizing a stopping point along the way. All of the southwestern pueblos have similar migration traditions, and they include specific references to the San Juan River Basin in what is now Utah and Colorado.

The first known human "footprints" in what is now known as San Juan County, Utah, were left some thirteen thousand years ago by nomadic hunters who probably passed through on their seasonal rounds as they stalked mammoth, ground sloths, bears, and maybe even camels.[1] Paleoindian sites have been found on Lime Ridge, near Valley of the Gods, near the northern end of Comb Ridge, and near Dark Canyon. Surely there are many others. Puebloan people started settling down in San Juan County two millennia ago and continued to do so into the thirteenth century. During that time populations fluctuated, clans moved around, architecture and agriculture evolved.

If you were to be zapped back in time a thousand years or so to the piñon and juniper forests of Cedar Mesa, you might encounter clusters of pueblos teeming with activity; men tending to hundreds of acres of electric-green fronds of corn, beans, and squash; women grinding corn and shelling beans on rooftops while dogs roamed village plazas and turkeys gobbled in pens. Groups of runners followed wide, carefully constructed "roads" from here to Chaco, perhaps the political and cultural center of the Pueblo world. Near the solstice, religious figures or deities may have emerged from canyons, danced slowly across plazas, and descended into great kivas to summon the sun or the rain. After a century or two, following a long dry spell, maybe, or a string of early frosts that damaged that year's crops, the clan or clans would move on to the next circle on its chosen path.

Near the end of the twelfth century, trouble arrived. Someone or something threatened the people, pushing them to cluster into bigger, more easily defended pueblos. And by the middle of the thirteenth century, the Puebloan communities of the Four Corners region were empty, although certainly not abandoned. After a journey every bit as epic as that of the Israelites, the people had moved on to place their footprints elsewhere, ultimately fulfilling the covenant and settling in their respective homelands, today's Hopi, Zuni, and Eastern Pueblos. "We have earned the right to be earth stewards," says Kuwanwisiwma. "That's why emotions run deep on these issues."

Many pieces are missing from the story of human habitation on this spectacular landscape, many specific details need to be filled in, but the purported mystery of the vanishing civilization is nothing but a myth, and a harmful one at that. The story is written on the land in the remnants of villages and communities, shrines and "roads," cornfields and architectural features whose function remains unknown. These aren't ruins, but memories, important cultural touchstones not just for the Pueblo people, but for all human beings. Picking up artifacts, digging up buried treasure, and vandalizing or otherwise disrespecting these touchstones is not only illegal, but an affront to our common story. "Many of these places were consecrated as homes, or as shrines, just as we consecrate our homes and shrines today," Jim Enote, of Zuni Pueblo, told me. "They are not ruins. They are not abandoned. Once consecrated, they are consecrated in perpetuity. They are holy forever."

CHAPTER FOUR

BEARS EARS GENESIS

COUNTLESS STORIES TELL HOW THE BEARS EARS CAME to be. All of them are true.

I

IT IS SAID THAT LONG AGO, BEFORE THERE WERE HUMANS IN this world, a great sea covered the land. The sea was shallow and salty and teeming with life, the shorelines sultry and lush. Utah sat near the equator back then, in the Pennsylvanian days, and the air was rich with oxygen. Dragonfly-like creatures with condor-sized wingspans plied the thick air, while huge millipedes slithered along the loamy earth under the canopy.

The sea grew, and the sea shrank, and the shorelines moved in, and the shorelines moved out.

Huge rivers carried massive loads of silt down from the highlands, dumping it into the sea, where it got mixed up with the zooplankton and the phytoplankton and settled to the bottom. One day those tiny creatures and plants would become oil, the lifeblood of the combustion culture and, perhaps, its death knell as well.

Millions of years passed.

The great mass of land known as Pangaea busted apart, the rivers stopped flowing, the lakes became stagnant and poisonous, the creatures of the sea perished. Utah shifted away from the equator, causing its tropical climate to get less tropical. Jungles became deserts.

Wind took the place of the old rivers, lifting up the sand—sand that had come from the Appalachian Mountains, that had been carried by the rivers to the north and to the west—and carrying it across the land, depositing it in the huge dune fields of the late Triassic and early Jurassic. These dunes would become the Wingate Sandstone with its deep, orange hue.

The climate shifted again. The streams, as one geological paper[2] put it, "were reactivated at this time and spread their sedimentary load ever more widely until a new onset of arid conditions, represented by the Navajo Sandstone, again forced their withdrawal." A sea of sand known as an erg covered most of Utah during this time and was hundreds of feet deep in places.

It's easy to lose the narrative thread. One's attention can only adhere for so many millions of years, and the eroticism of the Navajo Sandstone distracts. I can never remember which came first, the sand or the dune, nor which sandstone was sand dunes in its former life, and which was piled up at the bottom of the sea. But the stone remembers, and out here, in the desert, the stone tells the tale. There. See it? There's the wind, swirling around in those surreal patterns in the stone.

The long dry period dissipated. Playas splashed across the erg, and rivers cut their way through it. Allosauruses plodded about in the alluvial plains, sinking into the mud and the silt.

Another sea formed to the west of the Bears Ears, then receded.

Millions of years went by.

The Western Cretaceous Interior Seaway moved in from the east, and huge rivers, laden with silt and sand, slowed as they approached the rising sea, causing the silt to settle out onto the river bed and as alluvial fans along the seaside. Thick, fecund jungles and sultry swamps lined the shore. Giant bugs fluttered through the verdant canopy while possum-like marupiala, crocodilian scutes, and dinosaurs—from the "Bisti Beast," a horn-headed tyrannosaurus-like creature, to the *Dineobellator notohesperus*, a small, scrappy, pugnacious, feathered cousin of the velociraptor—cruised through the undergrowth among shallow, brackish ponds. Time would transform the silt-fans into the Dakota and Burro Canyon Sandstones that are so common in the Hovenweep area and further south and east around Chaco Canyon. And the peaty remains of the swamp would become coal, now exhumed by towering draglines with house-sized shovels before being burned up in the furnaces—spewing globe-warming gases in the process—to generate steam to turn turbines to send electrons dancing through high-transmission lines to run the air conditioners of Phoenix.

By the time the sea receded again, the whole area was like a layer cake of sedimentary rock, a three-hundred-million-year timeline plotting the power of erosion and transportation of sediment by wind and water. Meanwhile, in the Underworld, all was churn and bubble, flux and heat. Terrestrial plates nudged up against one another, and then one plate dived below the other, pushing the latter upward, a phenomenon known as the Laramide orogeny. Again, the land remembers this unhurried violence in the form of the sweeping wave of stone known as Comb Ridge, and the Technicolor serpent of the Raplee Anticline.

After the two plates collided, the one that was pushed downward likely snapped off of its parent plate and then rolled back at the bigger plate, causing magma to push up toward the surface and form pools called laccoliths. The Abajo Mountains, the La Sals, and Ute Mountain were formed in this way.

By this time, the Bears Ears were already in place, and over millions of years water and wind ate away at the surrounding rock and dirt, leaving behind the two buttes, capped with two-hundred-million-year-old petrified sand dunes known as the Wingate Sandstone.

II

IT IS SAID THAT LONG AGO, SHORTLY AFTER THE PEOPLE
emerged into this, the Glittering World, there lived around here
an intelligent, beautiful, strong woman who lived with her twelve
brothers. She spent her days weaving blankets and baskets, wandering along the hillsides and gathering herbs for her various
medicines, and trying to keep her pesky brothers occupied so
that they'd stay out of her way. Men, and even deities, came from
all over to court her. She rejected many of them out of hand. If
she happened to like one, she'd take him into her bed and ravage
him for a night. If he performed to her satisfaction she might
keep him around for a while, though that rarely happened. Each
one invariably staggered off across the mesa, broken and haunted
and forever changed by their short time with her.

Then Coyote showed up to try his hand. She turned him
down immediately. He persisted. So did she.

"Come on, baby," Coyote said, his long tongue dangling
from long snout. "Give me a chance whydontchya?"

Finally, exasperated, she said that if he killed one of the
giants that terrorize the people, she'd consider it. She knew quite
well that she was sending him to his death, which may have
caused a twinge of regret, but she was nothing if not sure of herself, and reiterated the challenge.

Coyote was a skinny, scruffy dude, but he was also the Trickster, endowed with wile and cunning, so he accepted the challenge with gusto. Confidently, he strode off into the mesas above
White Canyon, to the lair of the Gray Giant, a brutish, cruel, and
ugly monster who beat people and animals to death with a club,
sometimes in order to eat them, sometimes just for fun. Coyote
approached Gray Giant without fear, his sales pitch worked out
in his head.

"Hey, Gray Giant, you like to eat people, don't you?"

Gray Giant grunted in the affirmative as he calculated Coyote's gristle-to-meat ratio.

"Don't you hate it when they run away and escape because you're too slow?"

Gray Giant grunted again. Coyote would make a crappy meal, but he might be worth killing anyway, just for sport.

"Well, I have just the trick to develop some leg speed, and to get rid of some of that back fat of yours," said Coyote. "And because I like you, it won't cost you a thing."

Gray Giant looked back at his blubbery haunch, and decided that killing Coyote could wait.

"First," said Coyote, "we've got to build a sweat lodge." Gray Giant constructed the shelter with juniper branches, lining the whole thing with juniper bark and coating it with dirt, while Coyote built a fire and heated up some big, smooth river rocks. Once it was completed, they put the rocks inside and climbed in to the dark, cramped space together, the sweat dripping. Without Gray Giant's knowledge, Coyote had also smuggled a deer leg into the lodge.

"Okay," said Coyote. "The first thing you've got to do is snap your femur. Like this." He then snapped the severed deer femur. "Here, feel, you can feel how I broke my own leg."

Gray Giant reached into the darkness and, sure enough, felt the fracture in the bone.

Coyote then sang a little healing song and told Gray Giant to feel again, this time putting his own, unbroken leg where the deer leg had been. Sure enough, Gray Giant could feel that Coyote had healed his leg, making him faster than those furless humans.

"Okay," said Coyote. "Your turn. Break your leg."

Gray Giant held on to his own femur with two hands, gripped hard, and twisted. It snapped juicily, and Gray Giant let out a horrible wail of pain. That was Coyote's signal to clock the dumb brute over the head with a big, fat juniper branch. It took a few blows, but eventually Gray Giant succumbed. Coyote cut off his head and took it back to the woman.

When she saw him swaggering back to her house, Gray Giant's big, broken head in hand, the woman frowned.

"Well, well, you actually went and did it," she said. "I'm impressed. But that was just the first part of the test. Now, if you just die and come back to life four times in a row, then I'll consider letting you into my bed."

"But you said…"

"I know what I said. And now I'm saying this. Take it or leave it."

"Fine. Fine. But only if you kill me yourself."

At that, she jumped up from her loom and whacked him on the head with the club she kept around for suitors that refused to leave. She was powerful and skilled, and killed him with one blow, then tossed his carcass into the woods and returned to her art. No sooner had she gotten back to work than Coyote sauntered out of the woods. The woman jumped up and, in one swift motion, pulled a knife from a secret pocket on her chest and slit Coyote's throat. This time she kicked his body into the brush. A few minutes later, he reemerged again, looking bloody but otherwise spunky. Twice more she killed him, and twice more he came back to life, thanks to a trick he had learned back in trickster school that allowed him to split his heart in two, hiding one half in the tip of his tail and the other in the tip of his nose, places no assailant ever thought to maim or beat or stab.

He then attempted to claim his prize, her hand in marriage. She still refused. She didn't want to get married. After all, what's the point of being stuck with some stinky guy who is always cramping your style? Still, since he had gone through all that trouble, and since Coyote was not one to give up, she finally allowed him to lie down beside her on her animal hides. One thing led to another and soon they were passionately entangled, their bodies singing with joy. Over and over again they made love, until the sun rose over Dibé Ntsaa in the east. Even as they went about their daily chores, they would be overcome with longing and fall to the earth to gorge themselves on one another. Coyote was not just tricky, the woman discovered, but also a patient, gentle, passionate, and considerate lover.

But he also stunk and had a bad habit of marking "his" territory. And when the woman's brothers returned from hunting, they demanded that Coyote leave their home. Coyote was angry, and he knew he could outsmart the twelve brothers, but he worried that he might anger the woman if he antagonized her kin. So Coyote took his matted fur and his stink and headed out the door to find a new home. The woman went with him.

"Ah, what the hell," she said, "our bodies sang together in harmony. So I will now make you my husband, and we will live as one."

Coyote was a free spirit and a libertine, and not the marrying kind. Still, he was madly in love with the woman, and eager to spend his life with her. But he knew he'd look weak if he agreed too hastily. So he pulled his long and dangling tongue back into his craw and stood firm: he would marry her only if he could kill her four times. She was so enamored that she stood up and submitted to his blows without hesitation or complaint and died and came back to life—using some wile that she never revealed—four times. Coyote was impressed. They were thus married, and embarked on a life of bliss.

But it wouldn't last. Coyote, being Coyote, wanted to accompany the brothers on their major autumn hunting trip. He asked. They refused. He begged, and they refused again, saying it was too dangerous for a skinny guy like him. But Coyote was persistent and, with the woman's help, wore them down until they finally agreed. On a crisp autumn morning they embarked on their journey, headed for the rich hunting grounds of Forbidden Canyon, which originates on the slopes of Naatsis'áán. As the brothers stalked deer, jackrabbits, and bighorn sheep, Coyote became distracted. Hunting was never really his thing; he just liked it because it gave him an opportunity to walk around the woods meditating. He found a petrified tree and lingered over it, trying to decipher the magic that turned wood to stone. Then he saw the beavers having a great time playing the hoop game. He hated to be left out of things, so he sauntered on over to get in on the fun.

As he approached, the beavers collectively rolled their eyes as if to say, Oh, not this guy again. But they let him play the game and gamble away his hide, literally. His curiosity and thirst for adventure were not quenched, however, and pretty soon he came upon a group of rascally magpies, who were pulling their little black eyes out of their heads and tossing them into a juniper tree and then calling them back and reinserting them in their heads. Coyote thought that was pretty cool and that his new wife would be impressed by such a skill. So the magpies grudgingly let him in on the game and, well, they couldn't get his eyeballs back into his head, so he had to coerce some swallows into making him new peepers out of piñon pitch. He tangled with spiders and slid down cliffs on flat rocks with lizards—ending up quite a bit worse for wear and, somehow, even scruffier and mangier than before, but alive, nonetheless. Finally he got into it with a band of badgers, his biggest, and last, mistake. His trickery was not enough to save him this time.

When the brothers returned without Coyote, the woman broke down in tears. When she realized he would never return, she became enraged—at the world, at Coyote, and, most of all, at her brothers, whom she blamed for his disappearance. Her rage unearthed a long-buried magic within, one that allowed her to transform herself into a big, brown bear, with long claws and a teeth-filled maw. The men who tell this story like to think that she acquired this power from Coyote, that he had implanted it within her during intercourse. But that's a lie. She was and always had been Changing Bear Woman, it just took a moon-sized love and subsequent loss to bring this part of her to the surface. She killed one brother after another except for the youngest, who, with the help of Strong Wind and Knife Boy, was able to bury himself under a pile of rocks and stay hidden while he gathered up the strength to confront his ursine sister.

When he felt ready, he emerged from hiding and was able to outmaneuver Changing Bear Woman. He killed her with an arrow shot from his bow, and then found her internal organs buried nearby and killed them, too. Blood spurted from both, and Wind warned the boy that if the two streams of the bear-woman's blood met, she would come back to life, ferocious as ever. So the youngest brother dug a deep trench in the ground to keep them separate.

He then set about dismembering his sister, but also remembering her to the earth, throwing her body parts in all directions. Her nipples became the piñon nuts that the people still harvest today; her vagina is now the porcupine. The trench the brother dug to keep the blood from meeting is now known as Comb Wash and Comb Ridge. And most importantly, the crown of Changing Bear Woman's head became Shash Jáa', or the Bears Ears.

THE FIRST OF THESE INCREDIBLE STORIES COMES FROM GEO-logic papers, which draw from scientists' interpretations of what's written on the landscape. The second comes from a traditional Diné story and is derived from the landscape itself.

I find myself drawn to both. The former because it forces me to stretch my mind around a narrative that unfurls over hundreds of millions of years, and my mind doesn't want to do that on its own. And the second because it illustrates a potent bond that exists between humanity and the natural world.

The basic storyline of Changing Bear Woman was meant to be uttered orally, but over the past century has been written down repeatedly in its various versions, often by white anthropologists, who were recording what Diné historians had told them, but also by Diné historians. Sometimes the versions that make it to paper refer specifically to the Bears Ears buttes that protrude from Elk Ridge in San Juan County, sometimes they talk about other landforms, and just as often they are more generic and don't refer to any specific landform at all.

I first read the story of Changing Bear Woman in a book called *Coyote Stories of the Navajo People* that was published in 1975 by the Navajo Curriculum Center. My parents bought the book for me when I was eight, after a road trip through the Navajo Nation that culminated with a few days' visit to Canyon de Chelly. It rained the entire trip, and my brother and I had to ride in the back of a rundown old International Harvester pickup truck that burned through oil at an alarming rate. Nevertheless, I had been so taken with Canyon de Chelly, with the smooth, desert-varnish-streaked cliffs, the rain-swollen stream spread across the broad canyon bottom, and the peach orchards, that I cried most of the way home. As a consolation my parents bought me the book, a compilation of traditional stories put down on paper by Robert A. Roessel and Dillon Platero and illustrated by George Mitchell. The stories are raucous and humorous, with illustrations to match, and gave me an early appreciation for Coyote and for the Diné oral tradition.

Later, I encountered a racier version in *Diné Bahane': The Navajo Creation Story*, as recounted by Paul Zolbrod, and after that a slightly different version in Clyde J. Benally's *Dinéjí Nákéé Nááhane': A Utah Navajo History*. In more recent years, the story has been cited in legal filings by the Navajo Nation and the other members of the Bears Ears Inter-Tribal Coalition to illustrate their deep connection to the Bears Ears and surrounding landscape, and thus to make the case for protecting it as a national monument. The version here is based on a combination of these various accounts, with some obvious updating. I see the story as both a comedic fable and a tragic love story in the vein of Orpheus and Eurydice. There are common themes.

In both, the beloved dies and vanishes into the earth. Then the lovers—Changing Bear Woman and Orpheus—meet violent ends, as well, partly due to their reaction to loss. Just as Changing Bear Woman is torn asunder and scattered to the winds, so too is Orpheus torn to pieces by the maenads, his parts strewn across the forest. And both Changing Bear Woman and Orpheus live on, the former as parts of the landscape, and the latter as nature's song.

CHAPTER FIVE

SHASH JÁA SANCTUARY

I N THE SUMMER OF 1864 CAPTAIN JOHN THOMPSON AND
his troops marched among the desert-varnish-streaked walls
of Canyon de Chelly and destroyed thousands of peach trees.
It may sound like the premise for a quirky but sad Richard Brau-
tigan novel, *The Great Peach Tree Massacre*. It is not. Rather it is
a description of a war crime, one of a litany of atrocities perpetrated by the federal government against the Navajo, or Diné,
during what the Diné would come to call "The Fearing Time."

Nearly 140 years later, I sit and read an account of the crime
by the criminal himself, titled; "The Destruction of Navajo
Orchards 1864: Captain John Thompson's Report." The banal-
ity of the prose makes me uncomfortable, as does the fact that
the perpetrator's name is so close to my own. Serving as a salve,
however, is the knowledge of all that transpired in the years
since, and the knowledge that this story is not a tragedy, but ultimately is a tale of endurance, resilience, and hope.

THE DINÉ—THE FIVE FINGER EARTH SURFACE HOLY PEOPLE—
emerged long ago into the Glittering World at a secret place in
the San Juan Mountains of southwestern Colorado. Then First
Man fashioned the four sacred mountains that would bound the

homeland: Tsoodzil (Mount Taylor) in the south, Dookʼoʼoosliid (San Francisco Peaks) in the west, Sisnaajini (Blanca Peak) in the east, and Dibé Ntsaa (Hesperus Mountain) in the north. The land lying within the bounds of these mountains makes up Diné Bikéyah, or the homeland, and stretches across what is sometimes referred to as the Four Corners country. Dinétah, or the heart of the homeland, was originally in what is now northwestern New Mexico near the confluence of the Los Pinos and San Juan Rivers.

During their early days in the Glittering World the people had to contend with monsters that terrorized the land and people. They sometimes clashed with the Ute people, whose territory overlapped parts of Diné Bikéyah. And later the Spanish spilled into the region from the south, attempting to colonize and convert the Indigenous peoples who lived there using violent means, while also capturing Navajo, Ute, and Pueblo children, selling them into slavery on the auction block in Taos, Santa Fe, and Santa Cruz. In 1680 nearly every pueblo, from Taos to Hopi, took part in a coordinated revolt against the Spanish colonists, driving them all the way back to El Paso for a dozen years. The Spaniards returned and took a more humble approach, establishing uneasy peace with the various tribal nations whose territory they had invaded. Slavery, however, continued.

If anything, the situation only worsened when Mexico gained independence from Spain in 1821. In 1823 José Antonio Vizcarra, a trader and governor of New Mexico, led 1,500 troops westward out of Santa Fe and into Diné country for no other reason, it seems, than to systematically raid and kill and enslave whomever he encountered. The massive army crossed the fertile valley of the Rio Puerco of the East, passed the Puebloan structures of Chaco Canyon, and traversed the Chuska Mountains at Narbona Pass, dropping back down into a spectacular geological mélange of sedimentary red rock pierced from below by dark and shiny volcanic laccoliths near the head of Canyon de Chelly.

Vizcarra steered clear of the canyon, a wise choice, given that it was the Diné stronghold and invading it surely would have cost him his life, regardless of how many troops he had at his disposal. Had he ventured among the sheer walls of sandstone he would have encountered fields filled with a variety of crops such as corn, beans, squash, and melons, along with thousands of peach trees, their branches weighed down by small, juicy, sweet fruit. Peaches are native to China, were cultivated in the Middle East, and made their way to Spain via the Moors. The Spanish then brought them to the Americas and then to New Mexico, where Pueblo farmers adopted them. After the Pueblo Revolt, a number of people from Hopi and Jemez Pueblo, fearing reprisal for their roles in the revolt, took refuge among the Diné in Canyon de Chelly, bringing peach seeds with them. Soon the canyon bottom was covered in orchards, irrigated by the plentiful flow of water fed by Chuska Mountain snowmelt, and the peaches became a source of sustenance and currency for barter.

When Vizcarra and his soldiers came across a Diné rancheria, they'd attack, killing men, women, and children, and enslaving those who survived, actions that he would recount in his journal in a casually clinical way: "On my return, Colonel Don Francisco Salazar reported that nothing eventful had occurred, other than a party of fifty men...had succeeded in attacking a rancheria of Navajos, killing five women and capturing nine slaves of both sexes. Likewise, Captain Don Miguel Montoya reported having attacked the Navajos on his march, and succeeded in killing two women and capturing eight slaves of both sexes."

Even with his huge army, Vizcarra was no match for the wily Diné, who refused to engage with Vizcarra on his terms and instead "constantly were retreating, scattering, and vanishing into hideouts," as recounted by a frustrated Vizcarra in his journals. In other words, the Diné outsmarted the Mexicans, successfully keeping casualties to a minimum. Most often they were able to vanish into nearby hideouts, but on the rare occasions when Vizcarra and his men went in pursuit, the Diné headed for the "rough country" of Las Orejas, or the Bears Ears, and Navajo Mountain, both in present-day San Juan County. Some went overland through Monument Valley, others followed Chinle Wash all the way from Canyon de Chelly to the San Juan River, known by the Spanish as Rio de Nabajoo, and on to the other side. In either case the Mexican pursuers, dispirited by the twisted maze of canyons and the steep slopes of Navajo Mountain, soon gave up and headed back to Santa Fe, tails between their legs.

At the time, Bears Ears country was a place where tribal territories overlapped somewhat. It was frequented by the Weeminuche band of Utes and was home to bands of Paiutes (the Spaniards and Mexicans tended to conflate the Utes with the Paiutes). Diné clans also lived in the area surrounding Shash Jáa, or the Bears Ears, for centuries, and the landforms—Comb Ridge, Raplee Anticline, Douglas Mesa, Navajo Mountain—play leading roles in Diné history. So it was natural for the Diné to seek sanctuary in the region.

The United States went to war with Mexico in the 1840s, and in 1848 the Treaty of Guadalupe Hidalgo redrew the Mexican border more or less where it is now, putting a big chunk of the Southwest—including San Juan County—under US control, and opening the doors to wave upon wave of American invaders in search of gold and silver and forage for their cattle. Brigham Young led his flock of Latter-day Saints into the Salt Lake Valley to the north in 1847 about the same time, seeking religious refuge. The various bands of the Ute people were driven out of much of their territory when the gold rush came to Colorado's Front Range in the 1850s, and in 1860 Captain Charles Baker led a contingent into the San Juan Mountains in Colorado, where he set up camp and tried to spark another gold rush. The Americans, meanwhile, did nothing to curb the New Mexican practice of kidnapping Indigenous children and selling them into slavery, even after the Emancipation Proclamation had been signed. In 1863 an estimated two thousand Indigenous people remained enslaved in New Mexico. Since many of the territory's top officials were themselves slaveholders, they resisted any efforts at reform, and Congress didn't pass a law to end the practice—which they euphemistically referred to as "peonage"—until 1867.

The Diné weren't about to take these incursions onto their land and their lives sitting down, so they launched raids on the settlements that had encroached upon their homeland. Predictably, the US military reacted with disproportionate force. In 1862 Brigadier General James Carleton was given command of the New Mexico Department, from which he launched a brutal campaign to gain more land and resources for what he called the "great and advancing ocean of palefaces," particularly those intent on tearing the mineral veins from the flesh of the earth. "If I can but have troops to whip away the Apaches, so that prospecting parties can explore the country and not be in fear of being murdered," Carleton wrote to the secretary of the treasury in 1863, "you will without the shadow of a doubt find that our country has mines of the precious metals unsurpassed in richness, number, and extent by any in the world." Carleton was merciless, ordering his men to kill the Apache men, even if they carried the white flag of surrender, and threatening to burn all of Zuni Pueblo if any Zunis were found to be harboring or helping Diné fighters.

Carleton enlisted Christopher "Kit" Carson to lead his campaign of terror against the Diné. Carson was ruthless. He raided Navajo settlements, the cracks of gunfire and the staccato of horse hooves on pale red sandstone mingling with the agonized bleating of sheep and goats as they were slaughtered. He burned the corn, bean, and pumpkin fields, the inky smoke oozing into the hard blue sky. Then, in the depth of an especially cold winter, he invaded Canyon de Chelly and by spring had forced six thousand captives on the Long Walk to Bosque Redondo in the southeastern corner of New Mexico, hundreds of miles away.

But Carson hadn't captured or killed everyone, nor had he wiped out all of the food. Some had managed to evade capture and were said to be subsisting off of the remaining peaches of Canyon de Chelly. So in July and August of 1864, just as the peaches were ripening, Captain John Thompson was sent into the canyon and its tributaries with thirty-five men to destroy the orchards.

Thompson kept a diary[3] of his systematic slaughter, with entries like this: "On the 3d Moved Camp about 3 Miles to another Orchard. There I cut down 500 of the best Peach trees I have ever seen in the Country, everyone of them bearing Fruit. After this work of destruction had been perfected, I Marched through the Cañon a distance of 8 Miles to a Field of about 5 Acres of Corn which I had destroyed, and Encamped there that Night." All in all he cut down more than four thousand peach trees, leading to the surrender of hundreds more Diné, including leaders Barboncito and Manuelito. The crimes were carried out by Carleton, Carson, Thompson, and their troops. The ultimate overseer, the commander in chief at the time and he who was ultimately responsible for this attempted genocide was none other than President Abraham Lincoln.

"By the subjugation and colonization of the Navajo tribe," Carleton wrote in 1864, "we gain for civilization their whole country, which is much larger in extent than the State of Ohio, and, besides being by far the best pastoral region between the two oceans, is said to abound in the precious as well as the useful metals." Carleton's methods would one day serve as precedent and inspiration for the genocidal drive by the German Nazis to murder millions of Jewish people in order to gain more Lebensraum. In a 1928 speech, Adolf Hitler expressed his admiration for the American campaign of Indian removal, and the way Carleton's troops had "gunned down the millions of Redskins to a few hundred thousand, and now keeps the modest remnant under observation in a cage."

The Diné would not be defeated, however. Hundreds evaded capture and, like their parents before them, sought sanctuary in Shash Jáa country. Kit Carson and Carleton's other thugs weren't about to venture into that country. It was too intimidating, too dry, too twisted, too hard. Hoskannini, a Diné leader, settled on the rugged slopes of Navajo Mountain, and his grandson would still be there nearly a century later, recounting tales of his grandfather's fabled silver mine. Another Diné headman, K'aayelli, sought sanctuary near the Bears Ears. A canyon, a spring, and a Forest Service guard station are all named after him, and his descendants still live in San Juan County and take great pride in the fact that their ancestor never surrendered to Carson or anyone else from the federal government.

Carleton had intended the relatively minuscule Bosque Redondo to serve as a permanent reservation for the some nine thousand Diné people who had surrendered, a place where they would settle down, become self-sufficient farmers, and stay out of the way of progress. But in reality, it was a concentration camp, a barren, 160-square-mile swath of alkali soil and bad water, a place where, if their captors had their way, the Diné would slowly disappear. Carleton once wrote: "Therefore, place them upon reservations now, and hold those reservations inviolate. In the great and rising sea here prefigured, those reservations will be islands; and, as time elapses and the race dies out, these islands may become less and less, until, finally, the great sea will ingulf [sic] them one after another, until they become known only in history, and at length are blotted out of even that, forever."

The incarcerated Diné refused to disappear, however, and instead waged a quiet but meaningful resistance—some escaped, others refused to plant crops; the specter of revolt hung in the air. Carleton's cruel experiment was faltering. So, in 1868, the

Indian Peace Commission sent Lieutenant General William Tecumseh Sherman and Samuel Tappan to Bosque Redondo to come up with a solution.

Sherman, renowned for his scorched-earth policy in the South and for waging the brutal Indian Wars on the Plains, had favored sending the Diné to the Indian Territory to be established in Oklahoma. But when he arrived in Bosque Redondo and saw the deplorable conditions and then listened for days to Barboncito wax about his people's existential need to go home, Sherman changed his tune and established a reservation in the center of their old homeland.

The rectangular reservation mapped out in the Treaty of 1868 covered only about one-eighth of the pre–Long Walk homeland. It contained very little arable land, and its outer boundaries didn't even come close to the four sacred mountain peaks. Dinétah was left out, as was Huerfano Peak and Chaco Canyon and its surroundings, which had been Diné land for centuries. The northern boundary followed the Arizona-Utah border, cutting out Monument Valley, Navajo Mountain, the Bears Ears. Of all the treaties signed during that era, the one with the Diné gave the fewest acres per capita.

Those, however, were no more than lines on a white man's map, and for the most part the people who had been imprisoned at Bosque Redondo paid them no heed. Sherman told them they were free to go home. And that's exactly what they did, unconstrained by the purported reservation lines.

Over time, the federal government was forced to concede that the reservation they created was too small to support the largest tribal nation in the country, and through executive orders and acts of Congress, the Navajo Nation's boundaries were expanded to encompass some twenty-seven thousand square miles of land, including about one-fourth of San Juan County, Utah. Still, the return of the land remains incomplete. As often as not, efforts to expand the reservation to include the entirety of the original homeland were thwarted by white ranching interests, mining companies, oil and gas drillers, or, at times, the conservation community. The area that includes and surrounds Chaco Culture National Historical Park is a prime example.

AFTER THE 1868 TREATY WAS SIGNED, HUNDREDS OF FAMILIES flocked to the public domain land that lay outside the reservation boundaries, including into the Greater Chaco region in northwestern New Mexico. To solve the "problem" of the families living off the reservation, Major A. W. Evans, charged with overseeing the Navajos in the Pueblo Bonito Agency, suggested that the boundary of the reservation be extended eastward to encompass the entire area. It would have been a simple move, a mere flourish of the president's pen that would have avoided a great deal of future grief.

That didn't happen, however, and in the early 1880s white stockmen, spurred on by the government's General Land Office, the predecessor to the BLM, began to move into the Chaco region, staking out homesteads on land that was deemed public, even if it was already occupied by Navajo people. It was not uncommon for a Navajo family to return to their hogan after spending the summer at higher altitudes, only to find their land fenced off, their hogan obliterated, and a white man's cabin in its place.

When a region-wide drought in 1893 sparked an influx of white ranchers seeking new rangeland, Navajo leaders and Bureau of Indian Affairs agents renewed their call for a reservation extension. Officials in Washington declined, telling the Navajo leaders to instead file for allotments on the public domain, as provided for in the Dawes Act, or General Allotment Act, of 1887. Typically the Dawes Act applied to reservation land. The government would parcel up the common space into small, quasi-private parcels. Tribal members got first dibs on the parcels. Whatever remained was then opened up to white homesteaders. Ultimately, the federal government and white homesteaders would use the Dawes Act and similar laws that followed to usurp twenty-seven million additional acres of Indian land.

In the Chaco region, allotment was used in reverse fashion. There, the land had already been stolen from the Diné, and the government was offering to return it piecemeal to individuals by way of a process that looked a lot like homesteading, only open to Navajo as well as white people.

It didn't work out well for the would-be allottees. The Indian agencies lacked the skill and manpower to put together the paperwork for thousands of allotment applications. And the land office in Santa Fe—not to mention the territorial legisla- ture—was beholden to the white stockmen, who tried their best to hold up the application process, or to get allotments nullified by claiming that the Navajo allottees weren't making the proper "improvements" on the land in question. So allotment moved slowly, allowing white homesteaders to move in and stake their own claims, thereby pushing the Navajo people onto less desir- able land.

Among those doing the pushing was Richard Wetherill, the Colorado cowboy known for stumbling upon the cliff dwellings of Mesa Verde and exposing them to the world, and who also did early excavation in San Juan County, Utah. With cash from New York soap scions Fred and Talbot Hyde, Wetherill and archaeol- ogist George Pepper in 1896 began the extensive excavation of Pueblo Bonito, the spectacular, eight-hundred-room stone edi- fice constructed during the ninth to the twelfth centuries by the ancestors of today's Pueblo people.

Wetherill's team unearthed thousands of artifacts, most of which were hauled off to the American Museum of Natural His- tory. Others were sold to the highest bidder. The team occupied rooms in the pueblo and removed prehistoric timbers for use in their own structures, and Wetherill staked a homestead encompassing Pueblo Bonito. While Wetherill may have been following norms for the times, many of his contemporaries were horrified. Other archaeologists called on Washington to do something to protect Chaco's artifacts, a call that ultimately led to Congress passing the Antiquities Act in 1906. It's worth noting that while the act was created in part to preserve the artifacts of Indigenous cultures, the courtesy was not extended to the living members of those same cultures. Indeed, the Antiquities Act was often used as justification to steal more Indigenous lands.

In 1907, President Theodore Roosevelt wielded the act to establish Chaco Canyon National Monument to protect Pueblo Bonito and the other "Great Houses" nearby. Perhaps sensing an opportunity, just weeks later Navajo superintendent W. H. Harrison asked his Washington higher-ups to push Roosevelt to extend the reservation eastward in order to do the same for the Navajo people living in the region. "I have never met Indians… who seem to fear the loss of their homes and countries greater than do the Indians [in the Chaco region]," he wrote. "It is a fact that white and Mexican sheep and cattle owners are filling the country and actually driving many of these people from watering places that they have used their entire lifetime." In November 1907, Roosevelt issued Executive Order 709, withdrawing public domain lands in the Chaco region "from sale and settlement and set apart for the use of the Indians as an addition to the present Navajo Reservation."

But in 1911 President William H. Taft issued his own order putting all un-allotted lands in the agency back into the public domain, claiming that Roosevelt's order was never meant to be permanent. The families that had filed for and received allotments on the extension were able to keep their land, but hundreds of others had never received allotments for one reason or another, and thus became "unauthorized occupants" on public domain land. And even though the original proclamation creating

Chaco Canyon National Monument stated that Diné sheep herders should be able to continue to roam freely across the monument, it was eventually fenced off, and the allottees who had land within the monument were evicted and never received compensation. It was an echo of the federal government's theft of Ute Mountain Ute land to create Mesa Verde National Park. The distrust sowed by these betrayals rippled down through the years and played a part in motivating both sides in the debate over Bears Ears National Monument designation.

Today the whole Chaco checkerboard is a jurisdictional mess. State lands abut private lands that share borders with allotments. Tribal trust lands lie next to tribal fee lands. Much of the land is public land, managed by the Bureau of Land Management, of which about 90 percent is leased to oil and gas companies, giving the term "public land" an altogether new meaning. The lands that the Navajo Nation acquired in exchanges are split estate, meaning that the minerals underneath are controlled by the feds—so the tribe gets no royalties and little say over the exploitation of the minerals.

It's not just Chaco. Thousands more acres of the original Diné Bikéyah, including the Bears Ears and the four sacred peaks, remain outside the Navajo Nation's boundaries altogether and are managed as public lands by the BLM and the Forest Service, generally with no added protections regardless of their significance to the Diné and all the tribal nations that call the region home.

And what of the peach trees of Cañon de Chelly? Undaunted, the people replanted the orchards when they returned home, and by the 1880s, the peach trees were back. They continue to provide an abundant harvest to the descendants of their planters today.

CHAPTER SIX

BLIZZARD AT MOON HOUSE

I T IS PROBABLY A FOOL'S ERRAND FOR SOMEONE WHO IS pushing fifty to try to understand why he made a certain decision that led to near catastrophe when he was in his early twenties. We were young, I guess, and like most youngsters felt invincible. Maybe we didn't check the weather forecast, which, in our defense, was more difficult then because we had no internet. Perhaps we did check the forecast, and it called for a record-breaking snowstorm to be followed by a record-breaking cold spell, and we—David, Craig, and I—scoffed at the forecasters because what the hell do they know, anyway? After all, we had camped in canyon country at Christmastime for years, and we'd never had a problem. Why would this time be any different?

So, on a mid-December day in 1990 we threw our backpacks into Craig's Isuzu Trooper and headed west out of Durango. We arrived on Cedar Mesa a few hours later, went past the Kane Gulch Ranger Station, which was still in a doublewide trailer and closed for the season, and turned down the Snow Flat Road, which more or less follows the same route that the Hole-in-the-Rock party took in 1879 on their way to Bluff. Had we been a little more thoughtful, we might have asked why the road was called Snow Flat, and might have questioned the wisdom of driving down a path with that name on or near the winter solstice. We weren't all that thoughtful, apparently. The road at the time was un-graveled dirt and rocky-rough where it dropped off of the piñon-juniper-covered flats down the sandstone, but posed no problems for a Trooper when dry. After venturing nearly eight miles from the pavement on a backroad that got nearly zero use in the winter, we turned onto an even lesser-utilized two-track that, like many roads in this part of the world, wound erratically through the trees for about a mile or so where we would begin what was meant to be a brief solstice-time respite from the chaos of the world.

BY THAT TIME, CAMPING IN SOUTHEASTERN UTAH IN THE DEAD of winter had, for me, become a bit of a tradition, or perhaps a perverse, sadomasochist ritual. Once, in my years of early memory when I was around five or six, my dad took me camping at the mouth of Arch Canyon when there was a good eight inches of wet snow on the ground. I wore jeans. I always wore jeans, shitty jackets from TG&Y, and some stupid-ass moon boots, probably hand-me-downs from my brother, insulated only with foam rubber that held the moisture, and the cold, against my cotton-sock-clad feet. If I thought that crawling into my sleeping bag would help, I was wrong. It was little more than a sheath of nylon, with very little insulation, and probably also came from the sale rack at TG&Y. A giant bonfire might have fended off the chill that burrowed deeper and deeper into my bones, but my father refused to build a campfire for any purpose other than cooking, because campfires suck your attention away from the stars and the moon and the sounds of the night. I wasn't yet cheeky enough to point out that low-level, chronic hypothermia is not so conducive to stargazing, either.

A decade later, for Thanksgiving, my father and his friend Jim Whitfield took my brother, his friend, and me behind the Abajo Mountains so that we could backpack into Upper Salt

Creek in the Needles District of Canyonlands National Park. Typically one would access Salt Creek via a jeep road that led partway up the canyon, but Whitfield and my dad chose instead to drop into the upper reaches of the canyon from above, probably to avoid encountering any humans, particularly of the jeep-driving variety. At the time, a fight was raging over whether to put a nuclear waste dump nearby, and a decade later the Salt Creek road would become another focal point in the public land wars of San Juan County when the National Park Service would consider closing the road in order to protect the riparian ecology and limit access to the archaeological resources in the canyon. But at the time the road was getting more and more traffic.

We couldn't leave until after work, so most of the drive took place after dark, and when we finally arrived at Whitfield's "secret" car-camping spot for the night we encountered a bewildering sight: a vintage Toyota Land Cruiser parked in the little pullout, and a skinny, bearded guy standing in front of a campfire, looking as surprised to see us as we were to see him. Whitfield was enraged. Not being the type to drive away politely and find another campsite, Whitfield jumped out of the truck and confronted the man, while we watched tensely from the car, certain that this wouldn't end well.

Whitfield was an intense and brilliant and passionate man who didn't always mesh harmoniously with other human beings. He was an artist, a pioneer of Arizona rock climbing, and a follower of star-maps who lived in a rusty old singlewide trailer while he built a tower house up on the McElmo Dome west of Cortez, out where the bean fields end and the BLM land begins. His favorite aphorism, which he repeated often and in all kinds of company, was, "Fuck 'em if they can't take a joke. Fuck 'em if they can." We cringed as we waited for him to lay into the poor dude verbally, maybe even throw a punch or two.

But the situation de-escalated when Whitfield realized he knew the guy from his days as a boatman on the Grand Canyon in the seventies. The guy explained to Whitfield that he was now an adventure guide operating out of Moab, and he had two clients sleeping in a tent nearby, so if he didn't mind keeping it down as he drove away to find another camp, that would be great. Whit-field, smiling maniacally, slapped the man on the back in fare-well, jumped in the truck, slammed the door, revved the engine, and drove, horn honking, straight toward the tent containing aforesaid clients. As we careened toward the nylon dome two heads popped out, eyes wide open. Whitfield slammed on the brakes, kicking up a cloud of dust that hung suspended in the headlight beams, then tore out of there and pulled into another campsite just a few hundred yards away. Whitfield and my dad then started drinking tequila, and every ten minutes or so Whit-field led us in a howling session intended to drive the offend-ing party away. Whitfield wasn't angry at the guy for occupying a campsite on public land. He was mad because the adventure guide was making a business out of carting his clients out into lesser-known places on public lands and thereby profiting off of the solitude and the scenery.

We spent the next day on a long, chilly hike across the mesa and partway down into the canyon. The adventure guide and his customers were nowhere to be seen, much to all of our relief. My pack felt unusually heavy and cut painfully into my shoulders, but I stoically refrained from complaining or even inspecting the pack to see what the problem was until we arrived at camp under a drippy overhang below the rim. It turned out Whitfield had snuck a full-sized cooked ham into my pack before departure.

A year later, when I was sixteen, we left my dad's house north of Cortez, Colorado, in the pre-light dawn on Christmas Day in Whitfield's pickup. My father and Jim rode up in the cab, while I rode in the back with the two dogs, Chaco and Moqui. Before we started driving it seemed like a survivable, if not quite rational, situation. Sitting in the cab would have been warmer, sure, but I would have had to listen to the two adults argue while breathing my dad's cigarette smoke. So, my back pressed up against the cab, I wrapped myself in sleeping bags and put one dog on either side of me. As soon as we hit the highway and got up to speed I realized my mistake, and when we dropped into the San Juan River Valley and were enveloped by the fog there and ice crystals began forming on everything, including the exposed parts of my face, I thought I was going to die. But I was young and stupid and stubborn and proud, and there was no friggin' way I would break down and pound on the window and beg for rescue.

When we got to Page, Arizona, home of Glen Canyon Dam, the sun came out and the temperature rose above zero and I was able to unclench a few of my muscles just in time to see the colossal concrete plug: three hundred feet thick at its base, fifteen hundred feet long at the crest, a symbol of the effort to control what was once a muddy, wild, tumultuous river, that impounded billions of gallons of water and flooded hundreds of miles of sublime canyons—a crime against the gods. Like most sixteen-year-olds I was a bundle of angst and insecurity, of hormonal mania and uncertain identity. I was fragile and sensitive and flailing around for a sense of who I was. I was an ardent reader and devotee of Ed Abbey, despite all his flaws—even then he was a little too macho for my taste—and fancied myself as some mélange of Seldom Seen, Bonnie Abzug, and Everett Ruess. I even had a copy of *Ecodefense: A Field Guide to Monkeywrenching*, which probably put me on some FBI watch list. I often fantasized about some cataclysm prompting me to vanish behind the Slickrock Curtain, a la Ruess, the young man who headed into the canyons of the Escalante River drainage in the 1930s and never returned. In my fantasy I would one day reemerge as a stronger, more confident human being who had somehow managed to write several pseudonymous novels while feeding off of lizards in the bottom of a canyon. My resurrection would so delight and surprise my friends that they'd abandon their lives and join me in canyon country, where we would devise our plot to take down the electrical grid, to blow up the dam, to clear away the debris and help the world start anew.

We turned off of the highway onto a straight gravel road that followed a giant geological fold in the earth. After what seemed like days of driving we finally stopped in the small town of Escalante, went into a little store where a bunch of old dudes were hunkered around a stove, got some Fritos and a healthy serving of stink-eye, and continued down the Hole-in-the-Rock Trail to the trailhead. We shouldered backpacks in the afternoon sun, mine feeling especially heavy, and headed down a sandy wash. I reveled in the newfound warmth, but it wouldn't last. The wash soon hooked up with a deep and curvy canyon with vertical walls that kept the sun's beams at bay and the canyon bottom in a permanent, frigid shadow. At the first creek crossing I broke through the ice and soaked my cheap-ass tennis shoe and cotton tube sock and spent the rest of the hike with a numb foot. When we got to the first night's camp, Whitfield reached for my pack, opened it up, and produced a twelve-pack of Budweiser. He had done it again.

For the next few days we hiked down the bottom of the canyon in what would one day become a popular part of Grand Staircase-Escalante National Monument. But monument designation—and the resulting uptick in visitation—was still a decade away, and solitude was easy prey. Just as I was about to succumb to the chronic, low-level hypothermia that had first set in when we entered the canyon, we reached the canyon's confluence with the Escalante River and suddenly the sunbeams came back, emanating from brilliant blue. Chunks of ice floated lazily past on the murky green stream. I sat and listened to the soft gurgle of the current and soaked up the warmth of the sun. Then Whitfield said we should get to the night's campsite. I looked up at him curiously. He motioned with his head to a flat spot at the base of some cliffs—on the other side of the river. The water was thigh-deep. I was wearing jeans. As I struggled against the icy current, I envisioned my Ruess fantasy coming true, in the worst of ways: the frigid waters swallowing me up and carrying me down to Lake Powell, where my flash-frozen self would sink into the murky depths and the mythical giant catfish that lurk at the bottom of the reservoir would slowly devour my carcass.

I was just another hormone-addled teenager at the time, but I was also geeky and sensitive and sentimental and, though I've never been good at expressing it, full of emotional highs and lows. I was also madly in love, at least as in love as a sixteen-year-old can be, with a girl who was a year older and eons more mature than I. That dramatically changed my experience of that trip. At night, in addition to longing for a warm bed, I longed for J—'s warm mouth and soft skin. At the end of each day, after we set up camp and before night fell, I wrote letters to her, describing the beauty I saw and felt, the way the sandstone glowed far above me, the way a natural stone bridge framed a leafless cottonwood and, behind it, a burnished streak of desert varnish. I learned from those letters that, as much as I wanted to think of the desert as my metaphorical lover, my feelings for the desert were only complete when I was sharing them with someone else. But I also learned that the desert provided a bridge of sorts between me and other people, a medium through which I could express my emotions and thoughts and feelings. I learned both the power of words and their inadequacy.

On the last morning of that long trip in Escalante country, I awoke in the dark-blue light of dawn, and as I looked up at the canyon walls I noticed a break in the stone where a person could make it to the top. I got up, stuck my little notebook and a pen in my pocket, and started climbing. The top part of the climb was on a ramp of slickrock, which led to a sea of slickrock, pocked by potholes, hundreds of them. Navajo Mountain loomed to the southeast. A little more than a century earlier, just about a dozen miles from where I sat, members of the Church of Jesus Christ of Latter-day Saints' Hole-in-the-Rock expedition would gaze out trepidatiously on the same scene. Elizabeth M. Decker was one of the expedition members and described what she saw, writing, "It's the roughest country you or anybody else has ever seen; it's nothing in the world but rocks and holes, hills, and hollows." And a decade after I sat there those same lands would become the epicenter of the nasty and ever-escalating fight over how best to manage public lands.

All I could see and feel at that moment, however, was a beauty so overwhelming that it threatened to swallow me up, a beauty that blotted out the cold and struggle of the previous few days and the adolescent angst and the worries about the future. Instead of writing anything down, I simply cherished the sun's warmth, held it in, sat down on the stone, and was still.

I felt so much, understood so little.

On day six, we ran out of food, save for a few stalks of celery, a can of Vienna sausages, a tin of peanut brittle, and a box of freeze-dried potato-pancake mix. The powdered mix was supposed to be combined with eggs, flour, and oil to make it palatable, none of which we had. So, for the final night's supper and the next morning's breakfast, my father the gourmand combined celery, potato-powder, and "sausages" in a pot and warmed it over the fire. Thankfully, he left out the peanut brittle. The result was an insipid yet strangely rubbery and gelatinous gruel that positively slid down the throat—and not in a good way.

I choked it down with the knowledge that we'd soon be back out in the world of cheeseburgers and a warm bed. After breakfast on New Year's Eve we packed up and speed-hiked back up the canyon towards the truck. We stopped for a lunch of peanut brittle, our only remaining food, and as we savored the sweet crunchiness Whitfield proposed extending the trip by a few days. My dad was on board. They turned expectantly toward me. I broke down in tears, all the misery of the cold and my soaking socks and my sore shoulders and sleepless nights coming out in a torrent of sobs. They thought that was kind of funny, but they relented and we made it back to the truck and I rode home in the cab, triumphant, secondhand smoke be damned.

I'VE LONG HAD A STRANGE RELATIONSHIP WITH THE MORMON religion, formally known as the Church of Jesus Christ of Latter-day Saints. I'm an atheist, for starters. That's just how I was brought up. Religion was something other families had, and that we didn't—like a car that didn't regularly break down or a color television or a warm sleeping bag or vacations to seaside resorts. So all religious sects, including Mormonism, have always seemed a bit foreign to me. I like to think that gives me a clearer view because I lack the usual biases against Mormonism that tend to plague members of other Christian denominations. That Joseph Smith discovered the golden tablets in his well while using a top hat to "dowse" for gold is pretty weird, sure, but no more so than burning bushes and parting seas and turning water into wine. That Utah is a borderline theocracy is troubling because it violates the separation of church and state, but I don't believe it would be any better if 95 percent of the state legislators were, say, devout Baptists or Catholics, rather than Mormons.

As foreign as Mormonism may be to me, it also is a familiar, given how prevalent it is in the region where I grew up. I have aunts and cousins who are members of the LDS Church, and rumor has it that my father briefly converted to Mormonism in his youth, although rumor also has it that he did so only because he was in love with a Mormon girl. I can't help but wonder if his conversion also stemmed from the fact that Brigham Young chose the place that is now Utah to be the promised land, not because of the natural resources, not because of the riches that lay in the hills, but because of something less tangible and yet more real. Admittedly, I may be making this up. Still, I like to imagine that Young was drawn by the mysterious quality of light and illusion that characterizes the Great Salt Lake, or something even more mysterious, something akin to what I felt that morning on that Escalante trip on that sea of stone: a feeling of wholeness, of grounding, of tranquility.

There are those who argue that the Sagebrush Rebellion is rooted in Latter-day Saint theology. The ranks of the rebellion are rife with members of the church, and Cliven Bundy—the scofflaw rancher who has emerged as a figurehead of the latest anti-federal land management insurgency—counts as his influencers W. Cleon Skousen, an extreme right-wing pontificator and Mormon fundamentalist. One of the lieutenants of the 2016 armed takeover of the Malheur National Wildlife Refuge in Oregon called himself Captain Moroni, after the angel who guards the golden plates on which the Book of Mormon was written. And when Brigham Young and his followers from the Church of Jesus Christ of Latter-day Saints came over the Wasatch Mountains and into the Salt Lake Valley, declaring it the Promised Land, it looked a lot like the white colonization that was occurring all over the region at the time: an invasion by hostile outsiders; the removal, by force or the threat thereof, of the Indigenous inhabitants; and the subsequent occupation of stolen land.

And yet, Young's motivations were far different than those of the founding fathers of most other communities in the region, communities whose entire existence rested upon the presence of minerals in the nearby mountains, timber in the forests, or water and fertile soil on the plains. For the most part, the white settlement of the West was driven by greed for natural resources and the riches they could bring. Young, on the other hand, sought sanctuary where his people could find relief from intense and often violent religious persecution, and he sought a homeland in which their church could grow and prosper. Young would instruct his followers to exploit the resources that were so abundant, not for profit, but only to make the desert—and their nascent society—"blossom like a rose."

Young, like his martyred predecessor Joseph Smith, bristled

against not only greed, but also the pathological individualism that infected the gold and silver rush towns of the West. In so doing they were following the preachings of Samuel the Lamanite who, in the Book of Mormon, tells the Nephites of Zarahemla that the Lord said "ye are cursed because of your riches, and also are your riches cursed because ye have set your hearts upon them." Capitalism in general belonged in the category of the cursed, and the invasion of the western United States was a veritable orgy of government-sponsored capitalism—and the various iterations of the Sagebrush Rebellion were the love children of that greed-fest. In 1848, Young famously extolled: "There shall be no private ownership of the streams that come out of the canyons, nor the timber that grows on the hills. These belong to the people; all the people." In response to the rise of the Gilded Age, Young founded the School of the Prophets, which, writes Leonard J. Arrington, the late LDS Church historian, "countered an energetic and powerful laissez-faire capitalism with a vigorous, well-organized, socially minded and theocratically directed program of economic action." The school funded the creation of cooperative furniture and wool manufacturing, along with other businesses, to reduce reliance on eastern imports. It also created the Zion's Cooperative Mercantile Institution and instituted uniform pricing controls to minimize competition among Mormon merchants.

The Utah Territory successfully resisted becoming a mineral colony for the eastern industrialists, and the school disbanded in 1872. A year later the Jay Cooke & Company bank—one of the big backers of the railroads that were expanding their empire and enabling colonization—collapsed, validating Young's anti-capitalist approach. Other banks toppled like dominos, foreclosures were rampant, and the Panic of 1873 swept the nation and the world, leading to one of the worst depressions in history. Utah's mining towns were hit hard. But Brigham City, a settlement of about fifteen hundred people, actually thrived. It had organized a mercantile cooperative in the pre-railroad days, and, by the time the Panic hit, it had expanded into a major manufacturing enterprise mostly owned by the worker/shareholders. It built houses for the poor and widows and provided labor for jobless drifters, and its leaders instituted central economic and land-use planning and zoning, dictating where houses and factories and public transit should be built.

Novelist Edward Bellamy visited Brigham City after the Panic, a visit that inspired *Looking Backward*, his 1888 Utopian novel set in a socialist Boston in the year 2000, when greed and capitalism are no more.

Young didn't need to wait a century for Utopia. In the aftermath of the Panic of 1873, he set about spreading the Brigham City model, combined with an element of Joseph Smith's Order of Enoch wealth-redistribution plan, across Deseret. He started in St. George and worked his way northward, converting communities to the Order as he went. Each adopted the Order in its own way, but the core principles were the same: communalism, cooperation, and equal distribution of wealth.[4] That this occurred just after the *Communist Manifesto*, by Karl Marx and Friedrich Engels, had been published in America bears noting, if nothing else. The language in the St. George United Order Constitution gives a sense of what Young was trying to do, mentioning the struggle between capital and labor, bemoaning the "oppression of monied monopolies," and railing against "a growing…spirit for extravagant speculation and over-reaching the legitimate bounds of the credit system; resulting in financial panic and bankruptcies."

"It was clear to all that the United Order," writes Arrington in *Great Basin Kingdom*, "was an attempt to retard, and, if possible, to prevent the development of a market-oriented economy dependent on extensive importation and exportation." About two hundred communities implemented the Order. Some, like Brigham City, took a moderate approach. Others were quite radical. Young may not have been a Marxist—maybe he'd never heard of the guy—but he certainly incorporated a lot of ideas that jived with Marx's into his United Order. If he wasn't an outright communist, Young was certainly a communalist and opposed to free-market capitalism.

Young's relationship with the Indigenous peoples who called Utah home was more complicated.[5] He opposed the federal government's policy of removal, and, in 1850, he wrote: "We shoot them down as we would a dog. Now, this is all wrong, and not in harmony with the spirit of Christianity." Young stated that he preferred peacefully coexisting with the various tribes of the Utah Territory, yet he and his followers were at the same time taking advantage of the federal approach by occupying lands from which the original inhabitants had been forcibly removed. The church also sent missionaries to try to convert tribal members to Mormonism. While other Christian denominations have done the same, the LDS Church has been especially vigorous, and Young was willing to go to extremes to broaden the flock. The enslavement of Indigenous peoples by New Mexicans was still happening at the time, and in 1851 Young wrote a letter to his acolytes in Iron County, Utah, which then stretched all the way across the bottom of the state, advising them "to buy up the Lamanite children as fast as they could, and educate them and teach them the Gospel, so that not many generations would pass ere they would become a white and delightsome people." In 1852, the Utah Territorial Legislative Assembly passed a law making it legal for Utah families to "adopt," or purchase, women and children who had been kidnapped and forced into slavery, thereby giving them access to convert them to the Mormon faith. A more benevolent version of this practice would be repeated with the Indian Student Placement Program instituted after World War II, when the church would convince Navajo parents to send their children to live with Mormon families so that the children could attend better schools—and be brought into the church.

By the time of Young's death in 1877, his acolytes had established dozens of colonies across Deseret to propagate the faith and bring forth the bounties of the earth, with the most prized region being that of "Dixie" in southwest Utah and the communities of St. George, Cedar City, and Parowan. Yet on the maps of Deseret, the southeast corner of the state remained empty. An attempt to colonize the Colorado River Valley at Moab was cut short when the local band of Utes made it clear that the settlers were not welcome, and the rest of the landscape was deemed undesirable. But in the decade prior to Young's death, a hardrock mining boom had erupted in the ancient remnants of volcanoes in the San Juan Mountains of southwestern Colorado, and farmers and ranchers and merchants had followed to supply the burgeoning population. The wave was creeping westward—livestock operators had already begun driving their huge herds into San Juan County. This encroachment pushed the Ute and Navajo people off of their Colorado homelands and into Utah.

If they didn't act quickly, church leaders believed that the wave of humanity and greed would soon seep into Dixie. So they called on 250 churchgoers to pack up their wagons, tether up their cattle, and go east to colonize the southeastern corner of Utah. They were sent not to make the desert bloom, but to serve as human shields to buffer the colonies of Dixie against the potentially hostile Indigenous peoples and the greed of the cattlemen and gold miners.

In the spring of 1879 an advance party led by Platte D. Lyman headed south from Cedar City into what is now Arizona, crossed the Colorado River at Lee's Ferry, and continued onto the Navajo Nation before turning back to the north and ending up at what they called Allan Bottom, near where Montezuma Creek meets the San Juan River, and which Albert R. Lyman, Platte's son, later described as such: "Coming down from those heated sand stretches to the river bank, they recognized in the cool stream and spreading cottonwoods, the first real glimpse of what they had hunted during six long weeks, and all hands fell to fishing. The catch was of white salmon (Colorado pikeminnow), and one weighed twenty pounds." They established an outpost near where the Gentile Peter Shirts had already been living for a few years, "a lone hermit, subsisting on fish, and wearing vestiges of clothing which had been." The Navajo people they encountered had not been pleased with their incursion on their land, so the advance party returned to Cedar City by way of the Old Spanish Trail, going through Moab and what is now Green River before heading south again. Taking the larger party on that route would have been the most logical decision, albeit longer in distance. Instead, they decided to take what they thought would be a more direct, if unknown, path. It was supposed to be a six-week jaunt, which would have delivered them to Montezuma Creek while temperatures were cool but before winter had set in. It wouldn't work out that way.

THE SUN SHONE BRIGHTLY ELEVEN DECADES LATER WHEN MY two companions and I dropped into the canyon as if to go to Moon House, a Puebloan cliff dwelling built in the 1200s with a spectacular pictograph—rock art that was painted rather than chipped into the rock—that seems to show lunar cycles and perhaps a lunar eclipse. Had I written about the trip at the time, I wouldn't have mentioned Moon House, nor given anything resembling specific directions to it. It was still relatively unknown, and I had adopted my father's self-imposed prohibition against writing about "secret" places except in vague terms so as to keep them kind of secret. Not that it would have mattered, really, since there was no internet and I had no platform on which I might reveal the place. Nor was Moon House all that secret at the time. All the locals knew about it and weren't shy about directing visitors to the spectacular site. The artifacts that once sat in the pueblo's rooms and blanketed the ground outside had long before been pilfered and pocketed and carted away.

Now a Google search of "Moon House" will turn up hundreds of hits, detailed directions to it, and even YouTube videos. The site is now so popular that the BLM has instituted a permitting system and a twenty-person-per-day visitor limit. In 2016, during the drive to get Moon House and nearly two million acres around it protected as a national monument, Josh Ewing, the executive director of Friends of Cedar Mesa, told me: "A lot of people wish we had a time machine, and could go back twenty years. For a long time, the strategy of protection was to keep it a secret. The internet came. No more." Exactly. My ban on revealing secret places in my writing stands, but Moon House is secret no more.

When we passed by the pueblo thirty years ago, however, we saw no one. We decided not to visit the dwelling yet, because we needed to get camp set up before dark. So we continued down canyon until we found the perfect spot: a sort of stone cul-de-sac that sat a couple hundred feet above the canyon bottom and another couple hundred feet below the canyon rim. It was south-facing, protected from the wind, and offered some overhangs under which we could huddle if necessary.

We spent the next few days exploring, playing hacky sack, eating, and trying to stay warm. Craig and Dave were on winter break, but I was taking what would have been my sophomore year of college off—a gap year, as the kids call it these days—to try to figure out what I wanted to do with my life. I didn't figure it out then, and I still haven't figured it out now. Dave told us about bands he had seen in Olympia, Washington, and about the hippies at his college. We talked about the escalating tensions in the Middle East. The first Iraq War would break out a month or so later, the one with its own brand and slogans and marketing campaigns, as though it were a video game, and we were anxious about it. We had all been born during the Vietnam War. And we came of age during the Reagan era, and we all despised

just about everything that the era had produced: the conspic-
uous greed, injustice, imperialism, warmongering, dismantling
of the nation's safety nets, the celebritization of some cheeseball
millionaire named Donald Trump. We never could have guessed
that Reagan was only the beginning of the slide of America into
a populist and inequitable cesspool run by corporations. What
we did know is that if war did break out, and if the draft were
reinstated, we wouldn't go. Maybe we'd head down to Mexico, or
just hunker down out here, behind the Slickrock Curtain, until
it all blew over.

Daytime temperatures were in the forties but felt warmer in
the sun. Nighttime temps were frigid at best. I had long before
graduated from the TG&Y sleeping bag, but only to one from
Kmart, which continued to be woefully inadequate for the long
winter nights. I refused to sleep in tents. I told myself, and others, that it was on principle, that a tent formed a barrier between
me and the sky and the earth. Really it was because I was too
damned poor to afford a tent that was light enough to carry on
a multiday backpacking trip. So, instead, I'd put my sleeping bag
on a cheap foam pad and cover myself with a tarp to keep the
moisture out and a little bit more of the warmth in. When we first
started backpacking together in junior high school, my friends
usually brought tents. But I guess my stubborn stupidity rubbed
off on them, because by this time they were also equipped inad-
equately.

As a result, night became not a time to sleep and dream and
rest, but to endure. Days were oriented around that goal. We
hiked, climbed, and played hard from morning until sundown,
in hopes of wearing ourselves out and increasing the chances
that we'd pass out from exhaustion after we dared to crawl into
our sleeping bags. For dinner, we'd eat a lot of hot food, usually
consisting primarily of complex carbohydrates (ramen noodles).
Then we'd go to bed and shiver and pray for sleep, or for morning's light, whichever came first. Comfort came in the form of a

sky so dark and stars so densely packed together that there was nary any space between them. There are few places on the planet where light pollution is almost nonexistent. Some of those places can be found on Cedar Mesa.

On day three we woke up once again to blue sky and cold that eased once the sun blasted our camp. We did a morning hike, came back to camp, and ate some lunch, barely noticing the wispy sheet of clouds that drifted across the blue. Paradoxically, the clouds brought warmth, and the temperature rose a good ten or fifteen degrees, enough so that we could gleefully shed our jackets and heavy sweaters as we played hacky sack, ending up in shirtsleeves by late afternoon. It was so crazy that Dave, always the photographer of our expeditions, took a picture to remember it by. This was before cell phones and digital cameras and Instagram. In more recent times Dave would have climbed up onto the mesa top in order to get reception so he could post the picture to social media to gloatingly show our friends how damned lucky we were. Maybe he would have checked the weather forecast in the process, and maybe we would have hastily fled so as to avoid the coming tempest.

It was our last night, so we had a big dinner, using up as much of the remaining ramen as we could. We were so tired from a string of sleepless nights, and it was still so warm, relatively, that we didn't even bother washing our dishes or organizing camp, as we usually did after dinner. We just left the stove and our dishes and our food lying out on the rocks. Then we turned in, I under one overhang where I thought the radiant heat from the rocks would be strongest, and Dave and Craig under another. For the first night that trip I wasn't shivering or even praying for sleep: it came on its own, the bliss of oblivion softly overtaking me.

ONCE ONE HAS FINISHED SCOFFING AT THEIR FOOLHARDINESS, it's difficult not to admire the strength of the faith of the 250 acolytes that assembled at the town of Escalante in the autumn of 1879 and set out across an ocean of sandstone simply because they had been called to do so by the president of the church. The various members of the party converged near Forty Mile Spring, not far from where my dad and Whitfield and I would embark on our winter journey a century later. When the expedition members realized that they had reached the end of the road and were expected to travel into what at the time was still a big blank spot on the maps, many wanted to turn back. And when Platte D. Lyman returned from an advance scouting mission to report that crossing the Colorado River would be difficult, if not impossible, and that the going would get even worse after that, and that "there is no use of this company undertaking to get to San Juan this way," it seemed that this route was a no-go. But by then the mountains behind them were snowed in, making retreat difficult, and their cattle had eaten all the grass along the way, so would lack forage for any return trip—which, perhaps, should have been a sign that this country wasn't made for cattle grazing. And when their leader, President Silas S. Smith, declared that the mission would continue, everyone allegedly celebrated and "all was good cheer and hustle," according to a diary entry from the trip, and the group bellowed a hymn about the burning fire of God's spirit. How many of them were tempted to turn back, or just to stay put, has been lost to time. In any event, no one abandoned ship and, in early December, they set out with eighty-three wagons and more than twelve hundred head of livestock into what for them was the great unknown.

Even the first leg of the trip, a mere twelve miles as the crow flies, was rough and followed a curvy path across sandy dunes and around—and sometimes through—petrified sand dunes. Then they reached the two-thousand-foot-deep gorge of the Colorado River and what to any rational human being would have been the end of the road. These folks, however, were not guided by reason, but rather were impelled forth by something else entirely, call it devotion or delusion. Instead of turning back, they began the arduous process of building a road where no road should go. It was called Hole-in-the-Rock for the narrow chasm that opened up into a steep ramp down to the river. The entire journey was supposed to take six weeks. It would take that same amount of time and then some to complete the construction project. Again, no one got so bored of waiting that they turned back, and somehow the crew was able to get all of the wagons down to the river in one piece with only minor human casualties, though they may have lost a cow or two.

When Platte Lyman had climbed down to the river at the same point several weeks earlier, he had found a sort of Eden of stone and water, one that many years later would be inundated by the stagnant waters of Lake Powell. The current there was "sluggish and the water milky but of a good taste. The willow on the bank are still leaved in green.[6] One of the boys caught a fine fish called white salmon large enough for our breakfast and dinner." In all likelihood this was a Colorado pikeminnow. It's the largest minnow in North America, possibly the world, it evolved into its current form some three million years ago, and it can grow to be six feet long and weigh over one hundred pounds. During Lyman's time pikeminnow were abundant in the Colorado and its tributaries. But habitat degradation, dams, pollution, and overfishing have caused numbers to dwindle, and today they are listed as an endangered species.

The wagons were ferried, two by two, across the murky current, and the San Juan Expedition became the Hole-in-the-Rock Expedition. It was January, and what would turn out to be a very long winter canyon camping trip had only just begun.

I SLEPT DEEPLY AT LAST ON THAT FINAL NIGHT OF THE MOON House trip. And I dreamed. I dreamed I was in a supermarket, and I was walking up and down the aisles looking for something that would warm my cold feet. I went through the produce section and picked up an orange and realized it would not do the trick. I went down the cereal aisle and examined the ingredients of Lucky Charms. No dice. I tried the canned beans next. Finally I woke up to utter darkness. The flickery bright lights of the supermarket were gone. The produce was gone and the Lucky Charms. All that remained of the dream were my cold feet, even though the rest of my body was cozy and warm. And then there was the sound of water dripping very close to me. My feet were not just cold, it soon became clear, but also wet, along with the lower third of my sleeping bag—the part that stuck out from my little overhang. I found my flashlight and turned it on.

"Oh, shit," I muttered quietly. Snow fell in big flakes, and already the ground was covered with at least six inches of the stuff. I didn't have a watch, so I had no idea what time it was. I curled up into a fetal position so that my feet would be in the warm and dry part of my bag and clenched my eyes shut and tried to wish it all away. It did not work. After thirty minutes, maybe an hour, I heard Dave call out in a whimper. I yelled back, relieved to have someone awake with whom to share my misery. I got up, put my clothes on, stuffed my soaking, heavy sleeping bag into the stuff sack, and trudged through the snow to our kitchen. Everything was buried, the stove, our dishes, everything. We dug out what we could find and hauled it up to an alcove above the camp where we were able to get out of the snow and cook up our last three ramen packets while we waited for dawn's light and strategized our escape.

We determined, for reasons which I cannot remember, that the route we had taken to get from the car to our camp would be impassible in those conditions. Instead, we would climb straight up to the canyon rim, walk up the canyon to where it got shallow, cross, then double back to the car. We had gone up and down the sandstone benches that made up the canyon walls in the preceding days, so we weren't concerned about the technical difficulty. After all, it was just a bit of snow.

Soon after we started, however, we realized that it was not just a bit of snow. When the initial wave of the storm hit sometime at night, the stone was still warm from soaking up the sun all day. That meant that the first flakes melted upon landing and cooled off the stone enough that the ensuing flakes stuck and piled up on top of the moisture. Then that lower layer of liquid froze, creating a thin and very slippery layer of ice between stone and what was by now a foot or more of snow. What should have been a fairly straightforward friction-scramble turned into a treacherous expedition that involved hauling our full weight, plus that of our sodden backpacks, up a series of cliffs using only shrubs as handholds. Several near-death experiences later we clawed our way onto the rim where we were greeted with a parking-lot-flat plain of snow-covered sandstone. Having survived our own mini-Hole-in-the-Rock moment we gave each other gloved high-fives.

"Onward," I declared, setting off into the snow with green-chile enchiladas dancing in my head. I took one step, then another, but something was wrong with my legs or the earth or both, for the ground had tilted away from my foot, which landed on nothing but air. Soon the snow-covered stone plain rushed toward me and smacked me in the face. I lay in the snow, the weight of my pack holding me down, for a good fifteen seconds before looking up, only to see Craig repeat my actions. We had entered some bizarro world where gravity's pull was variable across space. In fact, the sandstone we were walking on was not flat at all, but undulated wildly due to the potholes all over the rim's surface, and the snow and the flat light rendered those undulations invisible. We were faced with a choice: either we could crawl back to the car, or stagger like drunks making their way across a ship's deck. We painfully chose the latter and lurched and teetered across whiteness, the snow dampening the sound of our anguished cries.

We didn't wear watches, cell phones were still the thing of science fiction, and the thick blanket of clouds had devoured the sun, wiping out its place in the sky, so we had no idea how many hours our journey took, nor how many hours of daylight remained. As we spied the red Trooper through the heavily falling snow, however, we knew that we had made it. I let the vision of a cheeseburger, this time with hot, greasy fries, fill my brain again. If I drooled, and I might have, the saliva would have iced up on my chin. When the engine fired up on the first try, we celebrated yet again. The celebration ceased shortly thereafter when we discovered that the two-track we had taken to the trailhead had vanished, the snow having totally obscured the unmarked path that wound through the trees. We may have followed the two-track back out, and we may have not. If it's the latter, I do hope that the snow buffered the impact the tires might have had on any cryptobiotic soil.

Obstacles that were hardly noticeable on the way in, before the blizzard, had become magnified by the snow. Take, for example, the barrow ditch we had to cross to get from the relatively established Snow Flats/Hole-in-the-Rock road onto the little two-track. On the way in, Craig just drove through it, probably not even bothering with four-wheel drive. On the way out, the front wheels made it through the ditch, but the back ones started spinning wildly, and the angle of the car took the weight away from the front wheels, causing them to spin as well. My shitty foam sleeping pad finally had a purpose. We put it under one of the back wheels, and sagebrush under the remaining three, then Dave and I pushed while Craig piloted the beast onto the road, where the tires regained traction. No sooner had Dave and I gotten comfortable, however, than the vehicle slowed to a stop, the tires spinning futilely once again. Craig killed the engine. All three of us, perplexed, climbed slowly out of the vehicle, trying to comprehend what had stifled our forward progress. The snow on the road was so deep that the Trooper's front bumper acted like a plow, pushing the snow until it piled up enough to stop the vehicle. We weren't about to surrender and, instead, developed a routine: We kicked the snow away from in front of the bumper, and while Craig drove, Dave and I pushed the Trooper from behind to get it going again. Once the vehicle was moving, we'd sprint around the vehicle and jump into the back seat. Thirty seconds or a minute later, the car would slow to a stop, and we'd jump out and start the cycle all over again.

It was frustrating and exhausting in two senses of the word: it was tiring *and* Dave and I were breathing in large quantities of exhaust. Each time I jumped back into the truck I grew progressively more lightheaded from fatigue and carbon monoxide inhalation. Which is perhaps why I might have only giggled deliriously rather than burst out crying when the Trooper, at the place where the road gets roughest and steepest, started spinning its wheels and fishtailing before sliding backwards off the road and into the ditch. In retrospect, I think we could have gotten the vehicle moving again with a little ingenuity and a lot of muscle. But by then, I think we figured: What's the point? Walking surely would be faster than all of this stop, start, exhaust-huffing nonsense.

We consolidated all of our remaining food—half of a box of Wheatena-brand gruel, a couple ramen packets, and a pack of peppermint chewing gum—along with a bottle of water, the camp stove, and a sodden sleeping bag, and put it all into one backpack and came up with a plan: Craig, who was the freshest among us, since he'd been driving, not pushing, would be our advance scout, breaking trail and plunging forward to the highway, where he'd flag down a passing motorist and have them wait for us. Dave and I would follow, slowly, trading off the heavy pack as we went. If we reached the highway and saw no cars, we would continue up the highway to the Kane Gulch Ranger

Station, which was closed for the season. What we'd do next was up in the air, but the possibilities included breaking into the ranger trailer where perhaps we could find enough warmth to keep us alive through the night. We'd worry about the consequences of breaking and entering into federal property if we survived.

Snow was still falling intensely when we set out on foot, but we were in high spirits, all things considered, thanks to having a plan. Although the going had been tedious, we did cover some ground in the car, leaving us just three or four miles to the highway, and another five miles or so to the ranger station. That would be easy, we thought, despite the fact that we were going on a good eight hours without caloric intake. In the beginning, the going wasn't too bad. The snow was maybe two feet deep at the worst spots, and the cloud cover kept the temperature high enough so that our extremities did not get frostbite. And then things took a change for the worse.

AFTER BLASTING AND ROAD-BUILDING THEIR WAY DOWN INTO the Colorado River gorge, and ferrying all eighty-three wagons across the mercifully low winter waters, the Hole-in-the-Rockers set out into what for them was the great unknown—the same country in which young Everett Ruess would descend into and never return from a half-century later and that would threaten to similarly devour my friends and me a half-century after that. When they set out on this route, they thought it would be more direct, and perhaps warmer and less snowy, than the northern route. They were wrong on both counts. In this country, there are no direct routes. There are simply too many deep canyons, wrinkles, landforms, spires, ridges, mesas, valleys, rivers, cliffs, and sundry other obstacles standing in the way, particularly when you're traveling in a caravan of dozens of big, heavy, unwieldy wagons. Platte Lyman described it thusly: "The country here is almost entirely solid sand rock, high hills and mountains cut all to pieces by deep gulches which are in many places altogether impassible. It is certainly the worst country I ever saw."

Take Grand Gulch, which reaches from just below the Bears Ears down to the San Juan River. It's a distance of thirty miles or so, but the canyon is so windy, doubles back on itself so many times, like a large intestine, that if one were to stretch it out into a straight line it would at least double, if not triple, that length.

While the expedition waited for the "road" to be constructed at Hole-in-the-Rock, a group of four men went ahead to find a route. Unburdened by the wagons and the families and provisions, they anticipated a quick and relatively easy journey. Instead, they found their way blocked by the various crinkles in the landscape, forcing them to backtrack and to spend an inordinate amount of time finding their way around the obstacles, the biggest being Grand Gulch. There was no feasible way to get people, cattle, and wagons through the gorge, so they had to go around it as their provisions were stretched thin. Two days before Christmas they found themselves in the midst of a raging blizzard somewhere near the south flank of Elk Ridge. They had never been to this part of the country, the maps of this area remained blank, and any recognizable landmarks had been blotted out by the storm. Their horses' hooves bogged down in the sticky mud, then in deeper and deeper snow. On Christmas Eve, one of the scouts, George B. Hobbs, wrote, "We had cooked the last food we had, consisting of a slap jack baked in a frying pan and about one inch thick." And the next day, things looked equally grim: "It was Christmas Day 1879, which found us on the side of the Elk Mountain without food, in the midst of a piercing cold…It surely looked like our bones would bleach not far from that point."

***

As we trudged through the snow in the days before Christmas in 1990, I kind of knew how Hobbs felt. That may sound like a stretch. After all, my buddies and I were doing this for "fun," not because some church leader ordered us to do it, we had a lot less ground to cover, and we weren't lost. Still, we were not too far away from a bleached-bones scenario.

The Snow Flat Road and the Hole-in-the-Rock Trail that we followed skirts a one-mile-by-one-mile square of private land as it makes its way across Cedar Mesa. From property line to property line, the entire square, save for the southwest corner, has been chained. Chaining is a particularly barbaric method of clearing a juniper and piñon forest. Two bulldozers drive side by side, maybe one hundred yards from each other, dragging a huge chain between them. The chain topples and uproots and tramples all in its path, whether it's the micro-world of cryptobiotic crust, tiny cacti, mariposa lilies, or centuries-old juniper trees. The purpose: to turn a living, vibrant, diverse forest into a pasture for cattle grazing. The aftermath, however, is not a green field where cows munch happily away, but a dusty plain that looks as if it was the site of an incendiary device detonation—and it remains that way for years, even decades, afterward, the grazing itself serving to keep the wound from healing. These apocalyptic parcels are neither uncommon nor confined to private or even state land.

On that December day, the chained area was a big, uninterrupted field of white spreading out to our left. Before we reached the area, as we walked through the forest, the snow had been shin- to knee-deep. But the chaining had destroyed the natural snow fence of the trees, allowing the wind to blow the snow from the chained area onto the road, where it drifted up against the trees on our right side. That meant that the snow, for that mile-long stretch, was thigh- to waist-deep, the pack was now saturated and heavy, and we were expending huge amounts of energy just to take each step forward. The snow had stopped falling, and the clouds were giving way to pale blue skies, which allowed us to finally see the sun just as it dipped toward the western horizon. We could literally feel the temperature dropping from somewhere near thirty degrees Fahrenheit down into the teens and, finally, as the sun disappeared, to below-zero frostbite territory.

One of the Hole-in-the-Rock party members later described that trip as "all harmony and hustle." I would not characterize our Hole-in-the-Rock Trail trip that way. We sure as hell weren't hustling, and the only harmonizing we were doing was when Dave and I would cry out various expletives in unison, followed by a verbal description of whatever vision of food had come into our heads—smothered green-chile burritos, French fries, pizza—followed by wailed whimpering. We were out of water. We hadn't eaten anything since daybreak, just prior to beginning our journey, and now, at day's end, we were reduced to pouring dry Wheatena, which had the consistency of sawdust with less flavor, onto our tongues and trying to wash it down with snow. We chewed our last pieces of gum and then swallowed them, desperate for whatever calories we could get.

As darkness fell, Craig's form, a quarter mile ahead of us, faded. It occurred to me that no one knew where we were. I had told my dad that we were going to Utah. He knew that meant somewhere in San Juan County, but San Juan County is as big as New Jersey—which is meaningless to me, since I've never been to New Jersey. He probably figured that his son was too intelligent to venture eight miles down an unimproved dirt road and backpack another few miles into an obscure canyon, so he wouldn't think to send a rescue party this way to find us. He figured wrong. Bleached bones, indeed.

DARKNESS HAD FALLEN BY THE TIME DAVE AND I REACHED THE highway. One lane of the road had been plowed, which lifted our spirits somewhat, but the fact that there were no tire tracks besides the plow's hurled us back into despair. The chances that anyone would choose to drive down the one lane of this road on a cold winter's night were almost zero. Craig was nowhere to be seen, but we could see his footprints leading north, to Plan B, as in Breaking into federal property and possibly setting it aflame. We followed. By now we didn't even have the strength to whimper.

After a half hour or so, we saw our shadows spread ahead of us on the glazed ice. For a split second I thought it was a hallucination. We both spun around. A pickup truck was behind us, slowing to a stop. "Get in," the driver said, and we complied. As I opened the passenger door I noticed that it was a BLM truck. The driver was a ranger. My father had called the Monticello Field Office and told them that we were out here somewhere and asked them to keep an eye out.

We drove up the road for about a half mile before encountering the tall, dark figure of Craig. The ranger drove within fifteen feet of him, the headlights on bright. But Craig, possibly hypothermic, possibly so determined to reach the destination, was oblivious. Finally, the ranger beeped the horn and Craig lurched to the side and spun around, his eyes as big as saucers.

On Christmas Day, 1879, Hobbs and party noticed a pyramid-shaped hill and climbed to the top. From there they could finally see recognizable landmarks, the Abajo Mountains and Comb Ridge, and they knew that they would survive to reach their destination. They called the hill Salvation Knoll.

Our Salvation Knoll turned out to be a ranger driving a Ford Ranger, something we probably laughed at since we were delirious and maybe close to death. The ranger drove us into Blanding and dropped us off in front of a hotel. I was a little out of it, but I think it was the Elk Ridge Cafe and Hotel, which had been owned by the notorious Cal Black up until his death several months prior. At this point we were still on hypothermia's edge. Our clothes had been soaked through with snow and sweat before the temperature crashed and froze them, and the truck's heater had not quite thawed us out. We didn't have enough money on us for a hotel room, so we asked, shivering and bedraggled, if we could use their phone to call our parents, collect, so we could get a credit card number and, by the way, do you think we could get some food? We got only the stink eye in return, and I suppose I can't blame them. At the time, the public land wars, even in San Juan County, had reached a lull, what with instigator Black dead and George Bush Sr. in the White House. Still, we were young, Colorado, enviro-hippy, atheist college kids who had materialized on a freezing winter's night. We could have been Satanists for all they knew, or liberal backpackers intent on destroying their way of life.

So we told them about our trek and the snow and the car sliding off the Snow Flat Road and our long walk and the BLM ranger picking us up, and maybe when we said BLM they flinched a little, but by then it didn't matter because we had told them a tale of woe and pleaded for help. And when it sunk in that we were in trouble and that they had the means to help this trio of pathetic, wet, stinky, frozen dirtbags, their collective demeanor shifted dramatically. Clearly they were the kinds of people who were inclined to lend a hand to those in need. I also like to think that they were swayed by the fact that our troubles played out on the Hole-in-the-Rock Trail, near where their ancestors had faced their own travails. They let us make phone calls, rented us a warm room, and even reopened the cafe and served us red-chile enchiladas, which was pretty much exactly what we had been craving.

And as we sat under the glare of fluorescent lights in the carpeted restaurant area, our plates stacked high with much-needed calories, I felt something welling up within me. It might have been gratitude, but then, it also might have been religion.

CHAPTER SEVEN

SAGEBRUSH REBELLION: ROOTS

THE HOLE-IN-THE-ROCK TRAIL BECAME AN ICON OF Mormon lore, a symbol every bit as significant as the more famous Mormon Trail, wrote Allan Kent Powell in a 1983 history of San Juan County, because it "illustrates the pioneer ability to conquer, to succeed, and to endure to the end—essential elements in any scheme to colonize and hold the deserts, valleys, and mountains of this vast land." The expedition had taken on some of the most rugged and remote terrain in the nation, its members drilled, chiseled, and blasted a wagon road into a cliff, and they suffered through an interminable winter camping trip and came out on the other end somewhat intact. They believed that gave them the right to the land that they had "conquered."

This same sense of entitlement to the public domain would serve as the seed for the movement and creed that would crop up in various forms over the years and, a century later, would be named the Sagebrush Rebellion. And the circumstances and location of the expedition's terminus would serve as the soil in which that seed would sprout.

The Hole-in-the-Rock Expedition was supposed to settle on the banks of the San Juan at its confluence with Montezuma Creek, a stream that gets its start on the east-facing slope of the

Abajo Mountains near Monticello. But they were so exhausted at the end of their journey that they stopped twenty miles short of their destination and established Bluff City, also along the river's edge. Situated at the mouth of Cottonwood Wash, Bluff seems like the most natural place to settle. The fertile river bottom hemmed in by pale-pink cliffs had long drawn people, from the Basketmakers, who built a village of pit houses there around 500 AD, to later generations of Pueblo people who built a thick-walled structure looking over the river, to the Ute, Diné, and Southern Paiute people who continued to gather and trade there even after the Mormon invasion.

Once they chose their location, the members set about to establish and build a more or less self-sufficient village, a small collective of subsistence farmers and craftspeople insulated from the outside world. They would treat the land as if it were empty, a blank slate on which they could impose their collective vision of a Deseret colony. But the land wasn't vacant, and the people who lived there already didn't take too kindly to the presumptuous encroachment. Although there was never any outright war between the Navajo people and the newcomers, there was almost constant tension and frequent skirmishes that occasionally resulted in the loss of life. Another element added to the unease. By the time the Hole-in-the-Rock party reached Bluff, the mesas and highlands of the county already teemed with cattle run by huge concerns and the Gentile cowpokes that watched over them.

Nor was Bluff quite the farm-friendly oasis it appeared to be. Cottonwood Wash only ran intermittently and so was an unreliable source of irrigation. At the outset, that didn't seem to matter—the San Juan River would provide more than enough water to fill the ditches and for watering the crops. Like most desert rivers, however, the San Juan was tempestuous and moody, dirty and mean, and refused to be harnessed or tamed without a fight. It could go from being so dry that one could walk across it and barely get their boots wet to a raging torrent in a matter of hours. It washed out ditches and dams and crops, sometimes even houses. It was almost always silty and brackish and polluted. Upstream towns dumped their sewage, blood and guts from slaughterhouses, trash, mill tailings, and sawdust into the river, most of it eventually making its way down to the little town of Bluff.

It wasn't long before a strain of discontent permeated the little community. "We have been here some nine years, struggling hard to hold and redeem this country," wrote Francis Hammond in the late 1880s, as recounted by Robert S. McPherson in his book *Comb Ridge and Its People*, "standing guard as it were, on the outpost, to protect our more wealthy, populous counties from the raids of the Indians and renegade white men, white renegades being far the worst."

The winter of 1883-1884 was particularly snowy and hard for the settlers and was followed by springtime deluges that carried away fruit trees and corn fields and topsoil and water wheels. That was also the year that President Chester A. Arthur signed an executive order extending the Navajo Reservation into Utah, with the San Juan River serving as its northern border, thereby making Bluff a reservation border town and making skirmishes more likely. It was all too much and proved more daunting even than the grueling Hole-in-the-Rock journey. Within a few years after arriving, nearly all the remaining residents of Bluff yearned to be "released" by church leaders from the mission so they could hightail it to greener pastures.

Church president Erastus Snow and Joseph F. Smith arrived that September to take stock of the situation. Initially they seemed ready to allow the settlers to abandon the mission, but then—perhaps remembering the importance of having a buffer on the Mormon-Gentile borderlands—they changed their tune. They declared that anyone who wanted to leave could go, but those who stayed would be "doubly blessed." Some accepted the challenge and stuck around, others departed. Still others aimed for the middle ground, staying put while also casting about for new, more amenable places within the county to base the mission.

In 1885 Francis Hammond ascended to the presidency of the San Juan Stake.[7] Upon his arrival he assessed the situation and concluded that the ideal of self-sufficiency was untenable, at least in Bluff, where the farmers had failed in their efforts to grow grain and other staples. Meanwhile he saw that the "white rene-gade" ranchers, working for huge operations that ran their cattle across the county's mesas and mountain slopes, did pretty well by fattening up their herds on free, public grass and then driving them to market and making a hefty profit. So Hammond urged his congregation to grow crops for trade in Durango, which by then was a flourishing smelter and mining-supply town. More significantly, he suggested they branch out into ranching, not as individuals, but as a cooperative effort. The result was the Bluff Pool, owned collectively by a good portion of the residents of Bluff, which went about building up its own herds of sheep and cattle, which it turned out on the public domain. "This change from agriculture to livestock," wrote Powell, "meant the abandonment of Brigham Young's home industry-self-sufficiency economic philosophy in favor of an export economy dependent on national markets."

The economic swerve into ranching also placed the San Juan Mission into a new relationship with the public lands and the federal government. The 1862 Homestead Act was created with subsistence farming in mind and allowed a prospective farmer to stake out a 40- to 640-acre claim[8] on the public domain, work it for five years, and then patent[9] it, or take title to the land. It was a buyer-seller arrangement between the federal government and the farmer, even though the land cost the farmer virtually nothing. Once the claim was patented the farmer was a landowner, no longer a tenant on government land, and therefore had no beef with the feds, so to speak.

This setup doesn't work for ranching, however, because homesteads aren't large[10] enough to support even a moderate-sized herd of cattle, especially in the arid West. Unless a rancher was able to buy up several contiguous patented homesteads, he had to run his cows on the public domain for much if not all of the year. Practically speaking that was no problem: the public's grass was free and grazing it a free-for-all. Yet on a symbolic level it put public ranchers into the position of being the federal government's tenants. No individualistic western rancher likes to have the federal government as their landlord; this was especially true for members of the LDS Church, who saw the feds as a hostile force intent on persecuting them for their religious practices, most notably polygamy.

The county's prime grazing lands were located at the foot of the Abajo Mountains, where in 1879 one of the members of the Hole-in-the-Rock advance party observed fields of waist-deep grass from which "many tons of hay could have been cut" along with plentiful "deer, sage hens, jackrabbits, and cottontails." But the big cattle concerns had been running their cattle on those lands for years and had even strung miles of barbed wire around the best grazing land, despite the fact that it was on the public domain. So the Bluff Pool drove their burgeoning herds of sheep and cattle further afield and onto Elk Ridge to find summer forage. Elk Ridge juts out from the lower southern slopes of the Abajo Mountains and stands sentinel over Cedar Mesa. Varying in elevation from eight thousand to nine thousand feet above sea level, it is home to a montane ecosystem that includes its namesake ungulate as well as mountain lions and bears and, before they were exterminated by cattlemen, wolves. Forests of piñon, juniper, ponderosa pine, scrub oak, and aspen cover much of its breadth, broken up by grassy glades and meadows and an occasional beaver pond. Early surveyor William Henry Holmes called Elk Ridge the Bears Ears Plateau for the two distinctive buttes that rise up from it. Dark Canyon and Arch Canyon both originate here and cut deep gorges into its slopes before making their way to the Colorado River and Comb Wash, respectively.

Elk Ridge had long been home to and hunting and gathering grounds for Navajo, Ute, and Paiute people. The Weeminuche band of Utes used the glades in the shadow of the Bears Ears and held its Bear Dance there, and the Navajo people still gather medicinal herbs and piñon nuts from nearby forests. By the time the Mormons came, the land already had been stolen and put into the public domain. Still, a band of Ute and Paiute "renegades," considered such because they ignored reservation boundaries and instead roamed freely across the public domain just like their white counterparts, was centered near the Bears Ears. The Mormons acknowledged that without the permission of the band, their cattle wouldn't forage in peace. So, the Mormons offered ponies, flour, and other supplies to the leaders, including a Ute man named Mancos Jim, in exchange for the privilege to drive their two-thousand-strong herd onto the plateau. The meadows and glades of Elk Ridge would never be the same.

A cow generally will consume its body weight's worth of forage each month. A typical, modern beef cow can weigh up to fourteen hundred pounds, while the smaller, more desert-appropriate breeds like the Criollo or Corriente weigh in at around eight hundred pounds. The bigger the cow, the farther it has to roam and the more energy it must expend to keep the weight on. According to the US Department of Agriculture's Agricultural Census, San Juan County was home to over seventeen thousand[11] cattle of varying breeds in 1890, making it one of the most bovine-populated counties in the state. That adds up to about seventeen million pounds of four-hooved hamburger factories chomping their way through seventeen million pounds of desert vegetation—every single month. Add to that another hundred thousand sheep gnawing on San Juan County forage each year between 1890 and 1930, and the result is utter destruction, a catastrophe that was not lost on the observers of the time.

"The way that mountain was eaten up by cattle and sheep from the day of that treaty," wrote Lyman, of the Elk Ridge deal, "probably made the old Indian's [Mancos Jim's] head swim, and he perhaps found difficulty in recognizing it as the same verdant forest where he hunted deer and hid from his pursuers." The San Juan County cattle historian, Franklin D. Day, reiterated the observation in 1958: "The vast San Juan ranges, with a plentiful supply of choice feed, were not to remain such for many years. Like everything else that goes uncontrolled or without supervision these ranges were used selfishly with the present only in mind [leaving them] in an almost irreparable condition." As the cows chewed the grass that once reached up to a pony's belly down to nubs the deer and elk herds diminished, leaving less game for the Ute and Paiute hunters and causing members of their community to go hungry and exacerbating tensions between the Indigenous and white communities.

Overgrazed landscapes—and the herds that depend on them—become more vulnerable to climatic vagaries. A multiyear drought settled over the region in the early 1890s, so diminishing the San Juan River that dying fish flopped around in shallow pools on the mudflats. What remained of forage on the range dried up, and clouds of dust billowed up from once-grassy meadows and drifted for miles and miles before settling on the San Juan Mountains.

Some of the big cattle operations, already dismayed at the fact that the new county assessor insisted on counting and taxing every head of cattle within the county lines, skittered away to grassier lands and sold their herds to the "Bluff Tigers," the nickname given to the cowboys that ran the Mormon-owned Bluff Pool due to their aggressive tactics. The Tigers had a reputation for harassing Navajo sheepherders and for driving their cattle, without permission, onto reservation lands along the

Paiute Strip. Even these methods wouldn't get the Tigers through the brutally cold and snowy winter that followed the drought, however, and more than half of their herd perished.

FOR THE PEOPLE OF THE SAN JUAN STAKE, THE FEDERAL GOV-ernment—along with their white, Colorado neighbors—would prove to be even bigger threats than climatic extremes. In the late 1880s, the Colorado congressional delegation launched an effort to turn all of San Juan County, which still showed up as a nearly blank swath on maps, into a reservation for three bands of Ute people and the Southern Paiute Tribe. The Utes, who had occupied a huge territory spanning all of present-day Colorado, had been forced onto smaller and smaller reservations beginning in the 1850s. They lost the San Juan Mountains in the Brunot Agreement of 1873, and then more land in 1880, when the northern bands were pushed onto a reservation in east-central Utah, and the southern bands—the Weenuchiu, Caputa, and Mouache—were squeezed into a sliver of land in southwestern Colorado along the New Mexico line.

Even that wasn't enough for Colorado business interests, who saw the remaining portion of the Colorado reservation as an impediment to their exploitation of the lands, waters, and minerals of the state, and who wanted for their own the farmable lands occupied by the Utes. Colorado senator Ed Wolcott led the blatantly racist charge in Congress, telling his colleagues in 1892, "Had the Indian offered the slightest evidence of capacity for civilization he too would have been taken by the hand and lifted up and planted on the firm ground of citizenship...but the Southern Ute Indian who now lives in Colorado is not capable of civilization in this generation or in this century." He went on to falsely claim that the Utes were recent arrivals to Colorado and that they had no attachments to land in the state. Wolcott argued that relocating the Southern Ute people to Utah would help rein in a "wandering band of renegade Utes" who lived in the Abajo Mountains and on Elk Ridge in San Juan County and who were, allegedly, "responsible for much of the stealing and for much of the bad blood and for many murders." Then he came to the crux of the matter, and the real reason behind the removal: "The land [the existing reservation in Colorado] has great value to the whites.... This tract is one of the most fertile in Colorado, and lies more contiguous to this mining section than any other belt of country."

Despite the underhanded motives behind the move, Southern Ute leaders mostly were in favor of it. The proposed reservation was larger than the strip of land to which they had been confined, and it also contained more potential for seasonal hunting and gathering, given the diversity of ecosystems and landscapes. More significantly, it was preferable to the alternative that the government would have forced upon them, which was to open up the existing reservation to "allotment in severalty" under the newly passed Dawes Act. Under the act, each individual tribal member could stake a claim to an allotment—a 40- to 160-acre parcel of land—from their reservation lands. The hundreds of thousands of acres that remained after allotment would go into the public domain. That land would then be opened to white homesteaders. The theory among the white politicians and thinkers behind the act was that it would force the Indigenous people to shed their "Indian-ness," become farmers and landowners, and assimilate into white culture. President Theodore Roosevelt in his first speech to Congress in 1901 praised allotment as a "mighty pulverizing engine to break up the tribal mass."[12] In reality it was just another way to steal Indigenous lands and to kill their cultures. Buckskin Charlie, a Southern Ute leader, said at the time that if the policy were applied to the Southern Ute bands, the tribe would be exterminated within three years.

The Indian Rights Association opposed the move, arguing that San Juan County was too barren to sustain the tribes and that the Mormons' failures had demonstrated how difficult farming could be. The group, formed by white easterners, favored allotment. The Utah legislature, which then as now was made up mostly of members of the LDS Church, was opposed to the move; they surely didn't want to give up the church's foothold in southeastern Utah, no matter how tenuous it might be. Virtually absent from the debate were the Mormon settlers of Bluff. In testimony before Congress, witnesses rarely mention the settlers, save for one woman who worried that putting the Utes in Utah might encourage them to become polygamists, and another senator who dismissed the settlers as a few dozen "squatters"[13] on public lands.

In some ways, the white colonizers were getting a little dose of karma. Just a decade earlier they had rolled into San Juan County and settled there as if it were vacant, with utter disregard for the people who had been living there for centuries. Now they were on the receiving end, as people thousands of miles away referred to their adopted home as a barren wasteland and debated the future of their communities with little consideration for them or their wellbeing. They were about to be forced to move not to make way for the Utes, but to give the Durango business interests access to the valuable Southern Ute Reservation. Although they may have deserved such treatment, it was bound to breed resentment of the kind that would later feed into the Sagebrush Rebel ideology.

The Senate passed the Southern Ute relocation bill, but it flailed in the House for months before finally dying. In the meantime, the Indian agent for the Southern Utes, a pugnacious newspaper editor by the name of Dave Day, reportedly told the Utes to go ahead and move to San Juan County, and in November 1894 they did just that, much to the consternation of San Juan county sheriff Willard Butt, who begged for federal troops to come help. The headline read: "INVASION OF UTAH: Southern Utes Grow Restless; San Juan Settlers Also Anxious;

Colorado Utes Driving Settlers Off Grazing Lands—The Situation Critical." No troops were sent, the "invasion" turned out to be benign, and the Ute people headed back to Colorado. In 1895 the Southern Ute Reservation in Colorado was opened to allotment to tribal members. Dozens made claims, getting little squares of land. Originally, the Dawes Act mandated that the federal government hold the allotments in trust for twenty-five years before issuing a patent, but the act was amended to allow the allottee to get the title much quicker, freeing it up to be taxed and sold, opening up another means by which Indigenous land could be taken from Indigenous hands. Between 1887 and 1934, when Congress ended allotment, that great sea of white men had inundated some ninety million acres of formerly tribal lands across the United States. The Weenuchiu, or Weminuche, band refused to be boxed in like that and headed westward to the area around Ute Mountain in Colorado and to White Mesa in San Juan County in Utah, where they eventually established the Ute Mountain Ute Tribe.

Buckskin Charlie's fears were not realized. While it's true that the tribe struggled for decades afterward, it also fought doggedly to get back a sliver of all they had lost. Beginning in 1896, a long series of lawsuits eventually brought multimillion-dollar judgments in the tribe's favor and stronger rights to water, land, and hunting grounds. "With each encounter," wrote Richard Young in *The Ute Indians of Colorado in the Twentieth Century*, "they became more confident in their ability to present their case and to maneuver among the various echelons of the vast and powerful federal government." Often the disparate Ute bands fought as one, but the Southern Utes were by far the most assertive. In the 1970s, the tribe rose up and seized control of the vast oil and gas resources that underlie their land and eventually leveraged it to become an energy and real-estate juggernaut worth billions of dollars and the largest employer in La Plata County, Colorado.

Across the state line in Utah, the white colonizers had managed to dodge the threat and that particular incursion by the federal government. But it wouldn't be long before the feds would invade their empire in more subtle ways.

By the end of the 1880s, huge tracts of public land had been handed over to the railroads, to mining interests, to states, and to homesteaders, yet across the West hundreds of millions of acres still remained in the public domain, and as was the case in San Juan County, nearly all of those lands were open to unrestricted grazing and the devastation that comes along with it. In hopes of mitigating the wreckage on at least some of that land, in 1891 Congress passed the Forest Reserve Act, giving the president the authority to withdraw areas from the public domain[14] as forest reserves, to be overseen by the Interior Department. Six years later Congress passed the Forest Management or Organic Administrative Act, which gave the previous law some teeth by providing a framework for managing the reserves. In 1905 President Theodore Roosevelt transferred management of the reserves to the Department of Agriculture and named the agency the Forest Service, appointing Gifford Pinchot as his chief forester.

Together, Pinchot and Roosevelt represented a major shift in the way the government managed and society perceived and treated the public lands. Roosevelt set aside some of the nation's most cherished landmarks as national monuments. Pinchot believed that humans should utilize the forests and grasslands but that they should do so in a more sustainable manner so as to save some of the timber and forage for future generations. This conservationist ethos came to be known as Pinchotism, a term spit derogatorily by western politicians who were beholden to the extractive industries, such as Republican senator Weldon Heyburn from Idaho. Employing the same rhetoric that would

later be used by the Sagebrush Rebels, Heyburn derided the forest reserve laws, suggesting that they amounted to theft of the
"people's forests." Heyburn and his western colleagues were able
to add a provision to the forest reserve laws requiring congressional approval for such withdrawals in Colorado, Wyoming,
Idaho, Montana, and Oregon.

Utah, however, didn't make that list because Utah's congressional delegation, namely Sen. Reed Smoot—a leader of the
Church of Jesus Christ of Latter-day Saints—strongly supported
the forest reserves, as well as the more moderate elements of
Pinchotism. During three decades on the Senate, Smoot pushed
a number of conservation-minded bills, including the establishment of Zion and Bryce Canyon National Parks.

While Roosevelt was creating the Forest Service in Washington, the people of the San Juan Mission were gradually moving
away from Bluff and the moody river to the newly established
towns of Grayson, which would later be renamed Blanding, and
Monticello, sitting at the southern and eastern edges of the Abajo
Mountains. But the mountain slopes—and source of the settlements' water—remained the domain of the big livestock companies, notably the New Mexico and Kansas Land and Cattle Company, or the Carlisle outfit. The combination of thousands of cattle
and sheep had reduced large swaths of the formerly abundant
grasslands in the Abajos and the La Sal Mountains to denuded,
dusty, gullied, flash-flood-prone wastelands. Plus, the sheepmen
and the cattlemen were constantly fighting over who got access
to what portion of range, a conflict that had disastrous outcomes.
At one point, allegedly out of spite, the Carlisle livestock concern
turned out thousands of sheep on the upper branches of Montezuma Creek, Monticello's source for drinking water.[15] Bacteria
from the sheep feces contaminated the water, leading to a typhoid
outbreak in Monticello that killed eleven people.

A number of residents of San Juan County got together and
petitioned the Roosevelt administration to create forest reserves

in the La Sal and Abajo Mountains to "augment the future pros-
perity of this region by conserving the timber and water necessary for mining and agriculture, and placing the public range
under judicious control." Roosevelt heeded the call, establishing the La Sal Forest Reserve in 1906 and the Monticello Forest
Reserve the following year. The two were later combined with
one another and with the Manti Forest Reserve to become the
Manti-La Sal National Forest, which now covers most of the
higher-elevation land in southeastern Utah. Rangers, including a man named John Riis, were brought in to get a handle on
grazing by creating a grazing allotment system and limiting the
number of cattle and sheep allowed on the forest. "I was here
to tell them they must pay hard cash for the use of the range
and their herds must be limited to the capacity of the range,"
Riis later wrote. Despite the fact that the new rules did little to
dampen the number of livestock on the range, the local ranchers
resisted, on principle. "They had settled [the region] and felt it
was theirs," Riis added. The sentiment was echoed on a larger
scale by the ranching, mining, and logging industries across the
West. Ultimately the backlash to Pinchotism elevated Warren G.
Harding, a friend to the industries that wanted free rein over the
public lands, to the presidency. Harding chose Albert Bacon Fall
to be his interior secretary, who immediately went about rolling
back regulations and doing his best to erase the legacy left by
Pinchot and Roosevelt, including opening up the public domain
and Indian land to coal mining and oil and gas drilling.

In 1934 Congress passed the Taylor Grazing Act to help
slow the wholesale destruction wrought by the millions of cattle
and sheep on public lands that had not been set aside as forest
reserves. A new agency, the Grazing Service, would manage a
permitting and fee system on about 140 million acres of land,
mostly sagebrush country in the arid western US. Mining claims
could still be made on the Grazing Act lands, along with oil, gas,
and coal leasing,[16] but homesteading was prohibited in order

to reduce the fragmentation and land-use checkerboarding of the range. The lands were divided into grazing districts, each of which had an advisory board mostly made up of ranchers within that district, thus giving it an element of home rule and easing concerns that the federal landlord was taking too much control.

Utah had nine grazing districts in 1939, more than any other state, on which 2.85 million sheep, cattle, horses, and goats ranged. Nearly 12 million animals were permitted to graze on Taylor Act land across the West that year, yielding just one million dollars in revenue—meaning ranchers were paying, on average, just eight cents per year to fatten up each of their bovines or ungulates on taxpayer-owned grass. Seventy-five percent of the revenue went back to the states and grazing districts, where the advisory boards determined how it would be spent. Nearly all of the funds went to so-called range improvement projects, which ultimately benefitted the ranchers, such as killing predators and rodents and construction of stock trails and diversion dams.

In retrospect, it would seem as if the Taylor Grazing Act might have been the first shot fired in what would eventually become the public land wars, in that it represented a flexing of the federal landlord's muscle. Still, even though many ranchers were in denial regarding the true causes of the ruination of the range—they attributed it to drought—they were generally ambivalent towards the act because it imposed order on the chaos that resulted from competing uses of the public domain. San Juan County stockmen weren't pleased with paying fees for grass that they considered theirs. But they were also able to use the new law to drive Navajo sheepherders off of the public domain,[17] thereby opening up more forage for their cattle.

Besides, a much bigger threat to the San Juan County cattle industry loomed on the horizon.

CHAPTER EIGHT

J. A. SCORUP:
PROTO-SAGEBRUSH REBEL

I N THE EARLY SPRING OF 1891, NINETEEN-YEAR-OLD JOHN Albert Scorup crossed the turbid waters of the Colorado River at Dandy's Crossing, near where the defunct Hite Marina now sits. With just a couple of blankets and whatever chuck his saddlebags could carry, he then headed up White Canyon into an area that few white people had ever seen. The tall, blue-eyed son of Mormon, Danish immigrants had made his way from his home in Salina, Utah, to pursue his lifelong dream of becoming a cattleman. All he had to do was round up 150 cattle that were roaming, in a quasi-feral state, through the "maze of cracks, washes, creeks, and cliffs that split and hedged" the White Canyon country where a Salina rancher had left them. In return, the rancher would give Scorup one-third of the calves that were born.

Scorup had a tough time, to say the least. He struggled to find the cattle, he ran out of the food he had brought, and he didn't have a gun for hunting game. His social life was limited to brief encounters with a grizzled old prospector named Charlie Fry. A less tenacious soul might have relented at that point, but not Scorup. Instead, he saddled up his horse and made his way eastward and followed the Hole-in-the-Rock Trail down into Comb Wash, skirted around Comb Ridge and then rode north until he came across a big livestock operation that needed help running its herd from the La Sal Mountains to Ridgway, Colorado. Because Scorup's fellow Mormons rarely associated with cowboys and almost never engaged in that line of work, Scorup became an anomaly. His Gentile colleagues coined him the "Mormon Cowboy." The earnings from the job would keep Scorup's dream alive and ultimately would propel him to the helm of one of the biggest cattle concerns in the region. His name would become synonymous with public lands ranching in the West, and it's fair to say that he was perhaps the prototype of the Sagebrush Rebel.

SCORUP WENT BACK TO WHITE CANYON WITH A POCKETFUL OF cash to tend to his adopted herd. When he arrived at his camp, five armed Texas cowboys from one of the big cattle outfits were sitting around his fire playing cards with Mancos Jim, Poke, and Posey, the leaders of the coterie of Utes and Paiutes who lived in the area. The Texans told Scorup that he was on their range and that he'd better get a move on if he knew what was good for him. Scorup knew he was outnumbered and outgunned, so he hightailed it back to Salina, not to surrender but to gather reinforcements. He managed to pull together three hundred head of cattle and roped his brother Jim into joining him on the three-hundred-mile journey back to the Colorado River and to the vast and labyrinthine White Canyon drainage.

After coaxing and prodding and dragging the cattle across the ice-choked river, the brothers drove them into the mesas and plateaus north of White Canyon, country so broken up and creased that it must have been horrific to try to move one cow, let alone a few hundred of them, over, across, and through it. Yet by sticking to the most rugged areas, they could avoid the Texan ruffians and their huge herds.

In the months that followed, the Texans no longer pestered Scorup and his brother. Still, the Scorups had other problems to deal with, including mountain lions, bears, and wolves that feasted on Scorup's cattle. Legend has it that Ol' Big Foot, a notorious wolf, killed 150 calves in one fell swoop—surely an exaggeration woven to justify mass extermination of predators. A giant herd of wild horses had also taken up residence in the area, and the agile ungulates had the upper hand on slow-moving bovines in the competition for scarce forage. For this reason, wild horses and burros, including free-range animals that belonged to the Navajo, Ute, and Paiute people, would become anathema to public land ranchers and a pawn in the public land wars. Scorup saw them as a threat to his livelihood and he dispensed with them ruthlessly: according to one account,[18] the Scorup brothers spent entire days shooting horses, killing as many as seven hundred at a time.

Today these tales of big predatory fauna may seem fantastical, given how rare it is even for the seasoned modern canyon-country wanderer to catch sight of a bear, bobcat, or mountain lion. Livestock operators, more than anything else, are to blame or thank for the scarcity of the toothy beasts. During Scorup's time ranchers killed predators and competing wildlife of all shapes and sizes indiscriminately, and livestock operators and governments hired bounty hunters to supplement the slaughter, successfully wiping out the wolf and grizzly populations in the Southwest. The task was later turned over to the bizarrely named Wildlife Services, a division of the US Department of Agriculture. Each year Wildlife Services kills two million or more animals for a variety of reasons, including because they compete with or prey on cattle that graze on public land. In 2019, for example, Wildlife Services exterminated 62,000 coyotes, 2,400 foxes, 800 bobcats, 300 mountain lions, and 400 bears—and that doesn't include the thousands that ranchers killed themselves.

Drought, snow, rugged terrain, and blazing heat would prove even greater threats than hungry wildlife, but the Scorups endured through sheer grit, herding their cows into sheltered canyons during blizzards and to food and water, one by one if necessary, during times of scarcity. They outlasted most of the large operations in the county, but their herd was still too small to earn them enough cash to build up the business.

So, once again Scorup went looking for work, this time as a bounty hunter tracking down a herd of longhorn, bovine bullies that had been brought in by a Texas outfit a few years earlier and put out to graze in Comb Wash. When the Texas livestock operators had bailed, they deserted their herd, and the cows had gone feral. The second generation was even rowdier, a veritable gang of "incorrigible 'pinion-busters' for which the San Juan rough country would sometime be notorious," as Albert R. Lyman, chronicler of Mormon settlement in San Juan County, wrote. "This indestructible Texas stock would crowd the Bluff cattle against the rims, starve them to death, and predominate over them by their native toughness."

The Bluff Tigers were fed up with the scrappy piñon-busters, and offered ten bucks a head to anyone who could round them up. The Scorup brothers hired some local kids and went to work. They may have rounded up two hundred cows or two thousand—the accounts vary. Either way, they ended up with enough cash to finance a larger operation, buying up cattle from smaller concerns that couldn't hack it anymore, including the Bluff Pool's when it collapsed in 1898.

From there, the Scorup empire slowly expanded, and in 1918 they teamed up with the Somerville family of Moab to purchase the Indian Creek Cattle Company, which included the Dugout Ranch just outside what is now the Needles District of Canyonlands National Park, to launch the Scorup-Somerville Cattle Company. Their timing was awful. Cattle prices crashed following the First World War, and a nasty strain of influenza, misnamed the Spanish Flu, spread across the world, extinguishing the lives of tens of millions of people. Jim Scorup's wife fell victim to the pandemic, throwing Jim into despair. Soon thereafter Jim Scorup was infected and died, too, perhaps as much from heartbreak as from influenza. John Scorup's trials were not over. A brutal winter came just as the nastiest wave of the pandemic ebbed, taking at least two thousand of Scorup's cattle. But he held on, cattle prices eventually went back up, and by 1927 Scorup-Somerville had permits to graze 6,800 cattle on US Forest Service land, more than any other permittee in the nation, along with an uncounted number on the public domain—where they continued to get fat, free of charge.

THE TAYLOR GRAZING ACT BROUGHT NOT ONLY RULES AND fees, but also an accounting of the approximate numbers and locations of cattle out on the public lands. Those data show that Scorup had cows scattered all over Standing Up Country. Virtually no part of the county remained un-grazed or un-trampled, save perhaps for the small areas protected by Rainbow Bridge and Natural Bridges National Monuments, and other places that were simply inaccessible to cows that lacked the ability to rappel or fly a helicopter. In 1936 the Scorup-Sommerville company's herds were distributed as such:

> 1,500 head of cattle in Cottonwood, Indian Creek, and Needles;
> 500 in Beef Basin;
> 600 in Dark Canyon;
> 100 in Red Canyon;
> 600 on Wooden Shoe and in White Canyon;
> 50 cattle in Grand Gulch;
> 1,000 between Bears Ears and Hole in the Rock; and
> 7,000 sheep in Harts Draw and Dry Valley.

Scorup's livestock occupied nearly two million acres of some of the nation's most spectacular, remote, and rugged public land, in an area that Bob Marshall and Althea Dobbins of the Wilderness Society deemed in 1936 the largest roadless area in the United States. It was also land that federal officials were eyeing for preservation, and in 1936 Interior Secretary Harold Ickes and the National Park Service lobbed a big missile in the public land wars by proposing the designation of a massive swath of that area as a national monument, frothing Scorup and Utah politicians into a fervor. By that time, a number of national monuments had been designated in canyon country by various presidents under the Antiquities Act of 1906, including Natural Bridges, Rainbow Bridge, and Hovenweep in San Juan County, and Arches, Zion, and Dinosaur in surrounding areas. "Wayne Wonderland," aka Capitol Reef, would be designated as a monument in 1937. Most of those were relatively small and targeted, limiting protection to a group of specific archaeological sites or landforms. The newer monument, however, would span an entire landscape—more than six thousand square miles, or 4.5 million acres, along the Colorado River in southern Utah. It was to be called Escalante, after one of the Spanish priests who ventured into the region in 1776, but newspaper articles from the time referred to it as Colorado River National Monument and the Great National Wilderness. After flying over the area, Grand Canyon National Park superintendent Minor Tillotson said, "There is no single section of the entire southwest which offers a greater variety or a more interesting array of spectacularly scenic effects than does the area under consideration."

From the point where the Colorado River crosses the Utah-Arizona border, the southern boundary of the proposed monument followed the San Juan River to Comb Ridge. From there, the boundary jogged northward to encompass all of what one day would become Bears Ears National Monument and Canyonlands National Park. It would have included a similar-sized area on the west side of the Colorado River, including the Henry Mountains and most of what is now Grand Staircase-Escalante National Monument. At the time, a single, unimproved road reached from Blanding, Utah, to Natural Bridges National Monument. The new monument would increase the likelihood of federal funds being appropriated to pave, widen, and extend the road through the new monument, thereby linking Mesa Verde National Park with what would soon be Capitol Reef National Monument. But, according to various press accounts, unlike other national monuments and parks, this one otherwise would be kept largely roadless and undeveloped. There would be no concessions or other development along the sole highway cutting through the monument, and travel beyond the highway would be restricted to foot or horseback.

Utahns had generally been in support of the new national monuments because they would draw more tourists to the area, thus diversifying the region's economy. The Utah Planning Board, which had been created by the state legislature to work with federal agencies to help chart the economic future of the state, issued a report in 1936 saying: "An extension of authority, especially of the National Park Service, would be beneficial to the people of Utah."

So Ickes was somewhat taken aback when opposition bubbled up among Utah's leaders. Governor Henry Blood, a Democrat, went on the offensive. He didn't like the idea of the area being shut down to mining and oil and gas development but was most concerned about the fate of water development projects being proposed for the Colorado River—a 1916 USGS study had located several potential dam sites within the proposed monument, including three different possibilities in lower Glen Canyon, one at Dark Canyon, and even a dam on the San Juan River where it meets Chinle Wash. Ickes ensured him that water development wouldn't be affected, but Blood was distrustful of the federal government and wouldn't budge. In a note to the

Utah congressional delegation he wrote: "Some morning we may wake up and find that…the Escalante Monument has been created by Presidential proclamation, and then it will be too late to forestall what we in Utah think would be a calamity." He unwittingly foresaw sixty years into the future, when President Clinton would spring the Grand Staircase-Escalante National Monument on an unsuspecting Utah populace.

Ranchers were even more furious. According to Park Service estimates at the time, 144,000 sheep, 26,000 cattle, and 2,600 horses grazed on public lands within the proposed monument. Grazing wouldn't be shut down immediately upon monument designation, but gradually phased out, giving the ranchers time to adjust and the tourism industry time to take hold, offsetting some of the economic losses. That did little to ease the anger. In 1936, eighty-seven people, more than half of them from San Juan County, showed up at a public meeting on the proposal in Price, Utah, rather than in Moab, Monticello, Green River, or any other community that would be most affected by the monument. One after another stood up and blasted the proposal. Charles Redd of San Juan County said that the withdrawal would bring "financial ruin to a majority of the people of five counties" and insisted that the "people of this region, who pioneered the way by building roads and schools should be considered when their basic industry is put in jeopardy." Another man, identified[19] only as a "prominent San Juan County cattleman," probably J. A. Scorup, said that he had been in favor of the designation of Arches National Monument, but he felt tourism was overvalued. "I was sorry that Mr. Ickes made the inference that this area could be closed," he said. "This is still a democratic country and we proposed to discuss this matter and petition in the manner of democratic government."

"This is just a little harder rap than we can take without putting up a battle," another stockman said. "You can make it legal but you can never make it moral." In the end, every member of the public at the meeting voted to oppose the designation.

Opposition of a different kind also bubbled up from unexpected places. In 1936, H. Dodge Freeman, a geologist from Chicago who had spent a good amount of time in southeastern Utah and the previous summer riding from Kanab to Moab on horseback, penned a letter[20] to the editor that appeared in the *Moab Times-Independent* (along with a cheeky note from the editor) and other newspapers. "I certainly hope they [ranchers] raise heaven and earth to retain their rights," he wrote, going on to deride the "Roman Holiday in land withdrawal and territorial expansion" and to "doubt the intelligence of the 'brass hats' in Washington." Freeman, though, wasn't worried about the government locking up the land—he feared the opposite:

> To me the charm of the wilderness along the Colorado rests far more in its inaccessibility and freedom from trodden paths than in its admitted wonderful beauty. I often asked myself last summer whether I would get the same sense of pleasure and enjoyment I got riding through that country on horseback if I were to go through by motor bus or auto with a lot of rubberneck tourists ogling around and making inane remarks.... It has always been encouraging to me to know that out there in your country there lies one large area, at least that represents something wild and remote, even in the material days we are living at present. What a pity it would be to destroy this—even to touch it. Why shouldn't the government take to move toward a new policy of creating so-called primitive areas whereby those few people who choose to can recreate for themselves some of the individuality and, to be trite, ruggedness of those gone before us?

Edward Abbey was just a nine-year-old growing up in a down-and-out family in Pennsylvania when Freeman wrote his comment prognosticating the industrial-scale tourism and recreation that Abbey would one day deride and that later would be held up as an argument against designation of Bears Ears National Monument. That year just four hundred people visited Arches National Park; now that same number passes through the park entrance every two hours. The Utah Planning Board, perhaps seeing that visitation numbers like those at Arches could not fuel an economy on their own, tempered its earlier enthusiasm for the Park Service and recommended that the proposed monument be scaled back and that any designation come with specific language saying that mining, grazing, and water projects would not be affected—it would be a monument in name only. Jesse Nusbaum, senior archaeologist for the Park Service, was horrified at the notion, saying it would defeat the whole purpose. In Utah newspapers Nusbaum waxed eloquently about the monument:

> In these days it seems we hear more about the recreational values of the national parks than we do about their spiritual values. They are related to be sure, but it is the potential capacity of our national parks with their inherent endowment to supply spiritual values which distinguish them from the multitude of the recreational areas. The canyons of the Colorado possess this quality to a marked degree....Here is desolation, solitude, and peace bringing man once more to the vivid realization of the great forces of nature.

Ickes backed off on the proposal, and he and the National Park Service came up with an alternate, vastly scaled-back plan: a two-thousand-square-mile recreation area that followed the Colorado River from near its confluence with the Green River to the Arizona line. It hewed closely enough to the river's deep canyon that it would have a negligible effect on grazing lands or potential mining or drilling. By then, it didn't seem to matter. The opponents no longer were opposed for practical reasons, but ideological ones, and the idea of any such withdrawals of "their" land were not acceptable. L. C. Montgomery, president of the Utah Cattle and Horse Growers Association, wrote that the recreation area proposal was nothing but "the same old ghost covered by a different sheet." They welcomed the tourism national monuments and parks brought, but only if it didn't come at the expense of grazing or mining or drilling, and only if it didn't infringe on what they saw as their right to exploit public land. State leaders pushed a bill that would require local approval for any future national monument designations under the Antiquities Act. It didn't go anywhere, but it served as a foreshadow of what was to come and the strident opposition was enough ultimately to kill the Escalante National Monument proposal, or at least put it into dormancy for decades. The controversy also sparked a primordial Sagebrush Rebellion that would flare up again in 1943 when President Franklin D. Roosevelt designated Jackson Hole National Monument in Wyoming. Wyoming lawmakers bitterly lashed back, even passing legislation to rescind the designation (Roosevelt vetoed it). The Utah Cattle and Horse Growers Association, with J. A. Scorup at the helm, declared Roosevelt's designation to be "un-American, undemocratic, and an abuse of executive authority."

The ranching industry was feeling emboldened on the one hand and oppressed on the other. And when the Bureau of Land Management, née the Grazing Service, endeavored to raise grazing fees on the public domain, the National Wool Growers Association and the American National Livestock Association gathered in Salt Lake City and launched a revolt that had the support of Sen. Pat McCarran, a Nevada Democrat, and Rep. Wesley D'Ewart, a Republican from Montana. They weren't ready to stop at a grazing fee ceiling, either. They wanted all of the lands governed by the Taylor Act to be transferred to the states or privatized.[21] "There is nothing in the law that says the public domain should not go back to private ownership," D'Ewart told the gathering of proto-Sagebrush Rebels. In 1947,[22] Bernard DeVoto described the attempted land grab: "Cattlemen do not own the public range now; it belongs to you and me, and since the fees they pay for using public land are much smaller than those they pay for using private land, those fees are in effect one of a number of subsidies we pay them. But they always acted as if they owned the public range and act so now; they convinced themselves that it belonged to them and now believe it does; and they are trying to take title to it."

The stockmen also demanded "that withdrawal of the public lands be immediately stopped, this to apply particularly to recreational type withdrawals." They were referring in part to public domain lands being taken by the military for rocket firing ranges and so forth, such as the three million acres withdrawn at Wendover on the Utah-Nevada border. They were also referring to lands withdrawn by the Forest Service and put off-limits to grazing, as well as by the president or Congress for national monuments or parks. The privatization effort reached Congress in the form of a proposed Senate bill that would "eliminate lands from national forests, parks, monuments, reservations and withdrawals in connection with such grants and for other purposes." In other words, the bill would not only stop future designations, but rescind all previous national monuments and parks as well. It didn't pass. But those who were pushing against what they saw as federal land managers overstepping their bounds gained traction. In 1950 Congress wrapped the Jackson Hole National Monument into Grand Teton National Park, while at the same time halting future national monument designations under the Antiquities Act in Wyoming.

J. A. Scorup ended up being a legend in southeastern Utah,

and deservedly so. He was an anomaly and the embodiment of oxymorons—Mormon cowboy, for one example, and a self-made cattle baron, for another. He started out as a salt-of-the-earth cowboy, living in caves and cowboy camps, enduring long winters and harsh summers, to eventually become a successful titan of the livestock industry. He served as San Juan County commissioner and even as the president of a Moab bank. But he couldn't have done it without the public lands, the stolen lands, and the American taxpayer's grass, on which he fattened up his herds for free, and on which he built his empire.

CHAPTER NINE

YELLOW MONSTER

I N LATE AUGUST 2018, IN THE HEAT OF ONE OF THE WARM-
est and driest years on record in the Four Corners country,
under a blanket of smoke emanating from wildfires burning
all over the place, I piloted the Silver Bullet—my trusty 1989
Nissan Sentra—to the quiet burg of Monticello. I was on my way
from one camping site on the Great Sage Plain to another on
Comb Ridge, where I would feed my misanthropic side with a
searing hike down a canyon, seeking out potholes that still had a
smitten of stagnant water leftover from the last rain.

I took a detour through Monticello to look into one of the
most contentious fronts of the long-running public land wars,
the battle over uranium mining and milling and even radioactive waste disposal. San Juan County's public lands played a
major role in what I call the Age of the Nuclear West, which
reached its multi-decade apex during the Cold War and which
hasn't ended yet. It was an era of innovation and greed, of hope
and harm, of faith in technology and the threat of annihila-
tion, of an almost miraculous source of energy, and of indelible
wounds on the land, water, and people. Today the ghosts of that
age lurk everywhere in the county, from the spires of Monument
Valley to the White Canyon mining district to the Lisbon Valley,
where a Texas prospector by the name of Charlie Steen staked his

Mi Vida claim and made a fortune. The ghosts continue to haunt Monticello, where for decades a uranium mill churned out poisons, and where residents are still grappling with the long-term health effects. And the last operating uranium mill in the nation, located just outside Blanding, has yet to give up the ghost.

THE NUCLEAR WEST DATES BACK TO 1898, LONG BEFORE ANYone had thought of nuclear power or nuclear bombs, when Marie Curie discovered radium in unrefined pitchblende. Radium is a radioactive "daughter" of uranium that was once seen as a sort of miracle substance, so much so that just one gram of the stuff could fetch upwards of $100,000. Paint it on watch numbers or even clothing and they'd glow in the dark. It purportedly could cure cancer *and* impotence and give those who used it an "all-around healthy glow," as one advertisement put it. During the early 1900s, it was added to medicines, cosmetics, and sometimes even food. The Denver-based Radio-Active Chemical Company added radium to fertilizers. The Nutex Company made radium condoms. Makers of the Radiendocrinator instructed men (and only men) to wear "the adapter like any 'athletic strap.' This puts the instrument under the scrotum as it should be. Wear at night. Radiate as directed."

Shortly after Curie's discovery, she received a sample of uranium ore from western Colorado. Curie found that it, too, contained radium, and she named the ore carnotite. A boom erupted in western San Miguel County, Colorado, just along the Utah border. Hundreds of mines were dug into mesas, and extraction plants built along the rivers, to get at the high-dollar miracle substance.

The boom busted in the early 1920s when huge mines opened up in the Belgian Congo that were able to supply the globe's radium hunger far more affordably. Radium's glow dimmed soon thereafter when the women who painted it onto watches began dying, and the inventor of the Radiendocrinator was stricken with bladder cancer. It is now known that radium is highly radioactive and a "bone-seeker," meaning that when it is ingested it makes its way to the skeleton, where it decays into other radioactive daughter elements, including radon, and bombards the surrounding tissue with radiation. According to the Toxic Substances and Diseases Registry, exposure leads to "anemia, cataracts, fractured teeth, cancer (especially bone cancer), and death."

Since uranium ore also contains vanadium, a metal that is used to harden steel and to color glass, a few mines were able to stay afloat throughout the 1930s. The Shumway brothers of San Juan County staked claims on the public domain in Cottonwood Wash and elsewhere during this time under the General Mining Law of 1872, which, like the Homestead Act, is a federal government land-giveaway. After staking the claims the brothers were able to patent them, thereby taking ownership of public lands. Today those parcels are private rectangles surrounded by public land.

When the Manhattan Project was launched to build the first atomic bomb, the carnotite-mining infrastructure was brought back to life, and the mines began kicking out ore once again. The old extraction plants also were revived and new ones built. In 1941 the Vanadium Corporation of America—the company that ran many of the mills across the plateau, including at Shiprock and Durango, and was therefore responsible for poisoning the earth and waters around those mills—constructed a mill on the edge of the small town of Monticello in cooperation with the Defense Plant Corporation. The mill was purportedly built to extract vanadium from uranium ore to supply the war effort. The real target was the uranium. Throughout the war, VCA secretly processed it for use in the Manhattan Project and the atomic bombs that would be dropped on Hiroshima and Nagasaki.

After the war ended, the mill—having served its purpose—shut down, along with many of the other facilities across the region. But when the Cold War and the arms race beckoned, the newly formed Atomic Energy Commission set out to manufacture a new uranium boom to provide the fuel for a massive nuclear arms arsenal and the nuclear reactors that would power cities, submarines, and even airplanes. The Monticello mill was retooled with a nearly $2 million upgrade and churned through about one hundred tons of uranium ore per day, crushing and grinding it up, then treating it with sulfuric acid, tributyl phosphate, and other nastiness. One ton of ore yielded about five or six pounds of uranium, meaning that each day nearly two hundred thousand pounds of tailings were piled up outside the mill, in or next to a branch of Montezuma Creek, along with the liquid waste, or raffinate, which is not only radioactive, but also chock-full of heavy metals and other toxic material. The mill was overhauled two more times over the next decade in order to up capacity and to handle different kinds of ore.

The federal government offered prospectors a cornucopia of subsidies, including bonuses of up to $35,000 for initial uranium ore production and grubstake loans to finance mining operations. Most significantly, the government agreed to be the exclusive purchaser of ore and yellowcake, and guaranteed a price to be paid for it, thus eliminating financial risk from what otherwise would have been a high-risk, high-return proposition.

A frenzied boom erupted on the Colorado Plateau, and San Juan County, which until then had been a fairly quiet place, was suddenly abuzz with humanity and greed. The mid-century equivalent of the gold rush infused popular culture. A 1949 cover story in *Popular Mechanics* instructed readers on how to build their own Geiger counters, and in 1953 a *New Yorker* writer penned a "Talk of the Town" piece about a New Jersey man who traveled to Moab to get into the uranium business. Several hundred words in a *New Yorker* feature article from that same year were devoted to an "alert-looking man named Calvin Black," who was working as a foreman at a uranium mine at the time. "Uranium is all I've bothered with since I left high school five years ago," Black told the reporter, "and I guess I've been lucky so far." A board game called Uranium Rush included a "Geiger counter" that "lights and buzzes your way to fun and fortune." Prospectors from across the demographic spectrum descended on the sparsely populated region, Geiger counters in hand, combing public lands in search for the next bonanza. In the mid-1950s some 750 mines were active across the Colorado Plateau. Ranchers were pushed off ancestral grazing lands, and quiet little Mormon towns erupted into boisterous, whiskey-soaked ones almost overnight.

To facilitate the craze, the Atomic Energy Commission, county bulldozer crews, and prospectors cut roads up cliffs, across mesas, and through washes. They didn't even need to ask permission, thanks to a provision in an 1866 federal mining law known as Revised Statute 2477, or RS-2477, which gave anyone the right to build a road across BLM land to anywhere or, for that matter, to nowhere, without getting a permit or even informing the federal land agency. Marshall and Dobbins's roadless area in America was soon covered with a web of roads.

San Juan County's population exploded, relatively speaking, as did the assessed valuation, going from about $4 million to nearly $140 million. Ranching was no longer the main economic driver, uranium was, followed by oil (development in the Aneth oil field and on surrounding BLM land ramped up during the uranium boom). If the shift from farming to ranching in the 1880s represented a deviation from Brigham Young's collectivist leanings, then the side-by-side uranium and oil booms pretty much nuked everything for which Young and Joseph Smith had stood. The Hole-in-the-Rock Expedition, sent to the corner of Utah in order to repel the advancing forces of greed and unbridled capitalism and who had been instructed to act as stewards of the land, was no more; the Hole-in-the-Rockers, themselves, were now fully invested in the avarice-driven society, and the county rose from one of the poorest to one of the wealthiest in the state.

The transformation in San Juan County mirrored that of a similar one happening simultaneously within the Church of Jesus Christ of Latter-day Saints, itself. When McCarthyism infected the nation in the 1950s, church leaders started an effort—perhaps concerted, perhaps not—to change their public image from borderline theocratic communists to full-on capitalists.

The ideological leader of this new, free-market Mormonism was Ezra Taft Benson, a rabid anti-communist who served as President Dwight D. Eisenhower's secretary of agriculture and was LDS president for fourteen years beginning in 1985. Benson was a contemporary, friend, and ideological twin of W. Cleon Skousen, the ultra-conservative political theorist whose teachings would influence the Sagebrush Rebellion of the 1970s, the wise-use and patriot movements of the 1990s, and the violent right-wing uprisings of the mid-2010s, including the armed occupation led by Ammon and Ryan Bundy of the Malheur National Wildlife Refuge in Oregon in 2016. Benson and Skousen both were strong supporters of the John Birch Society, which was considered extreme[23] even by the likes of hardcore conservatives such as Barry Goldwater. The society's founder, Robert Welch, derided Eisenhower as a communist and Benson concurred. And in 1963 Benson predicted that within the decade the United States would be ruled by a communist dictatorship, which would include military occupation, concentration camps, and the like. He then said, in what sounded like a call for violent revolution: "Words will not stop the communists."[24]

Neither Benson's nor Skousen's rhetoric was accepted by the entirety of the church leadership, by any means, but over time the resistance to it waned and the church and its membership moved much further to the right, thereby abandoning many of the principles of both Young and Smith.

DECADES BEFORE THE US BOOM GOT GOING, RESEARCHERS HAD firmly established that European uranium miners (before Curie, uranium was used to make dye) got lung cancer at much higher rates than the general populace—a phenomenon that had been observed as early as the 1400s. In 1942, W. C. Hueper, a German scientist who had immigrated to the United States, published *Occupational Tumors and Allied Diseases*, in which he theorized a link between radon—another radioactive daughter of uranium found at dangerously high levels in mines and mills—and the lung cancer in the European miners. A decade later, even as the uranium boom was in full swing, US scientists confirmed the theory by uncovering the mechanism by which radon caused lung cancer, and throughout the 1950s a variety of studies showed that uranium mining and milling was hazardous to workers' health[25] because miners and millers were inhaling both radon gas and radioactive nuclei that had attached themselves to dust particles. The same studies found that simply ventilating the mines would reduce risk. Yet the miners were never informed of the perils of their occupation, nor were meaningful protective measures taken until the sixties. In fact, the federal Atomic Energy Commission actively withheld or downplayed this information in a cover-up that ultimately benefited the corporations and sacrificed the lives and health of thousands of people in order to keep the nuclear weapons machine running at full throttle.

The government stopped buying ore in the 1960s and yellowcake in the 1970s, but continued to prop up the nuclear industry as a whole with a slew of subsidies. Many of the smaller uranium mines and mills shut down or were purchased by larger corporations and consolidated into big operations. The

Monticello mill was among those that perished in 1960, much to the dismay of the local business community, after having processed nine hundred thousand tons of uranium ore, churned out more than eight hundred thousand tons of tailings, contaminated the soil and groundwater with a litany of toxic and radioactive materials, and left a permanent stain on the land and on the collective health of local residents.

By the late 1970s the prospecting boom was long gone, and many of the smaller mines had shut down, giving way to larger strip mines in Wyoming or Grants, New Mexico. A handful of mines and mills across the Colorado Plateau were still operating at the time, but their days were numbered. In March 1979 one of the reactors at Three Mile Island Nuclear Generating Station in Pennsylvania experienced a partial meltdown, thanks in part to a stuck valve. While a devastating catastrophe was narrowly averted, the accident was enough to spark fear in a populace among which an anti-nuclear-weapon movement was already growing. A few months later an even more damaging, yet far less visible, accident occurred on the Navajo Nation, when a uranium mill tailings dam owned by the United Nuclear Corporation was breached near Church Rock, New Mexico, sending more than one thousand tons of tailings and ninety-four million gallons of radioactive liquid into the Puerco River, affecting livestock and contaminating the drinking-water wells of countless people downstream. *The China Syndrome* hit theaters that same year, and a rousing, star-studded *No Nukes* concert rocked Madison Square Garden, with Jackson Browne, Carly Simon, John Hall, and Bonnie Raitt imploring the world to "take all your atomic poison power away."

Even as public perception of nuclear power dimmed, and US utilities stopped building new reactors, uranium mining and milling operations were ramping up in other countries, leading to a global glut and a uranium price crash. With cheaper yellowcake flooding in from overseas, the domestic industry withered.

Uranium production in the United States peaked in 1980, then fell precipitously after that.

Monticello started life as a Gentile cowtown, not becoming a mill or mining town of any sort until the Second World War. Though it is the county seat, and though there is an LDS temple there, it still retains a smidgeon of that non-Mormon cowboy, mining-town flavor, with the only real bar in San Juan County—a speakeasy sort of place with a Mormon teetotaler mixologist who throws together complicated cocktails, including one called "The Best Blow Job Ever." It is home to the Four Corners School of Outdoor Education, started here in 1984, and the Canyon Country Discovery Center, founded in 2015. Then–San Juan County commissioner Phil Lyman called the center a Trojan horse for the pro-wilderness crowd, and others said it was a gateway drug that would lead to Monticello becoming a new Moab. Monticello also is home to Uranium Watch, founded years ago by a woman named Sarah Fields, who is currently the watchdog's sole employee.

During my 2018 stop in Monticello I looked Fields up and invited her to lunch on a shady café patio to talk about the nuclear West. The wind had blown the smoke away and the air was clearer than it had been for much of the summer, but the heat was as intense as ever.

In 1987, Fields and her husband and kids moved from San Luis Obispo—just a couple miles inland from the then-new Diablo Canyon Nuclear Power Plant—to Moab. There, the Atlas uranium mill, located on the edge of town along the banks of the Colorado River, was about to shut down for good, thanks to the crash of the domestic uranium market. The owners and the federal government had to figure out what to do with the sixteen million tons of radioactive tailings that sat onsite and that was leaching into the river—and the water supply of millions of people downstream. Fields jumped into the fray, watchdogging the process for the Sierra Club and Friends of Glen Canyon before starting Uranium Watch in 2006.

With a shy smile, big blue-gray eyes, and straight silver hair, Fields is tireless in her activism, most of which is funded by her. She puts countless miles on her decades-old Toyota station wagon driving to hearings and conferences and site visits. She has learned the art of activism on the fly, brought herself up to speed on the myriad technical complexities of her focus issue. She's often the only member of the public to attend public hearings held to consider permit renewals for uranium mines and mills. When others do show, they tend to make emotional pleas against permit renewal, recounting uranium-related health problems that have plagued their families, or for renewal, due to the economic boost it could bring. Fields's comments, by contrast, are always based in science, can be highly technical, and typically are aimed not at getting permits revoked, but at making sure that the facilities do as little harm as possible while still operating. And she's an expert at badgering agencies with Freedom of Information Act requests to get them to cough up pertinent documents such as letters concerning the twenty-six-thousand-ton pile of uranium tailings now inundated by Lake Powell. Over the years Fields has continued to monitor the Atlas mill cleanup—which won't be completed until approximately 2030—and fought hard to stop a proposed nuclear plant in Green River, Utah, while keeping an eye on the lingering pollution and health problems left behind by the Monticello mill.

In the late 1980s, the Department of Energy came to Monticello and spent $250 million in taxpayer dollars to clean up the mill mess—a mess that was made by the feds, too, and financed with taxpayer dollars. Mills all over the West were remediated at around the same time, from Uravan to Grand Junction to my hometown of Durango. Today you can find the former mill sites by studying satellite maps on Google Earth and looking for the telltale tombs—big, gray, featureless monoliths in which the tailings reside—out among the sage or the sandstone. You can find the memories of that time stored up in the silt of Lake Powell and the San Juan River. And the bodies and the cells remember, too—the bodies and cells of those who worked in the mines and the mills or lived nearby, and who played on the tailings piles, swam in the raffinate ponds, and put the sandy, radioactive tailings in their vegetable gardens.

A 1997 public health assessment found that in the fifties, sixties, and seventies, white men in Monticello suffered from tracheal, bronchial, lung, and pleural cancer at rates three to four times higher than in the general US population, and white women had similarly elevated incidents of breast cancer. A follow-up study in 2014 found, again, "evidence of significantly elevated risks for lung and bronchus cancer in residents of the City of Monticello...consistent with known exposures and are biologically plausible with prolonged exposures to the contaminants from the MMTS (Monticello Mill site)." An informal survey found six hundred incidents of people with cancer, twenty-six of which were leukemia.[26]

Citing these grim statistics, residents of Monticello and victims of the mill's pollution went after the federal government, demanding that it fund a cancer screening center in Monticello and create a fund for offsetting health care costs for victims.[27] Many of the victims were uninsured or underinsured and were unable to pay the tens or hundreds of thousands of dollars for medical treatment. Some were forced to take out mortgages on their homes or even go bankrupt. Residents here in the heart of the Sagebrush Rebellion—which is partly based on anti–federal government sentiment—had yet another reason to be disdainful of the government.[28] Indeed, when the BLM was looking to build a new headquarters in town, it originally chose the old mill-site, since federal officials had told townsfolk that it was no longer hazardous. They chose another location after Department of Energy officials verbally warned them away from the site.

Studies in Shiprock have found elevated levels of birth defects, kidney disease, cancers, and other persistent health problems. In Durango, a local doctor raised alarms in the seventies regarding what he saw as a lung cancer cluster in neighborhoods adjacent to the mill and the abandoned tailings piles. A recent study in Moab showed relatively high levels of lung cancer. Yet in almost every case, the researchers stop short of putting the blame on the obvious culprit, the nearby mill or the mines. They call for more monitoring. They attribute the illnesses to higher levels of naturally occurring radiation, or to cigarette smoking, even in a predominantly Mormon town like Monticello, where smoking is rare. And then they move the tailings, ship them off to where they can't be seen, "reclaim" the site, build dog parks or golf courses or wildlife refuges there, and hope that people will forget.

Yet no matter how many millions of tons of tailings are removed, and how many millions of dollars are spent to "reclaim" the land, the toxic legacy endures, somewhere, somehow. Radioactive, heavy-metal-laden water continues to seep into Many Devils Wash, adjacent to the site of the Shiprock mill, and then into the San Juan River, flummoxing scientists. Groundwater beneath the Durango dog park still swims with high levels of uranium, lead, and other contaminants. And, in Monticello, shallow groundwater is still contaminated with elevated levels of uranium, arsenic, and manganese, and every effort to clean it up has failed.

It's no wonder, then, that people like Fields are worried about what messes might yet be made by the industry, even one that appears to be dying. In 2019, US uranium producers kicked out a record low of just eighty-six tons of uranium concentrate, less than 5 percent of the fuel consumed by domestic nuclear plants (and 95 percent less than they produced a decade earlier). The industry employs about 265 people nationwide; it's not exactly a job-creator. Nearly all of the fuel for US reactors is imported, mainly from Canada, Australia, Russia, and Kazakhstan. These countries can supply uranium for far cheaper, in part thanks to government subsidies like those that propped up the US uranium industry from the 1950s to the 1980s. Plus, because of uranium's high energy density, it is relatively cheap to ship overseas. Energy Fuels, the owner of the White Mesa Mill outside Blanding, has lobbied the federal government to limit uranium imports in order to jack up the price and keep them in business. At the same time, the company has resorted to importing and reprocessing nuclear waste from Estonia to keep the mill clinging to life.

The Trump administration balked on the import limits, in part because it would hurt the nuclear power industry by increasing prices. Instead it proposed infusing the industry with cash by purchasing large quantities of uranium for a national reserve and asked Congress for $150 million for that purpose in 2021. If that proposal were to survive into the Biden administration, and if Congress gave it the go-ahead, it could immediately and substantially up demand and prices for domestic uranium, potentially raising production to levels that haven't been seen in decades. Meanwhile, a movement to turn to low-carbon-emitting nuclear power as a tool for fighting climate change is gaining steam, and the development of smaller, cheaper nuclear reactors could lead to a miniature nuclear-power boom.

If any of these developments were to breathe new life into the domestic uranium industry, it would be felt in San Juan County and the greater Four Corners region. Energy Fuels' Daneros Mine, located on the edge of the Bears Ears National Monument in the White Canyon drainage, is currently in standby mode and would surely be put back into operation, along with Energy Fuels mines near the Grand Canyon and La Sal, Utah. Residents of White Mesa, the Ute Mountain Ute community nearest to the mill, have fought alongside Fields and other environmental activists to get the company to implement better safety measures at the mill to ensure that it doesn't contaminate their groundwater. And the neo-Sagebrush Rebels have been there, as well, cheering on the industry. "I think it is a beautiful industry," said Lyman, in a hearing on the White Mesa Mill's permit renewal in 2017. "I think it holds the key to a peaceful and clean world and in the future, we will be a nuclear-powered civilization....Claiming to shut down the mill to protect the environment is akin to turning Bears Ears to an industrial tourism mecca in order to protect cultural resources."

Chapter Ten

Aneth Oil

I MAGINE THE SCENE: A DIMLY LIT ROOM IN A SANTA FE hotel, perhaps the La Fonda, on a crisp night in October 1923. A group of men sit around a table, wearing coats and ties, playing a game of poker, the smell of cigar smoke mingling with that of piñon burning in the fireplace. One of the men is Herbert J. Hagerman, distinguished-looking, perhaps a bit pompous, with a long face and hooded eyes. In 1937 writer Erna Fergusson will describe Hagerman as "a high-collared aristocrat with diplomatic experience in Imperial Russia, a big ranch in the Pecos valley, a turbulent career as governor of New Mexico, a love of calm and security, an unassailable integrity, a reluctance to fight, and doomed always to be the center of bitter controversy." He is the federal commissioner to the Navajo Tribe and will auction off a slew of oil and gas leases on behalf of the newly formed Navajo Tribal Council the following day. The other men around the table are potential bidders.

The poker players take a break, and Hagerman motions one of the players and a friend of his, railroad man C. S. Muñoz, to follow him to a private area. Hagerman asks Muñoz which parcels he plans to bid on. Most of the leases up for auction are in the Shiprock, New Mexico, area, where an oil and gas rush had erupted a few years earlier. Muñoz mentions the Tocito

structure, which geologists have deemed to be the most promising of the lot, as well as the Hogback. Hagerman raises his eye-
brows. Everyone will be bidding for the Tocito, which will surely
push the price up into the fifty- to sixty-thousand-dollar range.
"Maybe consider the Rattlesnake," Hagerman says, and then
walks back to the playing table. It's strange advice. The geologists
had ranked the Rattlesnake structure at the bottom of the barrel
because intrusive dikes would make it undesirable for drilling.
The next day, Indian Affairs commissioner Charles H. Burke
himself will preside over the auction, one of the first of its kind,
and made possible only by a major overhaul of the entire Navajo
structure of government.

PRIOR TO THE LONG WALK, THE TRIBE WAS DIVIDED UP INTO
political units of a dozen or more families, each governed by its
own *naataanii*, or headmen. While the headmen would gather
for occasional all-tribal councils, there was no central seat of
government, no chief who represented the tribe as a whole.
That was a source of frustration for those trying to make deals
or treaties with the tribe, yet it worked well for a highly mobile
and dispersed society that spanned tens of thousands of square
miles. After the return from Bosque Redondo, an ad hoc governing system slowly emerged that, in some ways, echoed what
had existed previously. Navajo lands were divided up into agencies, each of which had a white superintendent appointed by
the Bureau of Indian Affairs. Each agency also had a handful
of headmen who would come together to determine whether
to allow miners to prospect on their land, or perhaps lobby the
government on behalf of their constituents.

That system was in place in the early 1920s, when big oil
companies started poking around just inside the reservation
in the Shiprock Agency, near the banks of the San Juan River.
The agency superintendent called the agency leaders together to

consider allowing the companies to drill. The headmen at Shiprock, which remains a defiant chapter to this day, turned them down repeatedly. Finally they issued just one lease, to Midwest Oil, only after getting a number of concessions from the company.

Frustrated, the other companies appealed to Washington, which had just become more friendly to industry with the election of President Warren G. Harding. At the behest of the industries that had financed his campaign, Harding had appointed Albert B. Fall to be secretary of interior. Fall was a cigar-chomping, rapacious Republican rancher and friend to oil barons. He first entered New Mexico territorial politics in the 1890s, serving as a territorial representative and as attorney general. In 1912, he was elected as one of the brand-new state's first senators, and continued to serve until 1921, when Harding appointed him his cabinet.

In his first year as senator Fall went on tirades against the very idea of public lands and conservation thereof with rhetoric that would be echoed decades later by the Sagebrush Rebels. "The conservation of the natural resources of New Mexico means a restriction upon the individual," he ranted to the Senate in 1912. "And means that upon such forest reserves and Indian reserves the gentle bear, the mountain lion, and the timber wolf are conserved, so that they may attack his herds, his cattle, and his sheep." He went on to propose to his colleagues, "as an act of justice, to give those forest reserves to the charge of the people who know what a forest reserve is."

Fall was from the Manifest Destiny school of land use, and saw the West as a big grab bag of oil, gas, coal, timber, and minerals. "All natural resources should be made as easy of access as possible to the present generation," he once said. "Man cannot exhaust the resources of nature and never will." His early hostility towards public lands in general mellowed during his time in the nation's capital, probably because he realized that his oil baron buddies could exploit public lands even if they did stay in public hands, so long as regulatory hindrances were kept to a minimum. He eventually would come out in support of creating new national monuments, and was an architect[29] of the General Mineral Leasing Act of 1920, which brought some order to the drilling free-for-all on federal lands and which to this day guides public lands energy development. He no longer wanted to privatize all public lands, he just wanted private interests to have unfettered access to the resources embedded within those lands. And when he was appointed to Harding's cabinet, he was prepared to roll back and squash the conservation ethic that President Theodore Roosevelt and Forest Service Chief Gifford Pinchot had brought to the nation's lands two decades earlier. His ideology extended to the Naval Oil Reserves, which he managed to open up to general leasing, and to Indian reservations, particularly those created by executive order, which he considered to be the property of the federal government, not the tribes in question.

Fall put this credo to work in San Juan County, Utah, in the area known as the Paiute Strip. In 1884, President Chester A. Arthur signed an executive order adding all of the land in Utah south of the San Juan River to the Navajo Nation. Eight years later, in order to clear the way for the 1892 gold rush along the lower San Juan River, President Benjamin Harrison took about half of the Utah addition, the portion west of the 110th meridian, which contains Navajo Mountain, back, putting it into the public domain and thus opening it back up to mining claims and homesteading. That piece of land became known as the Paiute Strip because it was home to the Southern San Juan Paiute Tribe. When the gold rush turned out to be a dud, the land was returned to the Navajo Nation, and in 1907 it again became tribal land, only this time as the Southern San Juan Paiute reservation. But greed wouldn't let the Paiute Strip alone: in 1920, when oil prices shot sky high and wildcatters were descending on the region in search of Texas tea, a company called Paradise Oil applied for a lease on the land. Commissioner Burke told Paradise that a lease would not be possible until the land was taken away from the Paiutes—whose population had been ravaged by the 1918 Influenza in preceding years—and put into the public domain. In July 1922, Interior Secretary Fall did just that, stealing stolen land all over again.

Fall had to tread more delicately in regards to the Navajo Nation, since it was far larger and more powerful than the Southern San Juan Paiute tribe. In order to bypass the recalcitrant Shiprock Agency and get its oil flowing, Interior Secretary Fall first appointed a Navajo "Business Council" of three people to make leasing decisions for the entire reservation. Commissioner Burke—a well-known assimilationist who had banned Indigenous religious ceremonies—nixed that idea, however, since it was so blatantly undemocratic. He and Fall instead planned out a centralized, representative-style Navajo tribal council, with delegates from each agency. They assigned New Mexican attorney Herbert Hagerman to be the special commissioner to "negotiate with the Indians."

The Navajo voters elected twenty-four delegates, and in July 1923 the first tribal council was seated. The Navajo Nation had a centralized government for the first time ever, which should have been a step towards greater sovereignty and self-determination. Instead, the council promptly handed to Hagerman all powers to sign and negotiate oil and gas leases. Fall resigned around the same time under pressure for his involvement in the Teapot Dome Scandal as well as for his role in the Bursum Bill, which would have robbed Pueblo Indians in New Mexico of thousands of acres of land and water rights.

Hagerman organized the first Navajo lease sale to take place just a few months later in Santa Fe. Bidding on the Hogback leases was fierce, netting the tribe more than $80,000. The Rattlesnake, though, was thought to be a dud, and only Muñoz bid on it, paying just $1,000 for a 4,080-acre lease. Hagerman signed the lease on behalf of the Navajo Nation, and set a royalty rate of 12.5 percent, which was the same rate that the Mineral Leasing Act set for minerals taken from federal lands.

Later it was discovered that just two days before the lease sale, Hagerman had received the geological report on the Rattlesnake, showing that it was likely to be a bonanza. Yet he had kept the new information under wraps from all perspective buyers, save for, allegedly, Muñoz. After the sale Hagerman urged the Department of Interior to expedite approval of the Rattlesnake lease, which it did, and within a few months of the sale Muñoz's Santa Fe Co. had drilled multiple gushers. One Rattlesnake well would go on to produce millions of barrels of crude over the next decade, the grade so high that it was dangerous to pipe it to the rail line in Gallup or the small refinery then in Farmington. Soon after striking oil, Muñoz sold a percentage of his interest to Continental Oil for between $3.25 million, none of which went to the tribe that actually owned the oil.

Hagerman later came under attack in Congress for what appeared to be insider trading to the advantage of Muñoz—whom detractors referred to as Hagerman's "intimate friend"—at the expense of the tribe. Had that report been available to the public, bidding would have been far higher for the Rattlesnake, and the tribal government would have received a much larger payment. Hagerman also was accused of misrepresenting the Navajo Nation by supporting, on the tribal council's behalf, a congressional bill that would have slashed royalty revenues for tribes. The bill would have diverted 90 percent of the royalties paid for drilling on executive order reservations to the federal and respective state governments, leaving just 10 percent—or a royalty rate of 1.25 percent—to the tribal nation whose oil was being purloined by the petro-corporations. The bill had originated back when Fall was a senator, and hinged upon Fall's belief that reservations created by executive order, rather than by treaty or Congress, were the property of the federal government, and that the General Mineral Leasing Act of 1920 should apply to them. The bill bounced around in Congress for years, nearly passing in 1925, an indication that, among much of the federal government, the policy of Indian removal hadn't really ended back in the nineteenth century, but had instead just changed form. Finally, in 1927, Congress passed a bill that affirmed that all royalties would go to the tribe in question. It was an improvement, but it would not stop dishonest brokers from negotiating terrible leases for tribes for the next fifty years.

While Fall ultimately would be remembered for the fact that he was the first cabinet member to go to jail, his real legacy lies in his role in setting the groundwork for oil and gas and coal development on public lands and, to a lesser extent, tribal lands. The Mineral Leasing Act of 1920 that he helped usher through as senator still applies today. And a few decades after the Navajo Nation tribal council was formed, it signed off on some sizable oil leases in the Aneth oil field in San Juan County, Utah.

Oilmen began poking around in the Aneth area on the southern end of the Paradox Basin in the late 1940s. What they found proved promising, sparking interest far and wide. In November 1956 the Bureau of Indian Affairs held a lease sale for parcels on that section of the Navajo Nation, which would come to be known as the Aneth oil field, bringing in $27 million in lease bonus payments to the tribe. In return, the companies would get the right to extract the tribe's petroleum for the next ninety-nine years. A *Time* magazine article about the sale called the Utah Navajo a bunch of "lucky Indians."

The drill rigs arrived, roaring away day and night, the pumpjacks started their slow grind, and the oil flowed. The workers poured in, along with their high wages, to a place that had little infrastructure, law enforcement, or any other services to handle them. Few of the jobs on the rigs went to local Navajo people. Navajos who did get hired were paid less than their white cohorts, and were forbidden from speaking their native tongue. Most of the white workers lived in Cortez or even Farmington, commuting back and forth on the rough and narrow McElmo Canyon road. My father was a teenager at the time, living up the road in Dolores, Colorado, and he worked summers on a farm that grew melons and other crops in McElmo Canyon. The farm went belly-up soon after the oil rush began because the rough-necks would come by at night and trample the fields and steal the melons. It's one of a legion of ways an extractive boom can unravel the social fabric of a community or a region.

For the residents of the Aneth Chapter, things were much worse. Rig-hands stole sheep and sometimes took out entire flocks while speeding along the backroads in their oil company trucks. The workers brought drugs, alcohol, sexual assault, and sexually transmitted diseases. Noxious gases poured out of the processing plants and the rigs. Produced water—which occurs alongside oil, is often briney and contaminated with various hydrocarbons, and that is pumped out of the wells in massive amounts—was dumped onto the land or put back in shallow wells, allowing it to contaminate springs on which locals had long relied. In 1972 a pipeline leading out of the field burst, spilling nearly three-hundred-thousand gallons of crude, which ran down a wash and into the San Juan River. The oil slick floated two hundred miles downriver, through San Juan County. It killed countless fish and coated rocks, birds, and beavers on the way. The fledgling Environmental Protection Agency led the multi-agency cleanup effort on the San Juan branch of Lake Powell, one of its first big actions.

The first portion of the reservation north of the San Juan River had been added by President Theodore Roosevelt in 1905 by executive order. In 1933 the Aneth Extension was added to the Navajo Nation, along with the aforementioned Paiute Strip. They came with a unique provision: If and when oil was produced on the lands, the producer would pay a 12.5 percent royalty to the tribe, as was the case elsewhere in Indian Country. Royalties from Aneth oil, however, would be divided up, with 37.5 percent of it going to the State of Utah, which was to use the funds to benefit the people living within those lands; in 1968 the mandate was expanded so that the funds would be spent "for the health, education, and general welfare of the Navajo Indians residing in San Juan County." The other 62.5 percent would go to the Navajo Nation's central government. This arrangement would be a point of contention for decades to follow and would even seep into the controversy over the designation of Bears Ears National Monument.

As the oil flowed out—thirty-eight million barrels in 1959—and the damages accrued, royalty revenues flowed back in to the tribal government and the State of Utah, which had been designated as the keeper of the Utah Navajo's portion. It should be understood that "royalty" is a sort of euphemism that obscures what's really going on here. A royalty is not a tax or a fee imposed upon the oil company. Rather, it is the price the oil company pays to take the oil from its owner and sell it elsewhere for a profit. Yes, the owner. Federal minerals are owned by the American people and tribal minerals are owned by the tribal nation's citizens, just as the oil lying under private land belongs to the landowner unless it's split estate land. It's an important distinction to understand. When framed as a tax or fee, a rate of 12.5 percent of the sale-value seems rather high. But when a royalty is seen for what it actually is, the wholesale price, then the rate seems quite low, since, effectively, the oil company is turning around and selling the same oil that it pulled out of the ground at an 800 percent markup.

Even with the low rates, production from the Aneth field netted the Navajo Nation millions of dollars, and for years was one of its leading sources of revenue. Since a portion of the royalties also went to the Utah Navajos by way of the state's Indian Affairs Commission, the Navajo Nation didn't feel the need to redistribute much of its share back to the Aneth area. The San Juan County Board of Commissioners, made up entirely of white men, similarly refused to provide adequate services to its citizens that lived on the reservation.

Meanwhile, the state was spending the share intended for the Utah Navajos in ways that didn't match the mandate. In the 1970s, for example, the state spent over $200,000 on facilities and a private collection of pots and other antiquities for the new Edge of the Cedars Museum in Blanding. Some of the artifacts that were purchased had been taken illegally from public lands, and the big payout was criticized for incentivizing pothunting and looting. Cash from the fund also went towards building off-reservation roads and to the social services center and the College of Eastern Utah, both in Blanding. Most egregiously, the fund was used to purchase a shopping mall in a Salt Lake suburb, benefitting the white chairman of the board that chose how to spend the funds more than the Utah Navajos. The end result was that the people who lived in the oil field felt as if they were giving just about everything and receiving virtually nothing in return. They were getting screwed over by the oil companies, the feds, the state, the county, and even their own tribal government.

The situation boiled over when an oil-field worker shot at a sheepherder who tried to stop the worker from stealing his sheep. Long before the Standing Rock Sioux Tribe would rise up to try to stop a destructive pipeline from being built across their water source in 2016, bringing international attention to the cause of environmental justice and Indigenous rights, the people of Aneth took on the oil corporations. In March 1978, hundreds of Diné—men in jeans and cowboy hats, women in velveteen skirts, longhairs, shorthairs—set out across the spare landscape of the Aneth Chapter toward the Texaco pumping plant, kicked out the employees, and occupied it. They also blocked the only road into the area, ceasing production across the whole field.

Among those assembled were members of the Coalition for

Navajo Liberation, which had formed several years earlier to
fight against systemic violence in reservation border towns such
as Gallup and Farmington, where a group of white teenagers had
murdered three Diné men and were sent to a juvenile deten-
tion center rather than prison. The group soon expanded its
mission to include "protection of our natural resources against
white corporations, the protection of our Mother Earth, and the
protection of individual rights." The coalition held demonstrations in Farmington and was involved, along with the American
Indian Movement, in the 1975 armed takeover of the Fairchild
Semiconductor plant in Shiprock, where it issued a statement
saying: "It is time for Navajos to control their own domain and
their own destiny, rather than to remain victims of the white
man's industrial enterprises." The Aneth group wanted the oil
companies to stop wrecking their lands and livelihoods, but they
also wanted the Navajo Nation to start distributing the oil revenues more fairly. The occupiers demanded that the oil companies hire more Diné workers, that they provide scholarships for
local students, and that oil field workers refrain from bringing
drugs and alcohol onto the reservation. After seventeen days
of occupation, a settlement was reached, and the oil companies
were allowed to return.

Often left out in coverage of this act of resistance is the context in which it took place. There was the national context, of
course, which involved the rise of the American Indian Movement, the Wounded Knee Occupation, and the continuation of
the counterculture movement that rose up to protest American involvement in the Vietnam War. And tribal governments,
including the Navajo Nation's, were also working within the
establishment to wrest control of their energy resources from
the federal government's hands, forming CERT, or the Council of Energy Resource Tribes, in 1975. The local context bears
mentioning, as well: among the white population of San Juan
County, and much of the rest of the rural West, the Sagebrush

Rebellion was erupting at the same time. The Aneth uprising and the Sagebrush Rebellion were diametrically opposed to one another. Really, the Aneth group fit the definition of "rebel" far better than the Sagebrush Rebels. The Sagebrush Rebels were fighting to hang onto power and dominance, the Aneth group was rebelling against the established power structure. Yet they also moved in parallel. Both groups were pushing back against the federal government's policies and pushing for more self-determination. At that time, the Bureau of Indian Affairs was still negotiating oil and gas leases for tribal nations, a practice that had locked the Navajo Nation into century-long leases with relatively low royalty rates (in the early eighties Congress and a Supreme Court ruling would change that). And both the Sagebrush Rebels and the Aneth protestors were not happy with their respective central governments—in Washington, DC, and Window Rock—and the way they tended to treat outliers like them as if they were distant colonies.

The end of the occupation by no means marked the end of the problems, or protests, in the Aneth oil field. As the easy-to-get-at oil was depleted, drilling intensified along with the environmental effects. Oil companies started flooding old wells with millions of gallons of pressurized groundwater to push out more crude—this in a place where few homes have running water, and some people must drive for an hour or more to fill up tanks for domestic use. They then switched to shooting carbon dioxide into the wells, a practice known as enhanced oil recovery.

The web of oil infrastructure that is tangled up with the landscape and placed near homes leaks volatile organic compounds, methane, and sulfur dioxide. Spills of oil and produced water are common, still: between 2000 and 2014, San Juan County led the state for "accidental releases" of harmful materials, according to EPA data, with oil and gas companies reporting 2,200 such releases, four times more than in Salt Lake County, the second highest in the state. In 1992, a high-pressure oil pipe ruptured and sprayed crude all over someone's house. Mobil offered the owner less than $1,000 in compensation. In a story about it that year in the *Deseret News*, a Navajo Tribal Council delegate from Aneth was quoted as saying such incidents were common: "There are no environmental rules or regulations here. No one cares about the people who live here, just the oil."

The locals again demanded reform. "Something drastic has to happen," Rebecca Benally—who would later become a San Juan County commissioner and key player in the Bears Ears National Monument debate—told a group of protesters in 1992, as quoted in the *Salt Lake Tribune*. "You have to respect Navajo culture, otherwise we know you're here for the money and personal gain." Several months later, the resistance blocked a road to an oil facility in protest and then, after an oil field explosion in 1997, a group of locals set up a tepee in front of the Mobil offices, essentially shutting it down for seventy-two hours until a deal with oil field managers could be reached.

In the meantime, at the urging of the Navajo Nation, the Environmental Protection Agency launched investigations into the practices of the oil companies there. In 2002 the agency fined Texaco close to $400,000 for violating the Clean Water Act and required it to build a project to deliver potable water to area homes. In 2004 and 2005 the EPA made ExxonMobil pay $6.5 million for violations of both the Clean Water Act and the Clean Air Act. Shortly thereafter ExxonMobil sold its stake of the field to Resolute Energy and the Navajo Nation Oil and Gas Company, and Resolute later sold out to Elk Petroleum, which is in bankruptcy as I write this.

The Aneth oil field is mostly located on the Navajo Nation, so the public land wars don't play out on the sere landscape anymore[30]. But Aneth players and politics have significantly influenced the fight. Mark Maryboy was active in the Aneth protests, served as a San Juan County commissioner, and is one of the prime movers behind the Bears Ears National Monument designation. Rebecca Benally was Maryboy's ally in pushing back against the oil companies, but later joined up with the Sagebrush Rebels in virulently opposing national monument designation. While other Utah chapters would overwhelmingly support the national monument, the Aneth Chapter would become deeply divided over whether to support or oppose the designation, with the opposition usually prevailing.

Today, the Aneth oil field is a place of eerie and subtle beauty that most people miss as they are speeding through on their way to the narrow canyons and more dramatic topography to the west. But if you slow down and really open your eyes you'll begin to detect beauty in the subdued purple and ash hues of the buttes, in the massive blocks of desert-varnished sandstone that look like dice tossed carelessly across the earth by the gods. Horses range freely among the sage, ribcage ripples lining their sides. And everywhere one looks, there are the pumpjacks, looking like metallic cutouts of Tyrannosaurus Rexes, grinding their relentless languid grind as they pull out the three-hundred-million-year-old remains of phytoplankton and zooplankton caught up in mud and silt back when this was all covered by an enormous, shallow sea.

CHAPTER ELEVEN

THE THREE RS AND THE FIRST SAGEBRUSH REBELLION

[The] Sagebrush [Rebellion] comes into relief as what it really is — a murky fusion of idealism and greed that may not be heroic, nor righteous, nor even intelligent. Only one certainty exists—that Sagebrush is a revolt against federal authority, and that its taproot grows deep in the century's history. Beyond this, it is incoherent. Part hypocrisy, part demagoguery, partly the honest anger of honest people, it is a movement of confusion and hysteria and terrifyingly destructive potential. What it is no one fully understands. What it will do no one can tell.

— From *The Angry West*, by Colorado governor
Richard Lamm, 1982

IN MARCH OF 1977, CECIL ANDRUS, THE NEWLY APPOINTED secretary of the interior of the newly elected President Jimmy Carter, gave a rousing speech to a room packed with members of the National Wildlife Federation. He clearly wanted to let those gathered know that there was a new administration in town, one that would take a fresh approach[31] to public lands management.

"Conservation is no longer a pious ideal—it is an element of our survival, and my efforts will focus on curbing old habits of overconsumption and misuse, seeking instead to use less and to use better," he said. "I might as well begin with the [action] that has 'ticked off' the most opposition in this town—the deletion of dam building and other water projects from the upcoming year's budget [because] the environmental and safety consequences are more important than the dollars. Common sense dictates that we shouldn't dam up every river, stream, or creek in America."

He said this on the heels of a decades-long dam-building frenzy across the West, during which the once-wild waters of the Colorado, the San Juan, the Gunnison, and the Chama had been stilled, with the Dolores coming next. It was also a time of drought across much of the region, when the favored method of tackling dry years was to build a dam, a pipeline, or some other infrastructure that impounded, diverted, or channeled streams and rivers. So the words were clearly shocking. It didn't end there. "The initials BLM no longer stand for Bureau of Livestock and Mining. The days when economic interests exercised control over decisions on the public domain are past. The public's lands will be managed in the interest of *all* the people because they belong to all the people. For too long, much of the land where the deer and the antelope play has been managed primarily for livestock often to the detriment of wildlife." Had he been addressing, say, the National Cattlemen's Association, instead, he would have been torn limb from limb before he had a chance to step away from the podium. "At Interior we have begun to make sweeping institutional and policy changes to end what I see as the domination of the department by mining, oil, and other special interests."

And then he came to the kicker: "We intend to exercise our stewardship of public lands and natural resources in a manner that will make the 'three Rs'—rape, ruin, and run—a thing of the past."

Oh, to see Calvin Black's face when he heard or read that line.

Calvin Black grew up in San Juan County, the descendant of early Mormon settlers, and part of the big, tangled up family tree of Blanding and surroundings. You might say that he had bulldozers in his blood. His dad had been the state road foreman, back when there were very few roads in some parts of the county, and supervised construction of the road from Natural Bridges to Hite. As a young man Cal Black hauled ore for the uranium mines, then became a prospector and mine owner himself, as well as a businessman who started two radio stations, a mortuary, and owned the Elk Ridge Cafe hotel and restaurant in Blanding.

But he's probably best known for his politics. He was a San Juan County commissioner for more than two decades, a state legislator, and even the mayor of Blanding. And he was an irascible Sagebrush Rebel, the original, or so his sister once told me. Edward Abbey modeled Bishop Love, the antagonist that chases Hayduke and friends all over San Juan County in *The Monkey Wrench Gang*, after Black. Black grew up during a time when he and other locals, along with industries that invaded to get at the uranium or oil or whatnot, had pretty much free rein on the public lands. If they wanted to build a road, by God, they'd fire up the bulldozer and build a damned road, no permission necessary. If they wanted to mine for uranium, they'd file a claim and start digging. If they wanted to dig up an ancient village or grave to get at the "curios" hidden there, no one was going to stop them.

And so it was that when Black was still in his teens, there were only about seven hundred miles of county roads within San Juan County, which was fairly thin for a seven-thousand-square-mile piece of land, and the assessed valuation for the county was a mere $3.8 million. By the time Black turned thirty, oil and gas, uranium, and road-building had boomed, and the assessed valuation had jumped to $133 million, making rural San Juan County the second-richest in the state.

"All development was good development. It was bulldozers everywhere," Winston Hurst, an archaeologist who also grew up in Blanding, and also counts Hole-in-the-Rockers as ancestors, told me in the summer of 2016, during the buildup to the designation of Bears Ears National Monument. "You see the archaeological record of that time and mentality all over out there." The vandalism of the land extended to archaeological sites, too. "Back then the looting was on a scale that people have now forgotten. It was so out of control."

It wouldn't last. It couldn't last. Nationwide, an environmental ethos was gaining steam. The Sierra Club's membership blossomed during the sixties and early seventies, and their campaigns to halt dams and other development actually started working. Congress passed the Wilderness Act in 1964, the same year that President Lyndon B. Johnson signed the bill creating Canyonlands National Park, a tremendously downsized echo of the Escalante National Monument proposal from three decades earlier. Black's not on record opposing the designation, but when park superintendent Bates Wilson put forth a plan to keep development and roads within the park to a minimum, while upping preservation, Black lashed back, accusing Wilson of trying to make a park only for backpackers, one of Black's favorite pejoratives. He spoke out against the National Park Service proposal to enlarge Glen Canyon National Recreation Area to include portions of the Escalante and San Juan River drainages beyond the edges of Lake Powell. San Juan County sent a $50 million tax bill to the federal government in 1976, saying that was how much money they'd receive in property taxes if all of the public land was in private hands.

Black's mine-and-drill and bulldoze-at-all-costs ethos was getting crimped in other ways, as well. In the late 1960s the US Department of Labor finally proposed standards for controlling radiation in uranium mines for the sake of worker safety. Black said the proposal would cripple or shut down the industry, including the Markey Mine, which he owned, where radon levels were far higher than the proposed standards. In tackling lung cancer among miners, Black—who wore a uranium amulet around his neck—told a newspaper reporter, "It could be that we need to focus more upon smoking and less upon radiation."

Meanwhile, the preservationists were slowly making inroads into federal policy, with the Endangered Species Act, the Clean Water Act, the Clean Air Act, and the National Environmental Policy Act. Still, all of those were minor setbacks for the "rape, ruin, and run" crowd compared to what would come in 1976, when Congress passed the Federal Land Management Policy Act. FLPMA shifted the Bureau of Land Management's mandate from one of maximizing extraction from public lands, to preserving—to an extent—those same lands. Although it didn't overturn the Mining Law of 1872 or the General Mineral Leasing Act of 1920, FLPMA did end the longstanding practice of "disposing" of federal lands to states, corporations, or individuals. Significantly for southeast Utah, it also tossed out Revised Statute 2477, the provision in the 1866 Mining Act that granted anyone the right to build a road across the public domain without a permit. Plus, FLPMA opened the door to Wilderness designations on BLM lands. To critics, it locked in the absentee landlord relationship Washington had with much of the West, even though western members of Congress led the process of formulating the act.

FLPMA catalyzed the rise of the first Sagebrush Rebellion, or at least the first with that name. It emerged simultaneously across the rural West, with the most significant flare-ups in Nevada, Idaho, and southern Utah, with activity in all thirteen western states. The rebellion was in part a political uprising, with the big beef livestock lobby joining up with oil and gas and mining interests to push back against what they saw as hindrances to their ability to exploit public lands. But it was also an ideological and cultural crusade, a sort of counter-counterculture movement led by conservative, capitalist white men who faced a crisis of impotence. They were scared: not only

were environmentalists gaining strength, but so were Indige-
nous-power movements, from the American Indian Movement
to the Coalition for Navajo Liberation to the Native American
Rights Fund to the more staid, but still threatening, Council of
Energy Resource Tribes. On top of all of that Gloria Steinem
and Bella Abzug and Shirley Chisholm were storming male-
dominated Washington as politicians, protesters, publishers,
and lawmakers. The Sagebrush Rebels felt that their long reign
of dominance was coming to an end, and so they lashed back.

THE MOVEMENT HAD MANY LAYERS, TOOK MANY FORMS, AND
included a wide array of adherents. Some, like Black, Nevada
lawmaker Dean Rhoads, and Utah rancher and businessman
Bert Smith, fit the stereotypical mold of multigenerational rural
westerners from ranching or extractive industry backgrounds.
Others not so much. Orrin Hatch was a member of the LDS
Church like many of his fellow anti-environmentalist radicals,
but he grew up in Pittsburgh and didn't move to Utah until
matriculating in Brigham Young University. He was first elected
to the US Senate in 1976, defeating incumbent liberal Democrat Frank Moss, and his leadership of the Sagebrush Rebellion
would be one of the first major roles in a long, arch-conservative
career. Hatch, Black, and Senators Barry Goldwater and Ted
Stevens, Republicans from Arizona and Alaska, respectively,
launched the League for the Advancement of States Equal Rights,
or LASER, the biggest and most influential organization pushing
back against land-use regulations. It was a sort of western version of the right-wing American Legislative Exchange Council,
which was founded in 1973, and a predecessor to the American
Lands Council, which endeavors to transfer public lands into
state, county, and private hands.

On a legislative level the Sagebrush Rebellion had a single
aim: convey federal lands to the respective states. Lawmakers

in Nevada, Arizona, New Mexico, Utah, and Wyoming passed bills laying claim to BLM land, all of which were merely symbolic, since they lacked any legal basis. Hatch also introduced bills in the Senate in 1979 and 1980 that would have done the same thing. While some Sagebrush Rebels insisted that the states would hold on to the land and prove better stewards than the feds, it was implicitly understood that most of the land would eventually wind up in private hands. Hatch admitted as much on the Senate floor, saying that the land would go to the state, then the counties, before being sold off to the highest bidder. He later took a different tack, saying he couldn't imagine a state selling off its land. It was a clearly disingenuous statement given that Utah regularly auctions off its School and Institutional Trust Lands, which shows up on maps as 640-acre squares scattered randomly across federal lands.

On a larger scale, the Sagebrush Rebellion was anything but single-minded and proved itself to be a complex—or perhaps confused—movement rife with internal contradictions. In some cases, it even found itself allied with the enemy. Sagebrush Rebels, anti-nuclear activists, and affected tribal nations all joined up in opposition to the siting of MX missile launch facilities on public land in the Nevada and Utah deserts. Colorado congressman Ray Kogovsek, a Democrat, spoke in favor of federal land transfers so that states like his would have the power to slow or stop environmental degradation. In a 1980 congressional hearing on the Sagebrush Rebellion, Kogovsek said, "There are so few western congressmen that it is hard for us to win on any one given issue, because most of the things that are being done are being done to the West, whether it is nuclear energy, whether it is where we are going to put its waste, whether it is the MX missile, whether it is the development of oil shale…right now the only leasing going on is on federal property without the concurrence of the states and the local governments around them."

And Hatch, even while trying to open the way for more uranium mining in his state and deriding those trying to stop it
as "toadstool worshippers," fought tirelessly to get recognition
and compensation for downwinders, the people who suffered ill
effects of decades of nuclear weapons testing in Nevada. Many
years later he also managed to secure federal funding for Monticello residents who had been sickened by contamination from
the uranium mill that had operated there for twenty years.

The Sagebrush Rebellion never erupted into full-fledged
violence in the way that more recent uprisings have, but the
rhetoric definitely leaned that way. In response to inventories of
wilderness-quality lands, Black told BLM officials that he was to
the point "where I'll blow up bridges, ruins, and vehicles. We're
going to start a revolution." Black never delivered on his promises, but there was widespread vandalism of ancient Puebloan
sites in Utah that appeared to be politically motivated. In 1979
the Archaeological Resources Protection Act was passed, giving
more teeth to anti-pothunting laws and further fueling the rebels' fire. And in 1980, the Grand County, Utah, commissioners
led a group of hundreds of locals in bulldozing a road into a Wilderness Study Area in protest of what they saw as a BLM land
grab. No one was prosecuted.

The greater Sagebrush Rebellion reached its apex, and celebrated its last hurrah, in November 1980 at a four-day LASER
conference in Salt Lake City's Little America Hotel. Black, Hatch,
Rhoads, and all the other principles of the movement were
on hand to decry the "policrats" and the "colonization" of the
western states by the eastern bureaucrats. Various panels came
up with initiatives on which LASER should focus in coming
months, including public relations and trying to stock the federal agencies with people from the extractive industries. On one
of the walls hung a huge photo of Ronald Reagan, who had just
been elected president, emblazoned with his words from earlier
that summer: "Count me in as a rebel."

Reagan's election was a huge victory for the movement, and he staffed his administration with rebels, ranchers, and other members of what Andrus had called the rape, ruin, and run crowd. James Watt, a strident private property rights advocate, was named to head the Interior Department. In 1977 Watt had started the Mountain States Legal Foundation, which would become the legal arm of the Sagebrush Rebellion and continues to wage an ideological crusade against environmental protections, gun laws, and tribal sovereignty to this day. Reagan picked conservative Colorado rancher and politician Bob Burford to run the BLM, despite, or maybe because of, his lack of experience in land management. In 1983 Burford would marry Anne Gorsuch,[32] another arch-conservative Colorado attorney and politician who served as Reagan's first administrator of the Environmental Protection Agency, which she downsized and diminished from within.

Watt named Wyoming lawyer William Perry Pendley as his deputy assistant secretary for energy and minerals. "One of the worst things about going to work for the administration is to be referred to as a 'bureaucrat,'" Pendley said in a speech during the early days of his time in the administration, "but since I'm working for Jim Watt, I wear that badge with some honor and distinction."

Watt, protégé Pendley, and Burford set out to open up as much federal land as possible to development, drilling, and mining, while tearing down any regulatory "impediments" to the same. They attempted to allow oil and gas exploration in wilderness areas and eviscerated the newly created Office of Surface Mining Reclamation and Enforcement, preferring to let the corporations police themselves. The fees the federal government charges ranchers for putting their cows on government land have always been meagre, but the Reagan administration slashed them even more. The amount levied to put one cow-calf pair on public land for one month dropped from just above two dollars in 1981 to about half that in 1987, causing a steep decline in revenues as well.[33] In 1982 the department held an auction on federal coal leases in the Powder River Basin of Wyoming. Beforehand, Pendley encouraged his colleagues to lease out as much coal as possible, by whatever means necessary. The sale ended up turning over 1.6 billion tons of the American public's coal to huge mining companies at bargain-basement prices, ringing alarm bells in Congress. Ensuing investigations found that the mining companies had received confidential information prior to the sale, presumably from someone within the Interior Department, allowing them to bid below market value for the coal. They also found that attorneys for those same mining companies treated Pendley and his colleague to a lavish dinner at a Washington, DC, restaurant shortly before the sale. Pendley was never formally charged with ethics violations, but after Watt unceremoniously stepped down from his post for making bigoted remarks, Pendley was reassigned before he quietly departed the bureaucracy—for the time being. Pendley went on to head up the Mountain States Legal Foundation for three decades, whence he engaged in battle with federal land agencies before being chosen by the Trump administration in 2019 to lead one of those same agencies, the BLM.

With many of the key Sagebrush Rebels becoming government officials, there was suddenly a whole lot less to rebel against, and the nationwide movement ebbed. Reagan made moves to sell off small parcels of public lands but never went for wholesale land transfers of the kind that LASER had pushed. Meanwhile, what was left of the rebellion fractured on the issue of federal land transfer bills that were still alive at the state level. A study by the Interior Department found that states could end up losing millions of dollars if they were to assume ownership of federal lands. Also, the Payments in Lieu of Taxes program, or PILT, was just kicking in at that time. Under the program, the feds pay counties in order to make up for property taxes that the counties can't collect from public lands. That money would be lost if the state took over the land.

Many ranchers and miners had second thoughts about the states taking over federal land, as well. Hardrock miners have nearly unfettered access to federal lands and have to pay no royalties for the minerals they extract. FLPMA didn't change that. Oil and gas drillers still pay low royalties for federal minerals, and ranchers continue to get a prime deal for grazing on BLM lands. They were worried they'd lose those deals under state management since royalties and grazing fees for state lands can be 50 percent higher or more than for federal lands. In 2020 a livestock operator paid $1.35 to graze a cow-calf pair on BLM land for one month; they would pay at least $6 per month to put the same pair of cows out on Utah state land.

WHILE THE REBELLION FADED WEST-WIDE, AT LEAST FOR A while, it continued raging in San Juan County. Reagan's election may have put a damper on preservation efforts on public lands, but it didn't kill them. FLPMA remained in place, along with all of the landmark environmental laws. More importantly, San Juan County's economy hit its peak at about the same time that Reagan was elected, then it started crumbling, rapidly. This had nothing to do with environmentalists, or wilderness, or regulations, but with the market for commodities that were extracted from San Juan County. Uranium prices crashed due to globalization of the industry and the stagnation of the nuclear power industry, and oil prices cratered as the market corrected itself after multiple energy crises.

Instead of trying to chart new economic directions for the county to go in, Black and his fellow county commissioners demonstrated that they were just fine with federal overreach and incursion when it suited their needs. In the early 1980s, the Department of Energy settled on the Gibson Dome, a stone's throw from the eastern boundary of the Needles District of Canyonlands National Park, as one of the best places to build a giant repository for storing the nation's high-level nuclear waste. Many Utahns, having lived through decades of nuclear fallout from upwind weapons testing, were appalled. Black was delighted. The construction of the facility would employ over one thousand people, and the operation nearly as many, and Black believed that with a national waste dump in place for spent reactor fuel, the nuclear power industry—and therefore San Juan County's uranium mining industry—would be revived. In an open letter published in the *San Juan Record* in March 1982, the San Juan County commissioners wrote: "We support such a facility and are opposed to Canyonlands National Park or archaeological sites in the area used to preclude the repository." Black then went on to tell a *Salt Lake Tribune* reporter that tourists would enjoy visiting a nuclear waste dump, just as they reveled in seeing the gargantuan Bingham Canyon open-pit copper mine and the heart of the Mormon Church in heavily polluted Salt Lake City: "If pollution hurt tourism, then Temple Square in the heart of the state's worst pollution, and Kennecott, one of the worst blights on the environment, wouldn't be the state's number one and number two tourist attractions."

Even with that kind of marketing, Black wasn't able to enlist much support from outside the county. Former uranium boomtown Moab had by then grasped on to the tourism and recreation economy, motorized and unmotorized alike, and many of its citizens were not too psyched about having a nuke dump on their doorstep and waste-laden trucks rolling through the center of town. The Sierra Club, Earth First!, no-nuke activists, and national park advocates launched a campaign, Don't Waste Utah, to rally the public to oppose the plan. Utah governor Scott Matheson, a Democrat, went from being skeptical to outright opposed; his Republican successor ended up in opposition, as well. Black and his colleagues were enraged, and the county staked two thousand mining claims in the repository study area out of spite. It didn't work. Opposition to the dump continued to grow, and in 1986 the final environmental assessment was released, relegating the Canyonlands site low down on the list of possibilities, with Yucca Mountain in Nevada rising to the top.

Nineteen eighty-six was the year of discontent for Black and friends. The price of uranium was already in steep decline, and the Chernobyl disaster that year would further degrade public perception of nuclear energy. Oil busted so hard that drilling rigs were being chopped up for scrap. The Southern Utah Wilderness Alliance, created in 1983, was gaining prominence and was holding the local BLM field office's feet to the fire when it came to inventorying wilderness-quality lands in the state. A federal court had forced the county to redraw its voting districts to give the Indigenous majority better representation in county government, and Mark Maryboy, a Navajo from the Montezuma Creek area who tended to side with environmentalists, was elected as a commissioner and would face off with Black on numerous occasions.

The reaction to all of this, the wilderness inventory, in particular, showed that the Sagebrush Rebellion was alive and well in San Juan County. The mayor of Blanding at the time, Jim Shumway, blasted preservationists and the wilderness push. "We will give no more lands," Shumway said. "We have the legal right to have and bear arms. We shall." Shumway was outspoken in this regard, and in a public meeting on wilderness, he warned environmentalists and the BLM: "We know that you want our lands. You will not get them....We are tired of the wilderness terrorists....Those seeking the solitude of our beautiful lands shall now be expected to furnish themselves with armed guards while enjoying the serenity of our county."

Finally, the most visible of what Black saw as incursions on his county and his rights also went down in 1986. In early May federal law enforcement agents under direction of the Artifact

Looting Task Force raided homes of suspected pothunters and dealers in several states. Blanding bore the brunt of it, and many residents were taken aback and angered by the heavy-handedness of the action. Among the homes "invaded" was Cal Black's. "I've seen movies about gestapo raids and that's the closest it comes," Black told the United Press International, which referred to him as an antiquities collector. "They let my wife call me after they terrorized her. I think she was almost going to get a gun and run them off. I'd have to say now that if I read in the papers about agents being shot, I'd have to be on the side of the shooters." The reactions, and some of the same words, would be repeated after a similar raid in 2009.

It's no wonder that residents were shocked: many locals did not consider pothunting—even digging sites—to be a crime, and they saw pilfering a pot or an arrowhead as no different than picking up a pretty rock or a pine cone, albeit far more lucrative. An ancient basket and its contents taken from an alcove on Forest Service land in southeastern Utah netted a dealer $180,000 in the early eighties. And even if they did understand that pothunting was against the law, they made light of it. At the time of the raid, trinket stores in Blanding and Monticello sold T-shirts that said: "I dig San Juan County," and "Get Your Pot in San Juan County."

A number of ancient bowls were seized from Black's house, but he claimed they were from private land and there was no evidence suggesting otherwise, so Black was not charged. His son, Alan "Buddy" Black, however, was indicted and charged with aiding and abetting the sale and purchase of archaeological resources. But the attempt at prosecution fell apart and demonstrated one of the weaknesses of the then-new Archaeological Resources Protection Act. The judge in the case said that Black could only be found guilty if the prosecution could prove, beyond a reasonable doubt, that Black had known that the artifacts he was selling had been taken from public lands. If not, he wouldn't have known he was committing a crime, and therefore lacked intent. In this case, the government had an eyewitness who could testify that Black did know of the artifacts' provenance. The only problem was that it was notorious pothunter Earl Shumway, who had turned state's witness and informed on Black in exchange for immunity and possibly a reduced sentence on an unrelated crime for which he was serving jail time. The jury did not find Shumway credible, Buddy Black was ultimately acquitted, and the raid, which Hurst called a "giant federal fiasco," yielded no convictions. Even Shumway got off, for the time being.[34]

The laws regarding pothunting are flawed further in that they only apply to digging and collecting on federal land and Indian land. The basis of the law is this: since the land is owned by the federal government, then so is everything on that land, so when someone takes an artifact from public land, they are stealing federal property. Therefore it is a crime. By that same reasoning, if someone takes an artifact from land that they own, they are not stealing, because the artifacts are considered an extension of the land. This is problematic for a number of reasons. First, the artifacts were placed on the land in question long before the US government acquired the land via theft, treaty, or purchase, so they belong to the descendants[35] of the people who made the antiquities in question, not the government. Another law, the Native American Graves Protection and Repatriation Act, or NAGPRA, later codified this concept. Second, since the law only applies to federal and tribal lands it is difficult to prosecute pothunters without catching them in the act or getting them to admit that they knew the artifacts came from public lands. And third, and most importantly, since it is not a *crime* to dig up human remains, funerary objects, or other artifacts on private land, there is an implication that it is morally and ethically okay to do so. Yet, the end result of the pilfering is the same—disrespect for the dead and their descendants, destruction of the archaeological record, and larceny—regardless of who "owns" the land in question.

While the 1986 raid didn't accomplish much in terms of convictions, it seems to have led to an ebb in looting incidents in San Juan County during ensuing years, according to BLM accounts. It also served to further inflame the burning orb of resentment that the white old-timers of San Juan County harbor for the federal government, just waiting to be rekindled sometime in the not-so-distant future.

The end of the Cold War and the arms race a few years later dealt a harsh blow to what was left of the local uranium industry. The big buildup of world-obliterating weapons would slow, if not cease, and the existing stockpile of warheads could be dismantled, and the fissile material down-blended for use as fuel in nuclear reactors. Uranium mining, particularly in the United States, was no longer needed. That didn't stop the Sagebrush Rebels from fighting tooth-and-nail for the industry, however—and they continue to do so today.

In 1990 Black passed away, bringing an end to the first Sagebrush Rebellion. Cause of death: lung cancer.

CHAPTER TWELVE

F&^%$#LL CANYON

YOU WON'T FIND FUCKHELL CANYON ON ANY MAP, YET just about everyone who has spent a little bit of time out here in Standing Up Country has their own version. I'm sure even Al Scorup, the Mormon Cowboy, found himself up a slightly more mildly named canyon in a blizzard with some starving cows once or twice. We gave this particular place that name because those were the words that emanated from our mouths, pretty much in unison though not in harmony, just as we tossed our loaded backpacks to the ground on the edge of that canyon in disgust and exhaustion. We muttered the words in the opposite order, as well, but Hellfuck Canyon just doesn't have the same ring to it.

It was day one of a seven-day journey.

We were there because our maps sucked and because we hated guidebooks. Also because we had believed my father when he said that we could easily traverse this dry stretch of land and reach a perennial stream in less than a day. With that in mind, we had packed just enough water to get us through the day. Now we were left with no choice but to cook our beans in water that we scraped out of a shallow, stagnant pool on the canyon floor.

***

WE WERE IN COLLEGE, G—, C—, AND ME, AND SPENT FAR TOO
much time reading books written by white guys who were long
dead and we drank far too much coffee and thought far too much
and we all had weird imprints on our foreheads from where we
banged them on the tables after spending another hour trying
to decipher another Hegelian passage. So when spring break
came in early- to mid-March, we welcomed the opportunity to
leave the books and words and booze-parties behind and slip
behind the Slickrock Curtain for a while and stare at sandstone
and think about nothing at all. Naturally, we gravitated toward
southeastern Utah, where two of us had spent so much of our
youth, as it was an easy drive from our school in Santa Fe.

But spring in Bears Ears country can be tricky. Up on Elk
Ridge patches of snow might still cling to north-facing slopes
into May, and even the roads across the top of Cedar Mesa can
be muddy. Just about everywhere else can get crowded, since the
Salt Lake and Durango folks are likely to be on break, too. We
also wanted to go somewhere new to us. There were no smart-
phones or internet or Google Earth to look at, so we unfolded
a map depicting all of southeastern Utah and pored over it for
hours trying to find a good loop through canyon country. It
wasn't the ideal situation. The map covered a huge swath of landscape, and though it had contour lines on it, they would prove
mostly to be cosmetic flourishes, with little connection to what
was on the ground.

There was another option available to us: a guidebook. C—,
much to my dismay, owned a copy of Michael Kelsey's guide to
hiking on the Colorado Plateau. Guidebooks were—and really
still are—anathema to me. There's an old saying about the desert: never write about the places you love in enough detail to
lead your readers there. Guidebooks were made to violate that
mandate, particularly Kelsey's, which cover just about every
damned side canyon of a side canyon of a side canyon in the
whole region. Besides, Kelsey's tone could be a bit maddening.

He always referred to himself as "the Author," as in, "It will take an experienced hiker four to five days to traverse this stretch. It took the Author five hours." I suppose there was also a bit of envy on my part. The bastard had found a way to make a living, however modest, by hiking in and writing about canyon country.

So there was no way I would use the guidebook to find a route. However, I did consent to using it in a sort of backwards way: we could find a canyon on the map and then look in Kelsey's book. If the Author didn't write about it or hadn't been there, it would rise to the top of our list. In this way, we were able to come up with a few options that looked doable. The leading candidate was a canyon that G— and I had long wanted to check out but hadn't because of access challenges. Getting in from the upper branches required high-clearance vehicles, which we did not have, and getting in via the mouth only seemed possible via a boat on the San Juan River, which we also didn't have at the time. The map seemed to suggest another option, but we couldn't tell if it would go or not, and Kelsey had nothing on it. So I did what any twenty-two-year-old would do in this situation. I called my dad and asked if he knew anything about the route.

Funny you ask, he said. I was just there. I hiked to Xxxxxx Canyon and back in a day. You'll have no problem getting there, even with loaded packs.

With that information in hand, we plotted our route. We'd park our cars at J— Canyon and camp there, wake up early and get to the canyon mouth on day one, then proceed up the canyon, where water was plentiful, for the next several days, before coming back the way we had come. We would eat lentils, tortillas, peanut butter, and oatmeal. And this time, we had a new weapon in our sustenance arsenal: homemade instant beans. G— and C— had cooked up a huge pot of Dove Creek pinto beans, branded Anasazi Beans, and then laid them out on window screens to dry. This ingenious trick would allow us to carry large quantities of this nutrient-packed wonder food and whip it up in a few minutes on a camp stove without burning too much precious fuel.

Or so we thought.

WE GUILTILY PACKED UP TWO CARS FOR THE TRIP, G—'S 1975 Fiat and my 1967 AMC Rambler American station wagon. We felt guilty about it because one car would have done the trick except that we had planned on going different directions after the backpacking journey. We hit the road in our mini-convoy, stopping at the Española Sonic for our ritual green-chile hickory cheeseburgers and the resulting inverted chest burps before making our way north and west. We entered San Juan County near the Four Corners, passed through Aneth, Bluff, and Comb Ridge before finally reaching the dirt road leading to the trailhead.

Generally speaking, the fifteen-mile dirt stretch is suitable for two-wheel-drive vehicles, even ancient ones like ours. But a couple segments of the route are a bit dicey, in that the road is squeezed between a steep upward slope on one side and a precipitous drop on the other. These narrow and exposed sections occur where small washes cross the road, sans culvert, so the road tends to be rougher here. As I maneuvered my boat of a car through these spots I imagined driving the road after a good gully-washer, which would surely turn the hard-packed clay into something as slippery as snot and turn the roadbed into a high-centering zone. Any resulting anxiety was burned off by the sky, which was cloudless and blue as the sun set ahead of me.

We parked and camped alongside a stream, or more like a trickle of water that pooled up on limestone, each one a mirror reflecting the lilac-colored sky and the orange- and pink- and khaki-colored stone. We were in a broad, fairly flat-bottomed canyon—a valley, almost—bounded by towering sandstone cliffs. It was, like almost all of this county, cattle country, at least for part of the year. It's not hard to recognize the signs. The ground tends to be loose dust rather than coated with crypto-biotic crust, the vegetation, if any is left, is chewed down and gangly. Cow dung, desiccated or, worse yet, moist and mushy, lies piled next to the water.

My dad used to swear that he saw a UFO one night while camping here—lights that hovered overhead before zipping off at unnatural angles and speeds. That was back in the seventies, when all over the West ranchers were finding cattle that had been "bloodlessly excised," apparently by laser beams or some other alien instrument. He hypothesized that maybe the cattle muti-lators had come for the herd nearby and for whatever reason chose to go to other pastures for prey. He was on the South Per-kins allotment, adjacent to the grazing area that Rose Chilcoat and Mark Franklin were on when Franklin unwittingly closed a corral gate and got charged with attempted cattle mutilation as a result.

The morning dawned clear and chilly, but as soon as the sunlight hit the valley it warmed up quickly and, shouldering heavy packs, the three of us set off down the road. It was strange because on our map, which was admittedly a little scant on details, the road we walked on showed up as a trail. We found out why a half hour or so later, when we came upon a large sign, pockmarked with the requisite bullet holes, informing us that we were about to enter Glen Canyon National Recreation Area and that motorized vehicles were prohibited. I suppose this meant that the road became a trail at that point, by virtue of the sign, and by virtue of the invisible line delineating land managed by the BLM from that managed by the National Park Service.

It is possible that one or all of us spouted an expletive or two at the absurdity of it all. The sign was big; you couldn't miss it. But it was also meaningless. The road hadn't been gated or blocked or trenched to keep vehicles out, and there was no way in hell that a National Park Service ranger was going to make their way all the way over here to enforce the nonmotorized rule. At the time, in the early nineties, off-highway vehicles weren't nearly as numerous as they are now, and so we didn't have to worry about getting buzzed by a bunch of four-wheeling yahoos. Still it would be disconcerting and maybe even a little embarrassing to encounter some yuppies in their 4Runners and their coolers of beer while we trudged through the dust beer-less and on foot and in compliance of the rules.

More than that, we were reminded of the ubiquity of roads in this part of the world.

WHEN ALTHEA DOBBINS AND ROBERT MARSHALL PORED OVER maps in 1936 looking for America's remaining roadless areas, they found a nearly nine-million-acre swath that fit their criteria in southeastern Utah straddling the Colorado River. It was the same rugged landscape the Hole-in-the-Rock party had crossed in 1879 and where Everett Ruess had vanished just a couple of years prior to the Dobbins-Marshall inventory. Included in the count was pretty much all of San Juan County west of Comb Ridge with a little chunk taken out of the lower corner for Mexican Hat and its oil wells. If they were to do a similar inventory today, they'd still find relatively large road-free areas in the county in the most rugged and remote areas. But they'd also find that in the years since their survey, the people of San Juan County have built hundreds of miles of new roads, as well as labeled even fairly primitive cow paths as roads, too, so that a San Juan County road map looks like a chaotic, 7,700-mile spiderweb laid down over the landscape or, to use the county's own analogy, it appears as if the whole place has been afflicted with an awful case of varicose veins. From the county's master plan, written in 2008: "The County B and D road systems might be likened to a cardiovascular system with the generally higher standard B roads as the main arterial system and the D roads the secondary vessels branching out from the arteries. Just as the whole cardio-vascular system is necessary for the body to function properly, the whole Class B and D road system is necessary and each road is important for the County to function properly and provide the many services and needs of its citizens and visitors."

Where some counties might heap praise on the resident populace, San Juan County lauds its…road system? It borders on outright fetishization, going on to say, "Each road is necessary and each road is important." A 1983 history of San Juan County, mostly written by residents and published by the Utah State Historical Society, contains not one but three chapters on roads in the county, one of them penned by Calvin Black.

The Sagebrush Rebellion, and the ideologically similar movements that preceded it, has taken various forms over the decades. But ever since the 1990s, particularly in Utah, the focus has been on roads and motorized access, and counties and states have spent huge amounts of taxpayer funds to litigate their road obsession.

The counties' weapon of choice is RS-2477, which was passed by Congress in 1866 as one of a body of laws to encourage westward expansion by giving away the public domain for free or virtually free. The statute reads, simply: "The right-of-way for the construction of highways across public lands not otherwise reserved for public purposes is hereby granted." In other words, if you needed to build a road across the public domain to access your mine or house, you were free to do so as long as it didn't mess with anyone else's mining claim, homestead, or road. The intent was not to encourage road-building as an end in itself, but rather to keep open access across the public domain to mining claims and homesteads.

Congress repealed RS-2477 when it passed the Federal Land Policy and Management Act in 1976. But it wasn't until later, when the Forest Service, BLM, and NPS started closing roads crossing lands in their jurisdiction in order to preserve fragile ecosystems or antiquities, that counties started getting angry. One of the hottest flashpoints was in San Juan County, involving a ten-mile section of jeep road up Salt Creek Canyon, which crossed the only perennial stream in the area a number of times. By the mid-1990s, hundreds of vehicles per month made their way up the road. Vehicles often got stuck in the creek bed, leaked oil or transmission fluids into the water, and were generally wreaking havoc on the sensitive riparian system.

After considering closing the road altogether, in 1995 the Park Service decided, instead, to put up a gate and limit the number of vehicles allowed to travel the road. This wasn't enough for the Southern Utah Wilderness Alliance, which sued the Park Service on the basis that allowing any vehicles to travel on backcountry roads impaired park resources and therefore was a violation of the Organic Act of 1916, which established the National Park Service. In 1998 a court ruled in SUWA's favor on the Salt Creek Road—albeit not on other roads—forcing the closure of the ten-mile section. In 2000, the decision was overturned, but the Park Service went ahead and closed the road themselves, based on updated policies and a new environmental analysis.

County officials shot back, claiming that the road in question had been in existence long before FLPMA was passed, and therefore RS-2477 still applied. As their legal basis they invoked this clause from FLPMA: "Nothing in this Act, or in any amendment made by this Act, shall be construed as terminating any valid lease, permit, patent, right-of-way, or other land use right or authorization existing on the date of approval of this Act." Since the Salt Creek Road was "built" before 1976, RS-2477 applied. Therefore, it was a "highway" with a right-of-way that remained in place after FLPMA was passed. So, the county argued, the Park Service didn't have the authority to close the road, and the county also had the right to maintain or grade or pave the road as it pleased. In 1996 the county stood up for its purported RS-2477-given rights by running bulldozers and road-graders along a number of two-tracks, or rudimentary roads, that crossed federal lands. It sounded rather straightforward, but it was problematic. The purported highway up Salt Creek was not actually constructed so much as it was worn into the ground by Al Scorup's cattle prior to the 1964 designation of the Needles District of Canyonlands National Park. Aerial photos and maps from the fifties showed no road or even jeep trail in the canyon.

San Juan County wouldn't give in, however. In December 2000, San Juan County sheriff Mike Lacy, one of his deputies, and two other county employees removed the locks on the gate blocking the road, drove up the road, and declared it open to public travel. When Park Service officials locked the gate again, county staff returned and opened it back up. Bill Redd, then county commissioner, told the Cortez *Journal*: "We don't think that our road surfaces are subject to the wishes of some unelected environmental faction that wants to control them." The Park Service made the closure official and permanent in 2004, prompting a lawsuit from the county in which it made "quiet title" to the road right-of-way using RS-2477 as its legal basis. The county was joined by a host of motorized access advocates and Sagebrush Rebel ideologues, including William Perry Pendley and the Mountain States Legal Foundation. After a decade of back-and-forth in the courts, the county lost the battle when in 2014 the Tenth Circuit Court of Appeals upheld an earlier court's ruling that San Juan County had failed to prove that the road in question was a highway prior to the national park's designation. A number of similar lawsuits concerning other roads around the state filed by San Juan and other Utah counties are still pending.

The road my two friends and I walked on was constructed and it was in existence, in very rudimentary form, when Marshall and Dobbins reported on roadless areas. Unlike San Juan County, the two did not consider defunct wagon trails or two-tracks roads. The precise provenance of the road has been lost.

In my research I've found that the road may have been built in 1882, 1901, 1907, or "around 1920." Nevertheless, there is universal agreement that it was originally built by a prospector, originally from Ogden, named Emery L. Goodridge. In either 1879 or 1882 Goodridge traveled to Durango hoping to get in on the mining boom in the region and struck on the idea of floating the San Juan River in search of mineral wealth. He began his trip in Durango on the Animas River, joined the San Juan at Farmington, stopped in Bluff City for supplies, and continued all the way to Lee's Ferry on the Colorado River, now several miles downstream from Glen Canyon Dam, covering some three hundred river miles through some of the most diverse, scenic, remote, and beautiful country in the world. He didn't find much gold, but did find oil seeping directly out of the rock unbidden in a number of places.

After his trip, Goodridge went back to Oregon for reasons unknown, but apparently the San Juan oil bubbling up in his memory wouldn't leave him alone, so he returned a couple of decades later and started drilling wells, sparking the San Juan oil boom that would come to be centered in Mexican Hat, which was originally called Goodridge City. At some point in all of this, he built the road upon which we walked in order to reach the confluence of S— Canyon and the San Juan River, where Goodridge had spied some of the most prolific oil seeps during his boat trip. He then brought up a huge drilling engine from Gallup, presumably on a wagon, and hauled it out to his new, rather rough road. As he was lowering it down the cliff to the drilling site, it broke free, crashing and tumbling to the bottom and rendering it kaput and beyond repair, forcing him to abandon the project and all of the equipment. It seems like a good metaphor for natural resource exploitation in general: bulldoze a road to a remote place, wreck things, leave the wreckage behind.

Goodridge's road continued to be used over the years by prospectors and anyone else who wanted to access the San Juan gorge by foot, horse, or vehicle other than a boat. In 1952 the Don Danvers Co. hauled equipment along it to Goodridge's wreck site and drilled two wells. One was dry. The other, the No. 1 Jack Harris, produced enough—about twenty-four barrels per day at forty-degree gravity—to get a newspaper mention, but not enough to make hauling it back along the old wagon track worth it. Danvers seemed intent on drilling in some of the most scenic places. In 1953 the company drilled a well in the shadow of the Bears Ears, which "blew in and caught fire." It, too, was a non-producer, though over the years a few others would also drill wells in the vicinity, hoping for a different result. Roads were built to get to those wells, too, and even more were constructed around the same time to open up the landscape to uranium prospectors, all of it enabled by RS-2477.

My two friends and I briefly considered doing a little road construction—or rather, deconstruction—of our own to per-suade any tempted motorists to obey the aforementioned sig-nage. A few boulders strategically placed would have sufficed. But we had just started our trek and didn't want to destroy the momentum, so we kept going instead. Maybe that's for the best. Because in San Juan County, they won't only charge you with attempted cattle killing for shutting gates, they'll also go after you for shutting down roads, even if, especially if, you're a fed-eral official with jurisdiction over the land that the road crosses.

In 2011, BLM officials built earthen berms to block user-created trails that led to a dispersed camping site in the Indian Creek drainage of San Juan County. When county officials saw the closure they became enraged, mistakenly believing that the main road spur, which they had claimed as a county road, had been closed. Even after realizing their error—the main spur had been washed out by a rain storm—the county officials went on the attack in public meetings and a sheriff's deputy repeatedly called one BLM staffer a "liar," inciting locals in the process. A Facebook post from "A Voice for the People of San Juan County

Utah" included a photo of the local BLM staffer purportedly responsible for the alleged closure, with a caption reading, "… so everyone will know who [staffer's name] is when I talk about him closing the road in Indian Creek." In a comment on the same post, "A Voice" also posted links to the Great Old Broads and SUWA websites, noting, "Knowing your enemy is very important," thereby laying groundwork for the prosecution of Rose Chilcoat six years later. Shortly thereafter a young man rode a four-wheeler into the BLM official's yard and did donuts, leaving deep ruts in the grass. At the local public school, a student verbally accosted the same staffer's child, telling them that the BLM "are a bunch of idiots" for "illegally" closing a road.

San Juan County sheriff Rick Eldredge launched a criminal investigation into the matter. But instead of pursuing the ATV vandal or other bullies harassing public officials, he went after the BLM officials themselves for the "crime" of shutting down a road. "We do not want to be tread on by the federal government," Eldredge told KSL News.

THE FUCKHELL DESERT THAT WE WALKED THROUGH IS ON A bench that sits about halfway between the top of Cedar Mesa and the bottom of the San Juan River gorge. We were in a side canyon to the San Juan, and so our first objective was to get up, around the bend, and into the main branch. As in other places behind the Slickrock Curtain, time and space are distorted here, and it seemed as if we had been walking forever when we finally reached the bend. I suspect that has something to do with how much of it—space and time—is available to human perception here. It's a big place, a place where deep time lies luridly all around, baring everything. That cliff band above us, looking like a smooth, pale, corpulent thigh, represented tens of millions of years of wind and water and sand and silt. The shelf on which we walked was made of hard limestone, a sort of dividing line between Pennsylvanian and Permian. The realization is a bit frightening, like when you really think about how deep the ocean is when you're on it in a boat.

Human history is readily apparent, as well, thousands of years of it. When we got to a bend in our route we stepped out to a promontory to get a view of the milky green waters of the river a thousand feet below. A huge boulder stood among the scrub near the rim, coated in desert varnish. Several petroglyphs were etched into the side of the rock facing the river and the emptiness. One was of a V-shaped man—I know his sex because of the sizable phallus between his legs. A duck sat on his neck where his head should have been. This was just one of several such glyphs we'd see on the bench; they are spread up and down the canyon at the same level. The bench clearly served as a roadway, perhaps even a home or farming site, long before anyone came along looking for oil. We decided we should call the place the Duckhead Desert as a result, a name that other circumstances would eventually wipe out.

Soon the road got rough, washed out, partially blocked in places by boulders that had tumbled from the cliffs above and, to our relief, any old remnants of tire tracks vanished, too. There were just two sets of tracks visible on the road's surface: a human's and a dog's, which I took to be my dad's and those of his dog, Chaco. I silently thanked my father for the good advice. He had sent us to a place where we'd have our solitude. We walked and walked some more. My feet hurt, my shoulders hurt, we all drank the last of our water, the sun, harsh even in March, dipped toward the sandstone horizon. Several times we saw what looked like the canyon we were aiming for, but each time it turned out to be a smaller side canyon sans water. No better than a mirage. I silently cursed my father. What the hell was he thinking, anyway, sending us on this route? As the sun dropped behind the cliffs, and the temperature fell along with it, we all knew that we had to stop for the night. When we came to the biggest side canyon yet, I threw my pack down onto the limestone and yelled: "Fuck! Hell!"

The good news was, we'd get to try out our precooked, window-screen-dried beans. I had to walk up the dry wash to find a pool deep enough to dip a pan into. The water was stagnant and covered by some sort of film, and the entire creek bed was caked with minerally whiteness, indicating that the water was hard. This did not worry me. G— was fine with it, too. C—, not so much. G— and I had grown up drinking straight out of mountain streams, desert potholes, and a lot of sketchy water sources in between. I mean, sure, my parents had a water purifier of sorts that we'd take with us camping, namely an empty Clorox bottle. Maybe the redneck water purifier worked, maybe it didn't, though in the end it didn't really matter because sooner or later I always found myself facedown in the dirt guzzling straight out of a pothole, using my teeth to filter out any tadpoles. Chances were, G— and I already had giardia living in our guts. So why not add to the colony? Besides, the water in the desert is just rainwater that pools up in stone. It's not like it runs through areas rife with cattle or sheep, right? C—, on the other hand, was from the big city and also a bit more intelligent than us. So before he drank the manky water he ran it through his filter. I was a bit of an asshole back then, so I'm pretty sure I rolled my eyes at that.

We put beans and water in the pot, added some cumin and salt and pepper, and got ready to eat. Those guys didn't quite cook the beans all the way in advance, because they might have turned to mush during drying. So the beans that we cooked weren't quite instant, but it should have taken no more than fifteen minutes for them to get soft all the way through. After half an hour, though, the outer part of each bean was mushy, while the middle was hard like a rock—possibly the result of the hard water. We couldn't spare any fuel, so we ate the damned things anyway then went to bed, the stone on which we lay warm with sun-heat.

We got a nice early start the next day and upped our pace to get off the bench and into the canyon, where the going would be slower but also less monotonous. Probably a half hour into our walk it hit us all more or less simultaneously, a rumbling in the gut, followed by dynamic gas pains, followed, eventually, by pain-relieving release. I was fortunate enough to be leading the trio at the time of the first release and therefore upwind of my not-so-lucky fellows. G— let out an anguished cry. C— stumbled erratically, tripping over a boulder.

"Arrghh you stink!"

"It's not me, it's those damned beans. Whose idea was that, anyway?"

"It was a great idea. It was the water, not the beans. We've probably got giardia now."

For the rest of that part of the hike, when the way was wide enough we'd walk side by side, and when it got narrow, we'd put a good fifteen feet between us—we were social distancing way before it was cool. Even that only mitigated the stench. I'd like to take this opportunity to apologize to anyone who may have been within a two-mile radius of us that day, as surely they heard our verbal paroxysms that closely followed each intestinal one:

"Fuck!"

"Hell!"

"Fuckhell!"

By contrast, we all screamed in joy when we looked down to see the San Juan River at its confluence with S— Creek. We descended past Goodridge's wrecked equipment, which was slowly disintegrating and becoming a part of the landscape, and probably got quite near to the overhang where members of the Trimble party, who boated the river to study the geology and to look for dam sites, found a fully intact olla.

These days this particular spot likely would be crowded with river runners, the designated camping spots occupied. Rafters have to reserve the campsites at the canyon mouth in advance and then they can stay only one night; backpackers aren't allowed to camp there at all, a grave injustice if you ask me. It's the price of popularity. When we arrived, though, the place was empty. If anyone had shown up, they rapidly would have vamoosed when they caught wind of us and our bean expulsions.

We definitively decided not to return back the way we had come, as originally planned. Our map was pretty crappy, but it looked as if we could easily get out of the canyon we were in via a tributary, walk across the mesa top, drop back into the canyon where our cars were parked, and then walk back down canyon to our starting point. It would be a long adventure, but doable, and far more interesting than re-traversing the Fuckhell Desert in reverse.

Boulders and bushes choke the lower reach of the canyon, and the geology is prone to the formation of pour-offs feeding deep, green pools. Cottonwoods and willows rise up from fractures in the limestone, their branches covered with brand-new leaves of a green that exists only in springtime, only for a few days. The water was too cold for swimming, but we stripped off our packs and clothes and jumped in anyway, laying on the warm rock afterward and soaking up the warmth, adapting to the slow rhythm of the desert as we shed all the detritus and mind-clutter of the other life.

We are not quiet desert-goers, my friends and I. We sing and yell and tell stupid stories as we walk. We are not disturbing the sanctity of silence because there is no silence in the desert. Someone's always making a racket, whether it's wind, water, rain, cicadas, crickets, coyotes, magpies, ravens, mourning doves, or, my personal favorite, the canyon wren with its cascading whistle. And when we humans finally shut our traps the voices of the rocks, the trees, the ghosts whispering to one another can be heard. The breeze sings one song as it tickles the leaves of the juniper, another as it caresses stone.

We stopped for lunch: peanut butter and honey on tortillas

and some dried apricots. G— broke into song, that old folk tune by Peter, Paul and Mary about a lemon tree: "Lemon tree very pretty and the lemon flower sweet, but the fruit of the poor lemon is impossible to eat." C— soon joined in, and the canyon walls echoed with the sound of our harmonious voices as we danced a bacchanal jig, prancing, jumping, arms flapping, hips thrusting.

Just as we reached the crescendo the hippies came into view.

Maybe they weren't hippies, I don't know. But they were wearing tie-dyed shirts and one of the guys had long, scraggly hair. They passed by in groups of two or three, big packs on their backs. None of them said anything to us, and they all looked rather bedraggled, as if they had escaped from a cult. Their eyes emanated a strange combination of fear and fatigue. I was disappointed that we now had to share "our" canyon with someone else, particularly a group like that. G— seemed angry and started singing again, louder than before, as if that might scare the intruders away: "LEMON tree, oh so PRETTY!" After they passed by, we started speculating on their origins: they must have rafted to the canyon mouth and were taking an overnight backpacking trip up canyon. They'd be gone soon. There was no way they had backpacked in along the Duckhead Highway, that's for sure. Only we could handle that kind of trek.

In order to soothe ourselves we broke out some of our chocolate that we normally saved until after dinner. As we ate, two more figures strode up the canyon, two women, around our age, carrying huge backpacks. They both smiled big, toothy grins and, unlike the hippies, unabashedly approached us, eyeing us hungrily. Okay, they weren't eyeing us, exactly, but our chocolate. They were guides with the National Outdoor Leadership School, or NOLS, and were leading the hippies up the canyon.

"How'd you get here? Raft? We hiked across the Fuck— across the desert."

"No, no, we hiked up the river, from Grand Gulch."

"Huh?"

"Yeah. We came down Grand Gulch and now we'll go up to the head of this canyon, over the top, and into Lime Canyon. Hopefully our food stash will be there. It's a month-long trip. We're a little over halfway through."

"A month?"

"Yep," the blond one with muscular, tanned legs said, still eyeing my chocolate.

"Oh. Wow."

For the first time during the trip, we had nothing to say and instead just stood there gawking at these two canyon nymphs who could clearly out-backpack the three of us.

"Well, see ya. Hopefully our crew doesn't mess with your solitude."

And then they were gone, and I was left holding a melting piece of chocolate.

"Why didn't you offer her some chocolate, you idiot?!"

"What about you?"

"I was—I need this chocolate."

Flooded with regret, we continued up canyon, overtaking and passing the NOLS group and continuing at a stiff pace until we found a perfect camp site where a major tributary joined the canyon. We stayed there for the next three nights, rationing our other food in such a way that we didn't have to eat those stinking beans again. We did a lot of hiking and climbing and checking out some cliff dwellings that were remarkably intact. While I was friction-climbing a steep-angled cliff, my Teva sandal blew out, stranding me up there and forcing me to jump a good ten feet into a cliffrose. I was all scratched up and slightly bloody, but my leg bones were all in one piece, and when we got back to camp, G— gleefully announced to C— that I had invented a new climbing move called the "bush jump."

***

We broke camp on our last morning under overcast, but
not very threatening, skies and headed up the tributary, a narrow canyon in the Navajo formation with a stream running
down the bottom, willows and horsetail reeds growing from the
moist sand lining the pools. The water had a little bit of movement to it as well, fed by snowmelt up on the mesa top that had
worked its way through fractures and cracks in the stone and so
tasted fresh and clean. So much so, in fact, that C— finally gave
up his filtration urge and joined us in filling up our water bottles
straight from the pools.

"Don't worry, man, this is spring fed. And there aren't people
around and the canyon's too steep for cows. It'll be fine."

The map indicated that we'd have no problems executing our
plan to go up and over the mesa and the ease of the first leg
seemed to confirm it. Soon we were out of the canyon proper
and in a gully, still following the stream, which surprisingly still
had water in it up on the mesa top. We rounded a bend and came
to a dead stop: There before us was a corral. Inside the corral
were a dozen cows. The corral literally sat in the stream we had
just walked up, a dozen cows peeing, pooping, tramping around
in the mud of the very waters we had been drinking, unfiltered,
all morning. C— looked like he was going to puke.

We did not close any gates, open any gates, or do anything
else that might be construed as attempting to harm, maim, or
murder the cows, though we certainly considered it. We may
have let out a stream of obscenities—including a few that began
with F and H—in a tone that might have caused long-term
bovine emotional trauma. For that, I apologize. For the record,
we were not aiming our epithets at the cows, but at the livestock
operators who had put the cud-munchers out here in the first
place. Forget about the damage the animals do to the cryptobiotic soil and the fragile riparian ecosystems, forget the absurdly
low grazing fees, forget the unescapable cow shit, forget the fact
that those cows standing in that stream would probably cause all

three of us chronic intestinal distress. Consider, for a moment, the cattle themselves—they are not happy out here in the desert. These poor beasts are born, live for a few years, then get a bolt shot into their brain before going to slaughter. Why make their short lives a miserable trial of quasi-starvation in a place where forage is so scarce?

"You think those cows dream of moving to Iowa?" I asked. No one responded.

The blanket of clouds overhead thickened and the sky grew darker and we still had a long way to go. There was no time for waxing philosophical about the life of a cow. We headed off through the juniper and piñon in the general direction of the canyon where our cars were parked. On the map, in all its vagueness, the tributaries of our objective canyon looked no more intimidating than the canyon from which we had just emerged, so we were optimistic about our route. And we remained undaunted when we got to the edge of the mesa and found a sheer twenty-foot drop. This was expected; quite often the walls of these canyons are made up of giant stair steps, each one requiring a bit of lightly technical down-climbing. With a cheap nylon rope we lowered our packs to the bench. C— carefully climbed down to the bottom. I climbed halfway down, then employed my bush jump technique, landing in a relatively soft juniper. G— tried the same, but his landing was a little off, and he rolled to the dirt, clutching his knee and writhing in pain.

To our relief he jumped back to his feet, or at least to his good foot, and with clenched teeth assured us he was fine, but did anyone have any aspirin?

"Yeah, yeah, I got some ibuprofen. This'll do you good."

He opened the bottle, poured out a handful—eight, maybe ten—and washed them down with a big gulp of cow water.

"I'll be fine as soon as this kicks in." He grimaced as he shouldered his pack and limped lugubriously through the trees. C— and I looked at each other with concern and a bit of impatience.

At that rate, we wouldn't make the cars before dark. A couple grams of ibuprofen, however, can do magic, and pretty soon G— was walking along at a fairly good clip. He also babbled incoherently for what felt like hours, a stream of consciousness that involved fire-poking sticks, his mother's impulsive purchases, a bed-and-breakfast in Mancos, his undying love for the two backpacker women we had seen down in the canyon, and the emotional trauma he had suffered from eating too many peanut butter and honey sandwiches as a kid. He only broke from his monologue when the combination of painkillers and cow water went to work on his intestines and he ran behind a bush and evacuated his bowels while emitting howling moans.

With G— mentally incapacitated, C— and I were left to ponder our options, which were growing thinner by the moment. We had reached the next stair step into the canyon, the crux of the descent, and it had proved, thus far, to be an unbroken band of vertical cliff that was at least forty feet high.

"Bush jump!" G— yelled before launching into yet another soliloquy, this one having to do with working at a chuckwagon dinner place.

"No bush jump," C— replied anxiously.

"We could leap off the cliff into that ponderosa," I suggested, "then climb down it?"

C— didn't need to reply. It was an idiotic idea. We kept walking, not knowing what else to do, spirits flagging. Finally, G— stopped talking and we walked through a couple million years of geology to a point where the vertical cliff puffed itself out into the shape of a human thigh, and we were able to slide and friction our way down one layer after another. The final bench was passable only with a new maneuver, the pothole slide, which deposited us into a cold, shallow, silty pool left behind by the last rain weeks before. With wet shoes and wet pants we trod rapidly along the broad-bottomed, overgrazed canyon floor. Finally, in the waning hours of day, our cars appeared like beacons in the dust and sage and sandstone. The first drops of rain arrived as we hurriedly shed our packs and tossed them into the cars.

Oh, yeah, cars, plural. Our decision to take two vehicles was even more superfluous and more wasteful by then. The whole ibuprofen-overdose giardiasis thing had dissuaded C— and G— from continuing on to a new adventure, so we all would convoy back together, our tails between our legs. We had been conquered by the desert, by the canyons, by the cows, and by those goddamned dehydrated beans. I crawled into my Rambler, cranked the ignition, and the big American engine fired up on its first try. G— got into the Fiat, turned the key on that Italian jalopy, and…nothing. The battery was dead. He had left the dome light on.

"No worries, dude," I said, gloating just a little bit about my light-turning-off ability and our decision to bring two cars. "Grab your jumper cables and we'll get you fired up in no time."

G— gave me a look I didn't like.

"What kinda dummy doesn't bring…?" I stopped there, opened up the back of my car, and rooted around in the spare-tire/tool compartment. Nothing. "Never mind."

"Fuck!"

The rain was coming down a little harder. If it continued, the dusty road would become impassible before long.

"Hell!"

We all piled into my car and drove the hour or so to Bluff, where I got on the payphone and called my dad to see if he knew anyone from whom we could borrow jumper cables. He sent us over to Wild Rivers, where we were forced to explain how we had taken two cars but no jumper cables. They then sent us over to see a guy named Wolf. We met him in his front yard, which was a patch of dirt in front of his camper-trailer home, and he handed off the jumper cables. It was dark by then. We drove back to the dead car, jumped it, and without any additional hitches got it going again. We could have just camped out there for the night, but we were worried about the rain, the UFOs, vindictive cattle. We were out of food except for a few bags of those beans, and there was no way in hell we were eating those again. So we drove a little too fast for a road that was never meant for old cars like ours. The darkness by then was deep, but I could feel the towering cliffs on my left and the void of the Goosenecks on my right. I was pulled onward by images of a Navajo taco and a cold soda.

It wasn't to be. By the time we got back to Bluff, both the Dairy Cafe and the Sunbonnet were closed. That left the C-store for dinner. In the parking lot we piled into my car and ate stale crackers, rubbery slices of American cheese, and mystery lunch meat that was a month or two past the sell-by date. Then we headed back out to the Valley of the Gods road, pulled off next to Lime Creek, and threw our sleeping bags down on the dust next to the road, but not before kicking away piles of dried-out cow dung. We were still in cattle country, now on the North Perkins allotment, just a few miles from the gate that Mark Franklin would close more than two decades later.

Most of our adventure had taken place on land that would eventually become part of Bears Ears National Monument and then would be excluded from the monument before becoming part of it again. We were in the heart of the public land wars geographically, but in the temporal eye of the storm, a moment of relative calm falling between the wilderness fights and the pothunter raid of the 1980s, and the rise of the wise-use movement and the backlash to President Bill Clinton's environmental initiatives, including the 1996 establishment of Grand Staircase-Escalante National Monument, in the mid-nineties.

I lay down in my sleeping bag in the dirt and gazed up at the moonless sky, the stone forms of ancient Navajo warriors silhouetted against the splash of the Milky Way, and drifted away to sleep. The next morning, as the rising sun cast long shadows across the red earth, I found a local country radio station on my

car stereo and turned up the volume to full blast. Elvis Presley's
deep croon emanated from the speakers:

> There will be peace in the valley for me
> Well the bear will be gentle
> And the wolves will be tame
> And the lion shall lay down
> By the lamb, oh yes...

CHAPTER THIRTEEN

WISE USE?

A S THE COLD WAR CAME TO AN END, A RIGHT-WING, nationalist furor was fulminating in the Heartland. Billboards sprouted along rural roadsides decrying the United Nation's supposed takeover of America and the New World Order that President George H. Bush said was on the horizon. At about the same time, the latest iteration of the Sagebrush Rebellion, known as the wise-use movement, was launched by private-property-rights activist and timber lobbyist Ron Arnold, who, with Alan Gottlieb, had founded the Center for the Defense of Free Enterprise in the 1970s. Wise-use was far more than just the old Sagebrush Rebellion dusted off for the nineties. The wise-use philosophy was both more radical and more insidious than its predecessor, and the efforts of the movement's adherents were more precisely targeted. Arnold summed up his crusade's Western-civilization-centric ideology in a 1993 speech: "I see environmentalism as the destroyer of the economy, as the destroyer of material wellbeing—as the destroyer of industrial civilization—as the destroyer of individual liberties and civil rights. For those reasons, I fight against environmentalism as a matter of principle, as a matter of ethics, as a matter of survival. The same reasons for which I see environmentalists fighting against industrial civilization."

Wise-use put a nifty little twist on the land-transfer ethos of the Sagebrush Rebels: instead of focusing on privatizing public lands, they would extend private property rights—for livestock operators, corporations, and counties—to the public lands. One of the leading practitioners of this notion was Karen Budd-Falen, a Wyoming-based attorney and alumna of both the Mountain States Legal Foundation and the Watt Interior Department, who would go on to be chosen by the Trump administration to serve as the deputy solicitor for parks and wildlife at the Department of the Interior. In a telling article in the *Idaho Law Review* in 1993, Budd-Falen and her husband, Frank Falen, argued that grazing livestock on public lands was actually a "private property right" protected by the Constitution—a notion that would certainly make it hard for federal land managers to regulate grazing. Budd-Falen was instrumental in crafting a slew of ordinances for Catron County, New Mexico, declaring county authority over federally managed lands and, specifically, grazing allotments. While the ordinances and resolutions focused on land use, they also contained language influenced by the teachings of W. Cleon Skousen, an extreme right-wing author, Mormon theologian, and founder of the National Center for Constitutional Studies, née the Freeman Institute, known for its bestselling pocket-size versions of the US Constitution.

The ordinances were "about the legal authority of county governments and the legal rights of local citizens as regards the use of federal and state lands." They were intended to preserve the "customs and culture" of the rural West, which apparently included livestock operations, mining, logging, and riding motorized vehicles across public lands. And the Catron County commissioners were ready to turn to violence and even civil war to stop, in the words of the ordinance, "federal and state agents" that "threaten the life, liberty, and happiness of the people of Catron County…and present danger to the land and livelihood of every man, woman, and child." The National Federal Lands

Conference, a Utah-based organization launched in the late 1980s by Sagebrush Rebel Bert Smith, a contemporary and philosophical collaborator of Skousen's, peddled similar ordinances to other counties around the West.

A look at the organizations and thinkers behind the movement reveals that the culture they were rooting for was predominantly white, Euro-American, settler-colonialist, with a hefty helping of corporate influence thrown into the mix. Headlining sponsors of the inaugural wise-use conference in Reno, Nevada, in 1988 included Exxon, Mountain States Legal Foundation—with William Perry Pendley at the helm—several cattlemen's associations, the National Rifle Association, the Boise Cascade Corporation, and numerous ATV, snowmobile, and trailmachine groups. Wayne Hage, the public lands rancher who battled with the federal land agencies for decades, was in attendance, as was Smith. San Juan County, Utah, was listed on the attendance and sponsorship list, as well.

The patriot and militia movements rose up alongside wise-use, their members prepared to take up arms to stop the New World Order (another pet topic of Skousen's) and the mythical black helicopters that the UN or other shadowy organizations were sending across the nation to deprive people of their guns and liberties. Although the wise-use and patriot movements weren't officially linked, they shared membership and ideology. The National Federal Lands Conference's *Federal Land Update*, edited for a time by Hage, who also served as the organization's president, regularly ran rants against the New World Order and gun control legislation and in 1994 ran a long article touting the "need for the Militia in America."[36] Rep. Helen Chenoweth, a staunch Republican and Sagebrush Rebel from Idaho who would later marry Hage, once claimed that the black helicopters were being used to enforce the Endangered Species Act and that white, Anglo-Saxon males were the *real* endangered species.

The 1992 standoff at Ruby Ridge in Idaho, followed by Bill Clinton's election to the presidency and his appointments of Janet Reno and Bruce Babbitt as attorney general and interior secretary, respectively, was akin to throwing gasoline on the patriot-wise-use fire. The reactionary conflagration was further inflamed by the 1993 Waco fiasco and the passage of the Brady Handgun Violence Prevention Act, requiring people purchasing firearms to get background checks. Among other things, the act charged local law enforcement with conducting the checks until a federal system was set up. That provided an opening into which Richard Mack, then-sheriff of Graham County in southern Arizona, could step and propel himself into the glow of the inferno that was whipping up across America.

Mack grew up in southern Arizona in a conservative Mormon family, graduated from Brigham Young University, then joined the Provo, Utah, police force in the 1980s. While he was a police officer, Mack attended a class taught by Skousen that melded constitutional law with Mormon doctrine. In 2011 Mack told the *Arizona Daily Star* that the class had "converted" him to Skousen's way of thinking, and shortly thereafter he went back to Arizona, where he was elected sheriff of Graham County in 1988 and reelected in 1992.

When the Brady Bill was passed, Mack, with backing from the National Rifle Association, joined up with other county sheriffs to sue the federal government over the background-check provision. Mack's willingness to stand up to the federal government made him an instant folk hero among the anti-government factions, and he was soon headlining patriot gatherings, railing at Clinton and his attorney general, Janet Reno. In 1996, Mack lost his bid for reelection, but he still spoke for libertarian causes, and he cowrote a book with Randy Weaver, the man at the center of the 1992 Ruby Ridge shootout with federal agents. In 1997, the Supreme Court ruled 5-4 for Mack and his fellow sheriffs in the Brady Bill case, deeming it unconstitutional for the feds to force the state or its officers to execute the background-check provision in the act, giving Mack even more credence with the far-right.

Back in San Juan County no one stepped up to take Black's place as flag bearer of the new Sagebrush Rebellion until 1995, when the voters elected to the office of sheriff Mike Lacy, who in many ways was cut from the same cloth as Mack. Lacy gained national fame, or notoriety, in 1998, after a trio of young men who had stolen a gas-field water truck gunned down a Colorado state trooper. They abandoned the water truck, stole another vehicle, then fled into San Juan County, shooting their way across the Great Sage Plain and injuring more law enforcement officers, before ultimately abandoning the truck and heading out on foot. Lacy took charge of the manhunt. I happened to be on a rafting trip on the Dolores River not far from where it all happened at the time, and when my three friends and I emerged, we encountered a militarized zone combined with a media circus. We were stopped at two roadblocks. At one, a San Juan County deputy who looked to be about eighteen aimed an assault rifle at our heads, his hand quivering on the trigger, while they searched our truck.

Their caution was understandable. The three gunmen were, shall we say, exercising their Second Amendment rights and then some, armed with fully automatic AK-47s, pipe bombs, and sundry other armaments. Two were from Durango—I went to high school with them both—and the other from Dove Creek. Several years prior to their rampage, I encountered one of the fugitives at a Durango college party, and he had bragged to me about the archaeological "discoveries" he had unearthed in southeastern Utah—illegally. Another was active in a patriot-movement hate group. All three were anti-government and, in today's lingo, preppers, who had supposedly stashed food, water, and ammo throughout canyon country. They may have stolen the water truck in order to build a bomb not unlike the one that patriot-movement adherent Timothy McVeigh had used to destroy a federal building in Oklahoma City a few years earlier.

As the manhunt dragged on, Lacy became territorial, and thus open to criticism. He would not collaborate with other agencies, most notably the Navajo Nation police, and refused to give agencies permission to follow leads in "his" county. At one point, believing that the fugitives were hiding in the tamarisk alongside the San Juan River, Lacy proposed setting it on fire in order to smoke them out. One of the fugitives, Bobby Mason, was spotted near the San Juan River upstream from Bluff. When law enforcement converged on him, they found him dead of a self-inflicted gunshot wound. The other two remained at-large for years, something that would give me pause every time I went hiking or camping in southeastern Utah. It would turn out that neither of the gunmen had ever gotten more than a few miles from their truck. One of them died from a gunshot wound, perhaps self-inflicted, perhaps not. The other may have died just waiting. Their bodies were found many years later.

After all that excitement died down, Lacy turned his attention towards real crime: road closures by federal land management agencies. When the National Park Service closed a ten-mile section of Salt Creek road in 2000 to protect the fragile creek bed, it was Lacy, along with a deputy and two other county officials, who went in and cut the locks on the gate, declaring the road open. At the time, shock waves were still reverberating around southern Utah from Clinton's 1996 establishment of the sprawling Grand Staircase-Escalante National Monument in Kane and Garfield Counties to the east of San Juan. Apparently inspired by Lacy's actions, Kane County sheriff Lamont Smith protested the monument by going on an escapade across that county and removing more than two dozen BLM signs that indicated road closures or some other motorized travel restrictions. In 2004, after an off-road group failed to get a BLM permit for a jeep safari in Arch Canyon in San Juan County, Lacy and county commissioner Lynn Stevens led two dozen jeeps up the canyon in defiance of the BLM. "We're not here to send the BLM a message," Stevens told a reporter. "But if there's a statement being made, it's that this is a San Juan County road and anybody in America can drive it."

AT THE NOVEMBER 1980 GATHERING OF SAGEBRUSH REBELS IN Salt Lake City, panels were convened to discuss what the movement's agenda would look like now that they would have a friend and self-proclaimed Sagebrush Rebel in the White House. One initiative they came up with was to stock the public land agencies with people who worked in or for the extractive industries and otherwise infiltrate them with adherents of the Sagebrush ideology.

They succeeded to a degree that none of them could have imagined at the time.

Two decades after that meeting, President George W. Bush picked Dick Cheney, former CEO of Halliburton, to head up his Energy Task Force to develop policies guiding energy development, including on federal lands. Cheney then went about soliciting input from a cornucopia of oil, gas, and coal company executives and lobbyists and, based on their recommendations, managed to significantly undermine the regulatory framework governing energy development on federal lands.

Meanwhile, Bush's Interior Department staff resembled the attendance roster for a petroleum association gathering or a wise-use conference. They were led by Gale Norton, a disciple of James Watt's and alumna of the Mountain States Legal Foundation, the litigating arm of the Sagebrush Rebels and then the wise-users. Shortly after leaving she would go on to work for Royal Dutch Shell. Also on staff were J. Steven Griles, a lobbyist for energy companies; Rejane Burton, the former vice president of an oil and gas exploration company; and David Bernhardt, a lobbyist for the extractive industry.

Naturally, that played out on the public lands. During Norton's years in Interior, the BLM issued drilling permits at a record pace. Norton favored drilling in the Arctic National Wildlife Refuge, voided critical habitat on millions of acres, increased the number of snowmobiles in Yellowstone, and so on and so forth. Meanwhile, the Interior Department and its assorted agencies fell into a veritable orgy of ethical lapses, federal coffers were deprived of oil and gas royalties, fragile species denied protection, and industry given yet more power to wreck public land in the name of greed.

With so many wise-users in the government, the reactionary movement had nothing to push back against and therefore lost a lot of steam. The same went for the patriot movement. Mack's pulpit dissolved, and he became a used-car salesman. The movements weren't dead but rather had gone dormant. They would be back soon, as would Mack, his notion of "constitutional sheriffs" fully developed and ready to be unleashed on the world.

CHAPTER FOURTEEN

BACKLASH

I N THE SUMMER OF 2016 I VISITED WINSTON HURST AT HIS ranch-style house on a quiet, wide street in Blanding, to talk about San Juan County archaeology. Hurst grew up in Blanding and his ancestors were on the Hole-in-the-Rock Expedition, and like most white kids in San Juan County at the time, he liked to head out into the backcountry, find archaeological sites, and collect potsherds, arrowheads, and whatever other artifacts he could find. But then he went off to Brigham Young University, where he studied archaeology and had his eyes opened to the difference between looting a site and ethically surveying or excavating it. He has since become one of the foremost experts on the archaeology of San Juan County as well as an ardent preservationist.

On that hot and sunny day Hurst wasn't interested in talking archaeology with me. Instead, he wanted to talk politics, namely public land politics, with which he has been involved since the seventies, particularly on the preservation side of things. Hurst is tall, lanky even, and wears a long, wispy goatee and rectangular, black-framed glasses. He looks a bit like a Trotskyite revolutionary from another era. And yet, in a deeply polarized world, he now found himself "in a kind of quiet place in the middle" politically.

That's not to say that his fervor for preserving the natural and cultural landscape had died down any, it's just that he had become wary of using heavy-handed methods to accomplish those goals. "Whatever needs to be done to preserve, that needs to be done," he said. "We can win battle after battle, but in this county it needs to be done organically, or we've lost the war." Short-term successes, he said, tend to become long-term setbacks, each one deepening the polarization and lessening the chances of winning over the "hearts and minds" of locals. "We were in such a panic to save this stuff that we took a short-cut approach to these victories," Hurst said, as he sat next to a desk crammed with books, papers, and a couple of computer monitors. "Victories were always top-down. It fed right into the gut conservatism of the rural folks, not just in Utah, but across the West. These guys see themselves as the John Waynes of the American frontier. The far right has lethally turned every top-down decision into a club to beat us over the head with."

If President Barack Obama were to use the Antiquities Act to designate nearly two million acres of public land in San Juan County as a national monument, Hurst feared, it would ignite a furious backlash—another Sagebrush Rebellion—that would squash the more collaborative organic efforts that he and others had been working on for years.

History shows that Hurst was correct. But it also shows that he was too late. The folks of San Juan County have been in backlash mode nearly since the day that the Hole-in-the-Rock Expedition arrived in 1880. They lashed back at the land that beat and battered them and washed out their crops and ditches; they lashed back when the feds tried to turn the county into a reservation for the Utes and when thousands of greedy Gentiles descended on the place in order to get at the gold in the river's banks; they lashed back at forest reserves, at national monuments, at grazing restrictions, at road closures, at environmental policies. The Sagebrush Rebellion, a reactionary, backlashing movement by definition, constantly has raged in this little corner of canyon country for well over a century.

Still, the rebellion does have its waves and its troughs, usually building momentum nationally when Congress or the presidential administration move in more progressive directions, or locally by new public land restrictions of one sort or another. The most recent wave has been a big one, building up momentum in the mid to late 2000s, then crashing down across the land after the election of Barack Obama. Much of the action has been centered around a relatively unknown canyon known as Recapture.

RECAPTURE CREEK'S MAIN BRANCH BEGINS AT ALMOST ELEVEN thousand feet above sea level on the south face of Abajo Peak, where the slopes still show the signs of decades of overgrazing that began in the 1870s. It cuts a deep notch through the south end of the mountain range before spilling out into the mesas, where its upper branches come together in a wide valley that narrows down into a chokepoint. The Recapture Dam was constructed at the chokepoint in the 1980s and the resulting reservoir is used for fishing and boating, with a little bit of water going to a handful of irrigated farms. From there, the canyon continues in a southerly direction, widening as it goes into a spread-out U-shape, with sandstone rims bookending piñon-and-juniper-covered slopes and a green slice of cottonwood and willow and even beaver ponds meandering down the middle. Eventually the canyon sprawls into badlands of stone and clay before joining the San Juan River a couple dozen miles below its starting point.

Because of the large area it drains and because it originates in the high country, where snow piles deeply most winters, Recapture historically had a nearly year-round stream down its entire length. This has attracted humans to settle there for thousands of years, and the canyon is rife with Puebloan sites dating from the seventh century onward. When the Recapture Dam was constructed in the early 1980s, the requisite archaeological examination uncovered an extensive late-Basketmaker-era village. Cliff dwellings are scattered throughout the upper canyon, and there are no fewer than four village-scale Late Pueblo I to Early Pueblo II sites, along with dozens of smaller ones.

The Ute people could follow the entirety of the seasonal rounds within the canyon, hunting the lower reaches in the winter and the green mountain slopes in the summer, when grass grew so tall that an adult buck could hide in it—at least until the cattle and sheep showed up. A number of Navajo people lived and grew corn and other crops in the lower part of the canyon near where it empties into the San Juan.

And it was near the rim of Recapture Canyon that the Lyman family settled in 1905, leading to the establishment of the town of Blanding, originally called Grayson, the refuge for the Bluff Mormons who couldn't handle Bluff anymore. The new townsite on a windswept, sage-strewn mesa wasn't nearly as aesthetically pleasing as the riparian Bluff site, but since there was no rebellious river to contend with, the land was easier to dominate and control. Blanding "owes its existence to the foresight and persistence of Walter C. Lyman, the father of the irrigation project that brought the waters of the Abajo Mountains to some 3,000 acres of favorably lying land on 'White Mesa,'" wrote Herbert Gregory in a 1938 USGS report[37] on the geology of the region. "The site had been prepared by constructing a ditch line, clearing of rank sagebrush, and harvesting an experimental crop. In 1905 the first settlers arrived—chiefly those whose farms had been ruined by the San Juan River at Bluff and those driven from Mexico by political and religious persecution." An even more ambitious irrigation project was underway when Gregory wrote those words. In the 1920s, Lyman had gone up into the Abajos and noticed that the freshest, clearest, and most abundant waters of the range were flowing northward into Indian Creek. Lyman couldn't stand to see such water streaming unfettered

and unused into the desert, so he set out to build a tunnel to capture the stream and bring it through the mountains to Blanding.
It took three decades to build, but in 1954 the project was completed, the Blanding irrigation district purchased water rights to
Indian Creek from J. A. Scorup, and the trans-basin diversion
was done. Blanding would go on to become the biggest town in
the county and the unofficial epicenter of the Sagebrush Rebellion, although Monticello would end up with the distinction of
county seat and the Mormon temple.

Descendants of the early Mormon settlers tend to feel a
sense of propriety toward all the public lands within their county's borders, but the sentiment is especially potent with regards
to Recapture Canyon, given the fact that it is almost literally
in Blanding's backyard. Local kids play and go camping there,
and in the past locals have helped themselves to the antiquities.
During the excavation of Recapture Village, now inundated by
the reservoir, Hurst, who led the work, bemoaned the extensive
looting and collecting and digging that had gone on there since
at least the 1930s. He told a Moab *Times-Independent* reporter in
1981: "Despite popular opinion to the contrary, the digging of
the trash middens and burials for relics has permanently obliterated the amount of information not normally available from the
site's living areas alone."

Visitors from elsewhere tended to drive right through
Recapture—highways cross it in three different places—without even noticing it as they sped westward to the deeper, more
spectacular canyons on Cedar Mesa. Despite the archaeological
and cultural significance of the canyon, as well as its biodiversity,
environmental groups also tended to overlook it, devoting their
scant resources instead to getting cows or cars out of Arch Canyon or Fish Creek.

That all changed in 2005, when a woman named Lynell
Schalk came across a newly constructed OHV trail while hiking
in Recapture. It was no social trail, either. Old-growth juniper

trees had been cut down, a bridge built across a wash, culverts installed, and heavy tools and mechanical means were clearly used to construct the throughway. It ran right over archaeological sites, as well as the sensitive riparian vegetation. Schalk had worked as a BLM law enforcement ranger in southeastern Utah back when the agency's field offices had five to six times as many rangers as they do now. In the seventies and eighties Schalk was instrumental in a number of pothunting investigations. After retiring she bought a house in Bluff where she spends part of the year. When she spotted the construction and resulting damage she went straight to the Monticello field office of the BLM, where she got confirmation that the trail had been constructed illegally, without any permits or the knowledge of the agency.

Schalk didn't hold out hope that the BLM would do much. George W. Bush was president, and the Interior Department was headed up by Gale Norton at the time. Still, Schalk was alarmed when, in 2006, after the BLM had shut down its investigation without turning up any suspects or pressing any charges, San Juan County applied for a right-of-way to the trail, and the BLM seemed ready to give it to them. "This would be a case of turning over a felony crime scene to the perpetrators," Schalk told *High Country News* in 2007.

Schalk also brought the issue to the attention of the Great Old Broads for Wilderness, the Southern Utah Wilderness Alliance, and the National Trust for Historic Preservation, each of whom then enlisted their membership to pressure the BLM to take action and did their own assessments of the trail construction and damage it had done. The Great Old Broads, including Rose Chilcoat, were already active in efforts to get motorized vehicles out of Arch Canyon, and they soon moved into the leading role in the campaign to monitor and protect Recapture. In 2007, after those monitoring efforts turned up evidence of digging and pothunting at sites in Recapture near the new—or renovated—trail, the BLM finally put an emergency closure to motorized vehicles on the entire section of canyon and reopened the criminal investigation. The following year, the agency further riled motorized users by implementing a travel management policy. The prior plan had considered all trails open to motorized travel unless otherwise closed; the new one closed all trails unless specifically designated as open to motorized travel. County commissioner Phil Lyman would later compare it to changing the legal presumption of innocence to one of guilt, regardless of the fact that even under the new policy, and even with the section of Recapture being closed, there remained 2,800 miles of motorized routes in the county. Meanwhile, the BLM continued to move forward on the county's Recapture right-of-way application.

BARACK OBAMA RAN FOR PRESIDENT AS A MODERATE, WITH-out a smidgeon of a radical left-wing agenda. He had voted against the Iraq War, but was hardly a dove; he wanted everyone to have health insurance, but his plan was less socialistic than most of the New Deal. He ran without a strong policy on public lands. He had disparaged coal burning during his campaign and vowed to act on climate, but he also pushed natural gas as a relatively clean "bridge" fuel to facilitate the transition away from coal, which would help spur an oil and gas drilling boom during his term. He chose Sen. Ken Salazar, hardly a hardcore environmentalist, to be his secretary of the interior.

Still, he was Black, and that terrified large portions of the American conservative populace, who led themselves to believe that Obama would declare martial law, take away all the guns, and declare a war on coal and environmental destruction in general. To borrow Hurst's words, Obama's election "fed right into the gut conservatism" of America, giving rise to a loose-knit but widespread anti-federal-government crusade that included the Tea Party and patriot movements, the Sagebrush Rebels and federal land transfer efforts, anti-gun control and anti-immigrant groups, county and states' rights groups, and the Tenth Amendment-spouting sovereign citizens and self-proclaimed militias. All the groups had existed beforehand, in one form or another, but in the past they had tended to stay in their separate silos. After Obama's election, they were far more likely to mingle with one another.

More significant, and dangerous, this time the multifaceted movement was joined by another unified force: county sheriffs. As elected officials, sheriffs have long taken political stances and individual sheriffs have played a part in Sagebrush Rebellions of the past, mostly as lone renegades. Since 2008 many of them, particularly from the rural West, banded together in common cause, not only with one another, but also with the Tea Party-patriot-Sagebrush Rebels. Their self-appointed leader was "Sheriff" Richard Mack.

Overcome by "complete discouragement and feelings of hopelessness" at Obama's election, Mack wrote a fifty-page screed denouncing the federal government and its intrusion into individual and state rights. *The County Sheriff: America's Last Hope*, published in 2009, argues that the sheriff is the ultimate law enforcement authority and thus the "last line of defense" shielding individual liberties from out-of-control federal bureaucrats. The manifesto cemented his cause and made him one of the prime movers of the ad hoc reactionary movement that would come to be known as the Tea Party.

With his clear blue eyes, sweeping black hair, and easy smile, Mack looks like central casting's idea of the prototypical western sheriff. He shared his philosophy of the "constitutional sheriff" at dozens of Tea Party rallies as well as gatherings of the Oath Keepers, a quasi-militia organization founded in 2009. Had there been a true constitutional sheriff in Montgomery, Alabama, back in 1955, Mack told his audiences, that sheriff would have defied the segregation laws and protected Rosa Parks.

"Today, that constitutional sheriff does the same for Rosa Parks the gun owner," Mack said, "or Rosa Parks the rancher, or Rosa Parks the landowner, or Rosa Parks the homeschooler, or Rosa Parks the tax protester."

By refusing to enforce federal and state laws that they deem unconstitutional, whether they involve BLM road closures, gun control, drug laws, mask mandates, or bans against selling unpasteurized milk, Mack said sheriffs can lead the fight to rescue America from the "cesspool of corruption" that Washington, DC, has become. If need be, he said, sheriffs even have the power to prevent federal and state agents from enforcing those laws, thereby nullifying federal authority. If a particular sheriff doesn't rally to the cause, then the voters should kick him out of office.

Sheriffs do not derive their power, real or imagined, from the US Constitution. For the most part, the office of sheriff is defined and empowered by state constitutions (in Utah, it is a statutory office). Early American colonists established the office of sheriff, modeling the peace-keepers on sheriffs from Anglo-Saxon times. They would be elected by the people and would be given the power—*posse comitatus* (force of the county)—to enlist citizens to help enforce the law. Following the Civil War, in reaction to federal troops "occupying" the South to protect freed slaves, Congress passed the Posse Comitatus Act, which makes it illegal "to employ any part of the Army of the United States, as a posse comitatus, or otherwise, for the purpose of executing the laws."

That act was loosely interpreted by the late William Potter Gale to mean that the federal government can't engage in law enforcement at all, thus making the county sheriff the highest law enforcement officer in the land. On the basis of this faulty interpretation Gale formed the racist, anti-tax, county-first Posse Comitatus movement in 1970. Not wanting to be associated with Gale, Mack and his followers tend to avoid using the term posse comitatus, but they do adhere to similar beliefs.

Sheriffs like San Juan County's Mike Lacy had been acting out Mack's ideas for years. But Mack served as a glue that brought like-minded sheriffs from across the country together. And the constitutional sheriffs in rural western counties—I call them Sagebrush Sheriffs—provided a link between the Sagebrush Rebels and the other right-wing movements that were emerging.

In early 2011, Dennis Spruell, then-sheriff of Montezuma County, Colorado, appeared on a right-wing radio show based in Tennessee called *The Political Cesspool* and threatened to arrest BLM and USFS officials who closed roads in his county. "I took an oath to uphold the constitution," he said during the interview. "The sheriff is the ultimate law enforcement authority. I have an obligation to protect my county from enemies, both foreign and domestic. So if the federal government comes in and violates the law, it's my responsibility to make sure it stops."

Later that year, eight sheriffs from Northern California and Southern Oregon—an area sometimes referred to as the State of Jefferson—gathered for a "Sheriffs Stand TALL for the Constitution" event in Siskiyou County, California. Each of the sheriffs hammered on similar themes, namely that the federal land management agencies and their regulations were destroying the economy and culture of their counties. Tellingly, the only non-sheriff on the panel of speakers that night was Karen Budd-Falen, the wise-use attorney.

The event was hosted by Siskiyou County sheriff Jon Lopey.[38] A former military man who looks like a towering, slightly less demented version of Dennis Hopper, Lopey became one of the Sagebrush Sheriffs' most outspoken members and was always ready with anti-government bile. "Some of your federal and state agencies care more about fish, frogs, trees, and birds than you do about the human race. What's that all about?" he said at the 2011 event. "And one more thing, we're broke. Why are you doing stupid stuff to make us poorer? Why don't you let the people work?"

***

THE RECAPTURE SKIRMISH AWAKENED THE SLEEPING SAGE-
brush Rebellion of San Juan County. But soon an even bigger
catalyst would kick the movement into action. In June 2009 over
one hundred federal agents, some of them heavily armed and in
SWAT gear, came to town and raided homes of those suspected
of gathering or dealing in cultural artifacts found on public land.
The raid was the culmination of an undercover sting operation
known as Operation Cerberus that had been in the works for two
years and concerned hundreds of antiquities with a total mon-
etary value of $335,000. The suspects, many of them Blanding
old-timers, including respected physician James Redd and his
wife Jeanne, were served with warrants, handcuffed, shackled,
and interrogated. Sheriff Lacy's brother, David, was also among
those charged.

The next day, James Redd killed himself, leaving townspeople in shock and enraged. Lacy was one of the most outspoken
critics of the BLM tactics, comparing them to the gestapo's and
decrying the agency's lack of coordination with local law enforcement. Buddy Black, Cal's son, who was indicted and acquitted in
the 1986 pothunting raid, echoed his late father while talking to
a *Salt Lake Tribune* reporter after the 2009 raid: "Hitler had the
Gestapo and the US has the FBI. This has about put me over the
edge." For years afterward, townsfolk would blame the BLM for
Redd's death. Redd's son, Jay, has been known to show a photo
of a tiny bird pendant to reporters, saying that the feds had killed
his father over it, something that he claims is worth less than
seventy-five dollars.

It wasn't quite so clear-cut, however. Between the two of
them, Jeanne and James Redd were charged with receiving,
stealing, or selling a ceramic mug, an axe, four sandals, two
stone pendants, and the bird effigy, all taken from public land.
A few weeks after the raid, their daughter, Jerrica, was charged
with excavating three ceramic vessels. Jeanne and Jerrica both

ended up pleading guilty and were sentenced to jail time and probation, and federal officials seized more than eight hundred artifacts from their home.

It wasn't the first time. In 1996 James and Jeanne Redd were caught digging up a Puebloan burial in Cottonwood Wash on state land near Bluff and charged with "one count of abuse or desecration of a dead human body," a third-degree felony, and one count of trespassing on state trust land, a misdemeanor. The Redds claimed that they thought they were digging on private land, which makes the act legally, if not morally, acceptable. The judge didn't buy that. But in a blatantly racist ruling, the court dismissed the desecration count because he said the state statute was only meant to apply to the recently deceased or to digging around in cemeteries—read: *white*-people cemeteries—and not Puebloan burials because, "Anasazi bones are scattered all over this part of the country." The Hopi Tribe was understandably furious at the implications. Ultimately, Jeanne Redd pleaded no contest and was ordered to pay $10,000, while the charges against James were dropped because Jeanne was the one with the interest in collecting. The history shows that while James Redd was not convicted of the crime, he also had no moral or ethical compunction in digging up cultural sites or even human remains in order to get at the relics that accompanied them.

After another defendant and the primary informant also killed themselves, the case bogged down and the anger swelled up. The investigation had been launched during the Bush administration. Perhaps it would have had a different outcome if it had culminated under Bush as well; in 2008 Bush pardoned the first Utahn to be convicted as a felon under the 1979 US Archaeological Resources Protection Act, indicating that the president did not consider pothunting to be a serious crime. Since the resulting action had come just months after Obama took office, and was presided over by Interior Secretary Ken Salazar, Obama and Salazar are the ones who took the brunt of local resentment. It was a signal that the new administration wouldn't go easy on people who messed with the public lands and the antiquities therein, and it also gave locals justification to go after the BLM and the federal government, a sort of garnet of rage that they'd hang onto and that would fuel the resentment and rebellion to come.

There is no doubt that James Redd was well-liked and respected by just about everyone in San Juan County, white and Indigenous alike, for his kindness and generosity. His death was a deeply felt tragedy. Hurst was disgusted by the raid, and Navajo politician and community organizer Mark Maryboy told the *Salt Lake Tribune* that the feds had gone too far. Most observers agree that the agency's tactics were over-the-top and too heavy-handed, not unlike when a law enforcement agency sends a SWAT team to someone's home on a drug-possession charge. Redd's family would go on to sue the BLM for intentional infliction of emotional distress and wrongful death, but the case was dismissed and an appeal failed.

As is often the case, however, this story has another side to it. While Redd's family has claimed that one hundred agents in SWAT gear converged on their home, the record shows that it was only thirteen agents, and they were not any more heavily equipped than typical on-duty law enforcement officers. About ten more agents showed up in SWAT gear after Redd was taken into custody, but that was in response to what they believed was a threat coming from another family member. The feds had no reason to think that the Redds might respond violently to being served warrants, yet they did have a reason to think that other townspeople might. After all, it was only five years later that gunned-up men fancying themselves as members of a militia descended upon the Bundy ranch in Nevada and confronted BLM agents who were just rounding up some scofflaw's cows. And it's worth remembering that the local sheriff at the time, Lacy, had shown that he believed he was above the law when it came to the federal land management agencies, and thereby potentially prone to respond in kind to what he saw as the feds' incursion with force. Indeed, when archaeologists arrived following the raid to collect and meticulously inventory all of the looted artifacts, heavily armed sheriff's deputies stood outside the houses in an intimidating manner, as if there to protect the alleged criminals.

Probably without even knowing it, Lacy had joined the ranks of the constitutional sheriffs and the branch in the rural West that primarily targets federal land management agencies and their regulations, or Sagebrush Sheriffs. "I have an aggressive attitude against federal intrusion," Lacy wrote in the *San Juan Record* the following year as he unsuccessfully campaigned for reelection. "I have fought the battles with the federal agencies who have forgotten who owns the land. I have worked to stop road closures."

IT'S NOT EASY FOR THE VOTERS TO BOOT A SITTING SHERIFF. IN rural counties, among the only people qualified to replace a sheriff are the deputies, who risk losing their job by taking on their boss—the average sheriff's term is about twenty-four years. But in 2010, after serving for sixteen years, Lacy was unseated by Rick Eldredge, a local veteran Utah state highway patrolman. During his campaign, Eldredge, a Democrat, leaned on his professionalism rather than his politics and said he felt "the need to open doors" when it came to federal land agencies. Eldredge won, boosted by strong support from the southern, predominantly Navajo, precincts. Phil Lyman, not yet a firebrand, was elected to the San Juan County Board of Commissioners the same year.

Eldredge proved early in his first term to be much more moderate, and reasonable, than his predecessor, and he genuinely set about to mend fences with the BLM. But over time it appears that he got swept up in the ideological current of many of his constituents and of the nationwide constitutional sheriff's movement. His rhetoric and approach became remarkably similar to those expressed by Mack and the sheriffs at the Siskiyou convention.

In 2012 Mack's Constitutional Sheriffs and Peace Officers Association held its first gathering in Las Vegas, followed by a second event that September. By then, Obama was on his way to being reelected and Tea Partiers had triumphed in a number of Republican primaries. Mack's attendance rosters read like a Who's Who of Tea Party politics. They included Oath Keeper founder Stewart Rhodes and Sagebrush Sheriffs such as Spruell and Lopey. Bert Smith, aka "Mr. Sagebrush Rebellion," was on hand. Smith, who became wealthy from his giant military surplus business in Ogden, Utah, had provided seed money for the CSPOA and for the American Lands Council, created that year by Utah state representative Ken Ivory to push for transferring public lands to the states, counties, and private entities. Also speaking was Tom DeWeese, president of the American Policy Center, known for spreading fears that the United Nations, under Agenda 21, is taking over the world via bike paths and public transit, and Joe Arpaio, the notorious sheriff of Maricopa County, Arizona, whom Mack praised for launching an investigation into the validity of Obama's birth certificate. Ivory gave a rousing speech at the September gathering about the "revolution of ideologies" in which he and the sheriffs were engaged.

The Sagebrush Rebellion and the sheriff supremacy movements have meshed in state legislatures, where lawmakers have tried to pass laws codifying the "ultimate law enforcement authority" concept. "Sheriffs first" bills have been attempted in Montana, Arizona, and Washington. In 2013, Eldredge was on hand at the Utah legislature to help Rep. Mike Noel, a well-known Sagebrush Rebel from Kane County, Utah, introduce a bill to limit the ability of federal officials from land management agencies to enforce the state and local laws on public lands in the state. The "sheriff's bill" passed, but was later repealed after the courts stopped it from taking effect, and replaced in 2014 by this language: "The sheriff is the primary law enforcement authority of state law on federal land except as otherwise assigned by law to the authority of a state or municipal law enforcement agency."

The resistance to federal laws often extends to those concerning roads or even cattle grazing. Over the years, sheriffs in rural New Mexico, Colorado, Utah, California, and Oregon have threatened to arrest BLM or USFS employees who try to close roads. At the 2011 constitutional sheriff's forum, much of the ire was reserved for efforts to restrict travel. "The travel management plan…is a measure of the insidiousness and the calculated efforts that have been underway for a long long time," said Plumas County sheriff Greg Harwood. "I'll be damned if I'm going to enforce the travel management plan and criminalize the good folks of my county for doing nothing more than accessing public lands."

"When law enforcement refuses to enforce the laws, it sends a dangerous signal to extremists," Jessica Goad of the Center for Western Priorities told me. "It serves to embolden those who tend towards violence. This rhetoric and stance has an extremely chilling effect on the people who are doing their jobs—from park rangers to environmental activists. The thought that the sheriff doesn't enforce the law is scary."

Following the 2014 Recapture ride in Utah, Sheriff Eldredge was interviewed by *Breitbart Texas*, a conservative web outlet, under the headline: "Sheriff stands up to BLM." In the interview, the sheriff stated his opposition to a potential national monument in his county and implied that laws or closures to protect archaeological resources were unnecessary, because the people there "love Anasazi things and take care of them."

"I think there's a bullseye on San Juan County, Utah. This area used to be rich. It used to be the second wealthiest county in the state of Utah," he said. "But now it's the poorest in Utah, because everything's been shut down [by the BLM]. Worrying about trees and birds and these types of things rather than living human beings right now is just aggravating to the people.... We'd love to see the federal government give this land back to the states."

Eldredge was hewing to a now-familiar storyline: his county and the dominant, white culture that runs the place have become the victims—of political correctness, of multiculturalism, of voting rights movements, of environmental protections, of the gun-confiscators, of national monument designations. The Sagebrush Sheriff version of the myth is based in the false belief that counties with a lot of federal lands and natural resources are impoverished because the feds are restricting access to those resources. Since environmental regulations are hurting the county coffers, they argue, the hurt is trickling down to the sheriff's budget, meaning they have to cut personnel and even, in some cases, release prisoners from jail because they're costing too much to keep. Environmentalism, in other words, is an assault on public safety.

Rarely does the tale mention the part about San Juan County spending hundreds of thousands of dollars in legal fees to fight against voting rights, environmental protections, and the like. Rarely does it mention that the "traditional" ways of making a living, whether coal mining or ranching in arid lands, are disappearing due to free market economics more than rules or regulations. Rarely does anyone bring up the fact that public lands ranchers in the rural West are kept afloat by subsidies from the same federal government that they are always railing against: from 1995 through 2020, San Juan County farmers and ranchers received $69.4 million in agricultural subsidies from the US Department of Agriculture, including $7 million in livestock subsidies.

***

THE PLOT THICKENED IN SAN JUAN COUNTY. A FEW MONTHS after the pothunting raid, the Red Rock Wilderness Act, a far-reaching bill that, if ever passed, would put the highest level of protection on millions of acres of BLM land in Utah, got its first-ever hearing in Congress. Then, in 2010 a "secret" Interior Department list of western places worthy of protection was made public. The Cedar Mesa region in San Juan County was included. The document emphasizes in the short preamble: "The areas listed below may be good candidates for National Monument designation under the Antiquities Act; however, further evaluations should be completed prior to any final decision, including an assessment of public and Congressional support."

The tiptoe-esque tone didn't ease the backlash, however. The US Chamber of Commerce—notorious for its climate change denials—sent a letter to Congress urging it to remand the president's authority to create any new national monuments. The Congressional Western Caucus, led by nouveau sagebrush warrior Rep. Rob Bishop, R-Utah, ran no fewer than eight articles on its website bashing the document and its alleged intent, with titles like "War on the West II." For many in San Juan County, it felt like just another volley in the "War on Southeast Utah," coming on the heels of the Recapture closure and then the pothunter raid.

Sen. Bob Bennett, a Utah Republican, stepped into the fray, hoping to ease the tension. Bennett, who died in 2016, was once considered a hardline conservative, fiscally and socially, earning praise from the National Rifle Association and the American Conservative Union and low marks from environmental and social justice organizations. But when it came to public lands in his home state, he urged all parties to back down, give a little, and compromise, an approach that succeeded in Washington County, Utah, with a Bennett-sponsored bill that designated wilderness in sensitive areas and allowed for the sale of public lands on the fringes of the towns there in order to accommodate rapid growth. Environmental groups weren't thrilled with it, but eventually relented after concessions were made. Obama signed the bill—which was modeled after similar deals brokered by Sen. Harry Reid, a Democrat—in 2009. After the 2010 list went public, Bennett thought he could spread the Washington County model across the state. The county-by-county-level effort would establish wilderness on lands in need of protection, in exchange for various concessions such as land swaps that would allow for more development in urban areas or relaxing regulations to facilitate energy development for extraction-reliant counties. The ambitious goal? End the Utah land wars once and for all.

Bennett's conciliatory tone didn't fly so well in the venomous political climate that followed Obama's election, however, and he lost his 2010 primary to Tea Partier Mike Lee, now one of Utah's senators, pushing his deal-making into dormancy. It was one example of a tectonic shift within the Republican Party away from classic conservatism and toward the extreme right wing, a shift that left people like Bennett, Sen. John McCain of Arizona, and Sen. Mitt Romney of Utah looking like lonely moderates, at least when compared to the new majority of their party. San Juan County's Republicans had always been hardliners, but election results indicate that they, too, shifted further right after Obama's election. Phil Lyman, the San Juan County commissioner who would go on to lead the 2014 ATV protest ride into Recapture Canyon, is a manifestation of the shift. He was an early supporter of Trump and has been known to lambaste fellow Republicans such as Romney and Utah governor Gary Herbert for being too moderate.

Bennett's ouster effectively killed the land deal effort for the time being and reopened the door to a potential presidential monument designation of the kind that could, in Hurst's words, be used by the far right as a club to bash the progressives with. With that hanging over the county's heads, Recapture came back into the spotlight. In 2011 two locals, Kenneth Brown and Daniel

Felstead, pleaded guilty to damaging BLM land, a misdemeanor, by constructing the Recapture trail. They were fined $35,000 between them and given probation. It may have seemed to preservationists like a just punishment, given the damage done to the canyon and archaeological sites. But to the Sagebrush Rebels in San Juan County, it was the final straw.

THE SOUTHERN UTAH WILDERNESS ALLIANCE HAS LONG BEEN the Sagebrush Rebels' prime punching bag. The group was born in 1983, mainly to push for designation of more wilderness areas on BLM-managed lands in Utah. In 1989 SUWA put out a proposal that would ultimately become the Red Rock Wilderness Act, which the Sagebrush Rebels saw as an environmentalists' nuclear bomb. Since then the group has branched out from focusing only on wilderness to preservation in general, fighting tooth-and-nail to get motorized vehicles and cattle out of fragile canyons, including Recapture, Arch Canyon, and many others. There is even a "SUWA Sucks" Facebook page—more than one, actually.

But the multifaceted Recapture trail controversy put another group, one that hadn't gotten a lot of notice from locals previously, into the crosshairs: the Great Old Broads for Wilderness and two of its leaders, Executive Director Veronica "Ronni" Egan and Associate Director Rose Chilcoat. Although SUWA and even the National Trust for Historic Preservation had put pressure on the BLM regarding Recapture, the Broads emerged as the most blatantly targeted. Makeshift signs popped up in Recapture Canyon and other places with pictures of skulls and crossbones and "Wanted Dead or Alive: Members of Great Old Broads for Wilderness are not allowed in San Juan County, Utah." When they held a "Broadwalk" campout in San Juan County, the Broads' sign was vandalized, the gate that provided the only exit for them was locked, and a bloody mask and threat hung on the gate.

That the local sheriff seemed to be on the same side, ideologically, with whoever made the threats was especially frightening. "I don't want to get pulled over by the law enforcement there, especially in a Great Old Broads vehicle," Rose Chilcoat told me more than two years prior to being charged with attempted cattle-killing. "If I'm alone, and I don't go there alone, it would be a he-said, she-said deal. It's worrisome to not have trust in these areas."

When Egan retired from Great Old Broads, much of the ire was shifted from the organization generally to Chilcoat specifically.[39] She thereby joined Dan Love, the BLM special agent who had orchestrated Operation Cerberus, as San Juan County's top enemy. "Let's not forget Dan Love's role in prosecuting innocent men for the trail in Recapture," wrote Phil Lyman on Facebook in 2017. "He developed a strange accord with the great old broads [*sic*] executive director, Rose Chilcoat..." In another post, Lyman wrote: "This investigation should have started when Dan Love teamed up with Rose Chilcoat to defame, accuse, prosecute, and kill people in Blanding by creating a big fat lie about our friends and neighbors, Ken Brown and Dustin Felstead and the beginnings of the Recapture witch hunt."[40] It is troubling to see such unhinged accusations coming from an elected official, and especially scary given that it occurred against a national backdrop in which the atmosphere was growing more tense. "We now have a variety of militant groups that are networking, and I consider them to be much more dangerous than the more individualized, localized nature of the (past) Sagebrush Rebellion," Edward Patrovsky, a longtime BLM law enforcement ranger who now sits on the board of Public Employees for Environmental Responsibility, told me at the time. "The acts of violence are less random than they once were."

Add sheriffs that are openly hostile to both environmentalists and federal officers, and it magnifies the volatility and the intimidation felt by those who are on the other side of the political fence. "This is a pressure cooker and something's about to blow," Patrovsky said. And so it did on a public land rancher's spread in southern Nevada in the spring of 2014.

Cliven Bundy is the cowboy-hat-wearing, pugnacious, bigoted proponent of states' rights and owner of a ranch near Bunkerville, a tiny Mormon community near the town of Mesquite. He illegally had been running hundreds of cattle on public land that served as desert tortoise habitat since 1993 and had failed to pay a dime to the federal government for the privilege. He was, in other words, robbing the American taxpayer to the tune of several hundred thousand dollars while arguing that the land rightfully belonged to the state, not the federal government. The BLM, fearing a violent response, had hemmed and hawed and failed to enforce the law for two decades. The agency's hesitance spotlighted its inconsistency in enforcing its own mandates: in the 1990s, the BLM had gone after Carrie and Mary Dann, members of the Western Shoshone Tribe, confiscated hundreds of head of their livestock, arrested their brother, and charged them over $300,000 for grazing their horses and cows on BLM land that had been stolen from their ancestors. And in 2011 environmental activist Tim DeChristopher was sentenced to two years in jail for bidding on BLM oil and gas leases without intending to pay for them.

Finally, in early April, BLM contractors descended on Bunkerville to seize Bundy's cattle. Bundy's sons put out a call for help and soon dozens of self-described patriots had arrived, fully armed and ready to go to war, literal war, with federal officials. Sagebrush Rebel politicians showed up not to try to de-escalate the situation, but to aid and abet the lawbreakers. Richard Mack also arrived on scene. Mack and Bundy were linked by ideology as well as by the company they kept. Like Mack, Bundy and his sons were influenced by the late W. Cleon Skousen and Bert Smith, who penned a piece on the Bundy Ranch blog in which he called Cliven Bundy a "hero of the range livestock operator on public land" who had "a sacred God-given right of unalienable rights, private property rights" to graze his cows on the American public's land.

In an interview with Talking Points Memo shortly after the standoff, Mack railed about the federal government—Republicans and Democrats alike—"destroying farms and ranchers and mining and logging....It is the federal government that keeps shutting everybody down. And it is the federal government that has shut down 53 ranchers in Clark County alone, except for Mr. Bundy. He's the 53rd. He's the last one standing."

Chapter Fifteen

Recapture

I GOT UP EARLY ON THE MORNING OF MAY 10, 2014, LOADED up my camera and notebook into my 1989 Nissan Sentra with a duct-taped rear window, and headed west from my home in Durango, Colorado, to report on a protest scheduled for later that morning in Blanding, Utah. The weather was cool but not cold, the partly cloudy sky tempering the sunlight as I sailed along the ribbon of asphalt past the bean and sunflower fields of western Colorado toward the giant, phallus-shaped grain silo that serves as a locator for the down-and-out town of Dove Creek. Dove Creek was once known as the Pinto Bean Capital of the World, boomed a bit during the uranium years, got its collective hopes up when outside investors built a plant that would convert sunflowers into biodiesel, and then reverted back to depressed ag-town status when the venture went belly up.

On the west side of Dove Creek, just as a motorist starts regaining his highway speed, there's a little house on the south side of the road where the owner has put up all kinds of crazy signs emblazoned with either fanatical Christian slogans, or gun-nut slogans, or both, as if it were a billboard advertising cognitive dissonance. As I passed by, I rolled my eyes and chuckled a bit at the blatant display of extreme and unhinged hypocrisy.

Then I remembered what my mission was that day, and nervousness displaced my bemusement. I was on my way to cover the latest flare-up of the Sagebrush Rebellion, a protest in Recapture Canyon outside of Blanding led by San Juan County commissioner Phil Lyman. That I'd come face to face with similarly unhinged, and possibly heavily armed, folks was a given; that the protest would turn violent was a possibility.

The seeds of the protest were planted that February, when Lyman called a community meeting to discuss what he calls years of "unconscionable" actions by the BLM. Residents talked a lot about the 2009 pothunter raids, when dozens of heavily armed federal officers came in and arrested Blanding residents, and about public land issues in general. Lyman told the crowd that the county needed to "send a message that we do live here, that this is not a remote, desolate place, but it's actually our home." Someone suggested using Recapture Canyon as a "stage" for the cause, since the BLM had closed the trail to motorized travel back in 2007. "I have said a number of times," wrote Lyman on his Facebook page, "this protest is not about Recapture, or about ATVs, it is about the jurisdictional creep of the federal government."

It might have gone off quietly and without much notice from the outside world. On April 5 of that year, however, the Bundy Bunkerville standoff had flared up. The public land wars had taken on a terrifying new dimension, and images of angry white men aiming high-powered rifles at federal officials were splashed across the world's televisions and computer screens. After several days of tension, the BLM backed down and suspended its roundup. In the meantime, the Bundys and their supporters had received worldwide attention as well as backing from a number of right-wing western politicians. And some in the media speculated that Phil Lyman's little protest at Recapture could erupt into the next Bunkerville.

As the Bundy saga unfolded, Lyman wrote an op-ed in the

Deseret News explaining his lifelong connection to Recapture Canyon and inviting supporters to his "excursion" down the canyon. He prefaced it with a quote by that famous civil disobeyer Henry David Thoreau, beginning with this line: "The same soil is good for men and for trees. A town is saved, not more by the righteous men in it, than by the woods and swamps that surround it." He explained that as a youngster he had spent a lot of time hiking in Recapture Canyon. "Recapture, once alive and mysterious," he wrote, "now feels restricted and subdued. Where, once, you felt that you were treading on sacred ground and you started your descent into this canyon, you now find BLM closure signs. The trails have tree limbs and rocks dragged onto them by self-proclaimed 'Site Stewards' who have taken responsibility to 'protect' these 'treasured landscapes.'"

Lyman's sentiment about this being his home, about people actually living here, hit home for me. All too often communities that are surrounded by public land, particularly land ripe with recreational opportunities, are treated as if they are not real towns, and the people who live there are seen as no more than carnies in a giant amusement park, there only to serve the visitors' needs. And who could disagree about the human psyche's need for the outdoors, for wild spaces, particularly when it comes to children? Many of my childhood haunts on the fringes of my hometown were shut down, as well, only it was by private landowners and housing developments, not the BLM.

At the same time, no one was trying to keep Lyman from reliving his childhood by hiking, camping, or even riding horseback down the entire length of Recapture Canyon. He just couldn't ride an ATV down there. Somehow, I doubt that Thoreau would be all that jazzed about his words being used to argue for more motorized access. And when he mocks the "Site Stewards"—a thinly veiled jab at Rose Chilcoat and the Great Old Broads for Wilderness—and "treasured landscapes," he betrays his insensitivity for archaeological sites in the canyon. "I was very offended," Mark Maryboy would tell me months later in regards to Lyman's ride and rhetoric leading up to it. "I wonder how he'd feel if I went to the Blanding Cemetery and led a posse over their graves? Totally no respect. He refuses to believe that these people were alive and had feelings. He sees them as objects."

Soon it became clear that Lyman intended to harness the energy—the violent energy—fulminated by the Bundy incident. He had originally planned the protest for a weekday, but when the media started getting interested, he switched it to a Saturday to enable more people to attend. A few days before the protest he posted about it on the Bundy Ranch Facebook page, thereby subtly inviting Bundy's followers to join him. The comments on the post were vitriolic and threatening:

> *Drive those pricks of the BLM back to Washington DC so they can manage federal lands. They don't belong on state land. Feds are outlaws!*
>
> *The BLM is about to learn they can't push people around any more in the West. Our backs are up against a wall push back!*
>
> *Yet another case of the federal government taking tyrannical control of the people. They need to be put down and put down hard.*
>
> *I crossed the invisible line those clones made under the freeway in Bunkersville. Now, me and my wife will come from Provo, UT prepared for another showdown to route off the BLM from my own state by recapturing the canyon.*
>
> *The BLM has to engage first....If they engage it's illegal and we have the right under Common Law to defend ourselves against them.*
>
> *Wy is the BLM still around? If they so much as throw a stone in your way, light 'em up. Time to quit defending, being ever gnawed at, and go on offense....Strike while you are still strongest.*

These and other quotes, along with the news that a few days earlier some BLM employees in Utah had been threatened, ran through my mind that morning as I drove into Blanding, the county's biggest town with fewer than four thousand people. Blanding is about as Midwest, or maybe West Texas, as it gets in this part of the country. There are a few old, stone homes from the early days, but mostly it's all super-wide streets and low-slung ranch homes, lawns ranging from lush to patchy, and a quiet main drag that lives up to the town's name. The town is bone-dry, liquor-wise. All of Utah has some weird laws regarding alcohol, but in most places you can get a drink if you want to. Not Blanding. You can't even get 3.2 beer within town limits or a glass of wine to go with dinner at any of the restaurants. The best bet for excitement here is probably the combination gas station, A&W, and bowling alley at the center of town, which does a mean root beer float, by the way.

But that day in May, the action was unfolding on the unnaturally green grass of Centennial Park on the town's southern fringe. That's where Lyman and his followers, along with a sizable cadre of media, were gathered for a pre-ride rally.

IN PERSON, LYMAN DOES NOT COME ACROSS AS A FIREBRAND extremist. He resembles Cliven Bundy or his sons less than he does the comic actor John C. Reilly, more accountant and former high school football player than cowboy. His voice is deep and soft, his face boyish. He typically wears the uniform of western politicians and businessmen: blue jeans, a button-up long-sleeved shirt, comfortable shoes. All of this seems to have a tempering effect on the words that come out of his mouth or his pen, no matter how incendiary they may be. In recent years the pitch of his rhetoric has grown more feverish, but back then his tone, at least, was reasonable. Yet at the same time, by evoking the Bundy incident during the lead-up to the event, he had, intentionally or not, framed the protest ride as the next battle in the war over public lands and the very ideological soul of the Western United States.

When I arrived at the rally and saw the assembled crowd, and when Lyman began to speak, it became clear that this apparent internal conflict of Lyman's had manifested itself in this event. Quite a few locals milled around, perhaps thrilled by all the reporters and television cameras, something they probably hadn't seen since the 1998 manhunt. They were joined by a sizable crowd of out-of-towners, many of whom clearly were either a part of the Bundy group or had been drawn by the Bundys' involvement. A young couple from Provo, Dylan Anderson[41] and his wife, whose name I did not catch, held up signs that said "Tranfer [*sic*] federal lands to the states," and "Disband BLM Paramilitary units." They had traveled to Nevada to take part in the Bundy standoff, and Dylan—looking more like he was preparing to go on a Mormon mission than to war with federal agents—carried a six-shooter on his hip.

I was most surprised and alarmed to see Ryan Bundy, Cliven's oldest son. He circulated through the crowd in a weathered cowboy hat, flannel shirt, and Wranglers, handing out pocket versions of the US Constitution published by the National Center for Constitutional Studies. I meekly took one of the pamphlets and flipped through it, noting as I did the tidbits of scripture peppered throughout. Ryan Payne, who had been one of the leaders of the "militia" presence at the Bundy ranch, was there too. In a later interview with the *Montana Independent*, Payne described how during the Bunkerville standoff he had positioned at least one sniper, sometimes two, to be ready to pick off each BLM agent. "If they made one wrong move, every single BLM agent in that camp would've died."

"I have huge respect for what took place on the Bundy ranch," Lyman said, gesturing toward Ryan Bundy, a big Gadsden flag whipping in the wind behind him.

"Freedom's never free," Bundy replied in a deep, booming voice with a cowboy drawl. "It does cost."

Lyman went on to talk about the purported transgressions of the BLM, from the closure of the Recapture trail to ATVs, to the 2009 raid—"they target a community, they targeted Blanding"—to the subtle change in their resource management plan regarding motorized vehicles. "It's frustrating for a community to all of a sudden become confined to their own private property." With his emphasis on motorized access, Lyman showed just how much the focus of the Sagebrush Rebellion had shifted over the years. In J. A. Scorup's time it was almost all about ranching and public lands grazing. Cal Black and his ilk expanded the scope so that his generation of rebels were also defending oil and gas drilling and mining. Now motorized access has come to the fore, the purported right to ride ATVs and four-by-fours and side-by-sides unfettered across public land, which, by the way, is not mentioned in the Constitution, even the version handed out by Ryan Bundy.

Then Lyman abruptly deviated from the script. He expressed disdain for the BLM, sure, and even quoted Thomas Payne, but soon his voice took on a soothing tone, and he pleaded with the two hundred or so in the audience to forego the civil disobedience portion of the protest. He urged the group not to ride down Recapture at all and particularly not to violate the trail closure. "My fear is that this event is looking like conflict for the sake of conflict," he said. "I think we do more harm than good to actually cross that line today. It takes a lot of courage to go down that road, it takes a lot of courage to say you know it's going to do more damage than good for our cause today in the media."

Instead of pacifying the crowd, however, Lyman's words only seemed to rile them. The Bunkerville crew let out a collective grumble of dismay. "If we don't open it, then we might as well go home right now," hollered Ryan Bundy.

"It's not illegal. It's your land," said Ryan Payne. "To hell with the media."

I backed up a bit, looking for escape routes, ending up instead crowded against a guy with "REGULATOR" tattooed to his neck, wearing a "United States Militia…Molon Labe" ("come and take them") T-shirt and a black glock sidearm strapped to his belt. I had been a reporter for a long time and was no stranger to hostility, but this felt different.

"Let's hold the media accountable to the truth for a change. You guys get your pen and pencils out and write that across the nation we are in support of the people," hollered a woman who said she was with the Citizens Action Network, looking around the crowd and picking out members of the news media as the crowd applauded raucously. "And you people writing articles that are lies and slander, we're coming after your bonds and after your insurance if you harm any of these people out here with slander." I refrained from retorting with a lecture on libel and instead started heading to the edge of the crowd, just in case. What I didn't know yet was that I was witnessing the precursor to what would come just a couple of years later, when Donald J. Trump would be elected president and soon thereafter declare the "fake news"-spewing press to be the "enemy of the people."

Lyman nodded at the woman—one day his rhetoric would match hers—but then went back to his pleas for restraint, saying he didn't want to go down into Recapture at all, because counter-protesters would be waiting and the potential for violence loomed large. "We can carry out a good protest. We can do it without the threat of damaging archaeology and receiving trespass citations. It's not wimping out, it's an intelligent move to take this morning. Does anyone agree with that?"

The answer, generally, was no.

At that point, the audience collectively took the lead. One man, older, whose name I didn't catch, was clearly angry. "We have a treasure, a jewel, and it has been mugged. It's been stolen from us by people back east. They have stolen our treasure. We have to stop this BLM police state. They come into our town, raiding our town…"

"You've got guns, too, by God, that's what they're for," said a voice from the crowd.

Jay Redd, the son of James Redd, the doctor who committed suicide after the 2009 pothunter raids, also urged de-escalation. Again, it went unheard. "What's underlying all that we're seeing here is a religious war, the religion of environmentalism," said one man, his voice shrill. "They are manipulating the government to implement their gospels. They have taken over the mechanisms of government and they are running the show."

The roar of two-stroke engines revving brought an end to the rally. Lyman's pleas to remain out of Recapture had fallen on deaf ears, and even Lyman had resigned himself to that fact. Perhaps he was emboldened by the assurance San Juan County sheriff Rick Eldredge had given him prior to the ride. "I've got a sheriff standing next to me," Lyman had said in a video leading up to the event, later reiterating that the sheriff and his deputies "are our friends, and they support us."

I MANAGED TO GET TO THE TURNOFF TO THE TWO-TRACK ROAD down Recapture Canyon before most of the rest of the crowd, giving me a chance to build up my courage prior to the onslaught. It was remarkably quiet, for the moment, and there were no counter-protesters to be seen. The Great Old Broads had planned on doing something to push back, to show that they were watching. Rose Chilcoat would later tell me that they had relented at the urging of none other than Dave Foreman, the founder of Earth First! and a self-proclaimed monkeywrencher. "They want a target," he had told her, and Chilcoat knew that Lyman and friends had already put an imaginary bullseye on her back. "It's a lot scarier than it used to be," Chilcoat told me after the protest, long before she had been targeted by local law enforcement for reputedly trying to kill cows.

Instead of counter-protesters, I found only a tall, weathered man with a long, thin ponytail and a vest emblazoned with a somewhat threatening-looking San Juan County Sagebrush Rebel logo on the back, along with a Confederate flag patch with this text: "Try to burn this one, asshole." As I snapped a photo, a voice from behind me said, "My brother was the original Sagebrush Rebel." I looked over to see an older woman, Marilyn Lyman, sitting in the shade of a scrub oak, a smile on her face. "Calvin Black," she added, when she saw the question in my eyes. "We need another Calvin Black," she said, "and Phil [Lyman, her nephew] might be it."

As if on cue, the incessant buzz of the convoy of three- and four-wheelers alit on the air just then. I bid my farewell and trotted down canyon a bit to get a head start. Along the two-track road between the canyon's desert varnished walls, a man riding a four-wheeler sputtered by me, kicking up a mist of red dust, followed by another, and then another. The pungent aroma of sage mingled with the acrid smell of exhaust. Some of the vehicles held two people, some three; on one, a woman in a too-heavy-for-the-weather coat managed somehow to light a cigarette, her deeply creased face scrunching up even more, while she navigated a technical spot on the trail. A clean-cut man, who opted to walk rather than ride, carried his towheaded, American-flag-carrying child on his shoulders while his daughter, wearing a red plaid shirt and long blue skirt, walked alongside. It might have felt a little like a backcountry Fourth of July parade had it not been for the guns.

There were maybe fifty OHVs in all. Some of the riders wore helmets, others baseball caps with cameras affixed above the bill. Sidearms were common, from the antique six-shooter on the hip of an older man in a cowboy hat, suspenders, and a belt, to the semiautomatic glocks toted by others. Monte Wells, a Monticello town council member and local blogger, was dressed in full camouflage with a four-wheeler to match, a pistol strapped to his right thigh. A strapping young man in an "American Venom" T-shirt, looking more frat boy than cowboy, rode with one hand on the handlebars, the other on the trigger of an assault rifle. Henry David Thoreau was nowhere to be found.

A man driving a four-wheeler with a woman sidled up behind him slowed to a stop next to me, causing me to jump. "Hop on," the man said, motioning to the little cargo area on the back. To the handlebars a sign was affixed that read, on one side, "I support Commissioner Lyman," and on the other, "I support Sheriff Eldredge." I climbed on the back. After we started buzzing down the trail and it was too late for me to bail off, the woman asked who I was reporting for. I was on assignment for *High Country News*, a publication that isn't always well-received among this crowd, who are likely to consider even Fox News to be too left-leaning.

"I'm freelance," I lied.

"Are you for us, or against us?"

"I'm for the truth." That seemed to do the trick.

Soon we reached the wide spot in the trail where a large sign marked the line beyond which motorized vehicles are no longer allowed. Like the county line and the state line and all the other damned lines around here, this one was placed somewhat arbitrarily but was nevertheless significant: it also marked the place where a lawful group ride became an act of civil disobedience. The first riders had stopped here and a traffic jam piled up behind them. The guy driving the vehicle I was on stopped, too, and I took the opportunity to hop off on the pretext that I was going to get photos of the crowd. A group of sheriff's deputies stood off to the side, nodding to a few of the riders but offering no warnings or signs of resistance. Then a man with a mustache gunned his engine and, smiling, rode past the closure. The others, including Lyman, followed.

The sheriff's deputies, including Eldredge, who was on hand in faded blue jeans and a white cowboy hat, smiled casually and nodded a stoic greeting as the cavalcade rode by.

ELDREDGE WAS NOT REQUIRED TO ENFORCE THE BLM CLOSURE, since he was not under contract with the BLM, as some sheriffs are. He had set out to keep the peace and, he had said before-hand, "to protect the constitutional rights of everyone involved." Militiaman Payne had met with Eldredge before the ride and told the press that the sheriff promised "to protect us from the BLM." Eldredge also told plainclothes BLM officials, in the canyon to collect evidence for later prosecution, that he would protect them as long as they obeyed his orders. This approach would stand in stark contrast to law enforcement's response in ensuing years to Black Lives Matter demonstrations, when police officers garbed in gear and driving vehicles straight off the fields of war attacked protesters with tear gas and rubber bullets.

Shortly after the convoy passed into the unmotorized area, Eldredge ordered the plainclothes BLM observers to pack up and leave the canyon. But the protest—and the lawbreaking—wasn't over yet. After passing the nonmotorized line, the convoy continued to follow a well-established two-track road that is on the right-of-way of a water line and is used by the watermaster for maintenance and inspections. After it ends, a more primi-tive trail continues downstream. This is the section where two locals did some trail building back in 2005, ultimately leading to their conviction and the motorized closure. When Lyman got to the end of the road, he stopped and announced his intention to turn around and head back to town. They had made their point by coming down the road and into the closed area. Going any further would only damage their cause. Perhaps Lyman was also thinking about the legal ramifications of what he had already done and knew that he'd have a better case if he stayed off the more fragile trail.

The convoy coalesced among the sage and piñon. Some folks stayed on their vehicles, others mulled around and chatted. A group of local kids held up signs with slogans that seemed to have been kicked out by some sort of right-wing trope generator:

DON'T CLOSE S.J.C.hildrens FUTURE KEEP OUR TRAILS — OPEN
STOP AGENDA 21 ROAD CLOSINGS
RIDE 4 OPEN ROADS! Keep OUR Libertys!

It felt a little bit like the finish-line party of a running race, a celebration of a task completed. When the Bunkerville crowd realized what was going on, however, the mood was shattered by a rumbling of discontent and a revving of engines. They would have no more of Lyman's conciliation. The "Venomous American," AR-15 slung over his shoulder, led the charge down the trail, paying no heed to the sagebrush that had grown over it. He was followed by Ryan Bundy, sandwiched between his tow-headed son and daughter on his four-by-four, a big American flag flapping in the breeze above him. As many as half the participants followed while Lyman helplessly watched them go. Perhaps he was thinking about what Stefnee Turk of the San Juan Alliance, a local group that adhered to Sagebrush Rebellion ideology, said during the rally: "I want to ask that we be respectful and responsible…the consequences, negative and positive, will reflect on the people of this community," not on those who could just load up their trucks and go back home. It was an uncomfortable scene to behold, the organizer of this act of civil disobedience ignored by a notably uncivil group that essentially had bullied him into coming even this far.

***

THINGS WOULD ONLY GET WORSE FOR LYMAN. THE FEDS HIT
Lyman and three others, including Monte Wells, who runs *The
Petroglyph* blog, with a number of charges serious enough to net
them up to a year in prison and a hefty fine if convicted. Ryan
Bundy and his followers, meanwhile, were not charged for riding further down canyon, despite the fact that that's where the
damage had been done.

It seemed that Lyman would not only use Thoreau's words
as justification for his lawbreaking, but also might end up in jail
due to his protest, just like Thoreau. Thoreau, a pacifist and aboli-
tionist, acknowledged he was breaking the law by not paying the
poll tax, but said he was forced by his own conscience to do so
in order to prevent a greater wrong. The illegal nature of his act,
or the disobedience, and the stiff consequence thereof, is what
lent the act power. Lyman seemed to embrace this approach in
the weeks leading up to the ride. He clearly intended to violate
the BLM closure to make his point, saying, "It is only motorized
machines that are deemed unfit [by the BLM] for these trails. I
for one plan to be riding an ATV, carefully and respectfully, on
these well-established trails which have existed in this canyon
for many, many years." BLM officials warned him prior to the
ride that if he "uses a motorized vehicle within the closed area,
BLM will seek all appropriate and civil penalties." But in his trial
he abandoned the initial principles behind the act and instead
tried to argue that what he did was not illegal. At one point he
even told the judge that the ride was not an anti-government
protest, that in fact, "I love the federal government." In attempting to dodge the punishment, Lyman also succeeded in weak-
ening the power of his protest, and he drove a wedge between
himself and others in his movement.

Almost exactly a year after the ride, a jury found Lyman
and Wells to be guilty of conspiring to operate off-road vehicles
on public lands closed to motorized vehicles and of operating
vehicles on said lands. The two other defendants were found

not guilty. In his sentencing memorandum asking for leniency, Lyman and his attorney, Peter Stirba, singled out Chilcoat by name, as if she were the cause of Lyman's troubles. Also included in the memorandum was a statement by Eldredge to the effect that Lyman deserved a break because he is always "flying the American flag proudly." It was for naught: a judge sentenced Lyman to ten days in jail and thirty-six months of probation and ordered him and Wells to pay $96,000 in restitution for damage done to archaeological sites and vegetation by those who continued down the trail beyond the end of the road. A BLM investigation concluded that a total of eight cultural sites were damaged, including by "the displacement or alteration of the context of features such as cists [stone-lined pits used for storage and sometimes burials], midden areas, and ash stains."

Lyman's supporters, mostly comprised of fellow Utah politicians with a far-right-wing bent, such as Governor Gary Herbert and then-state Rep. Mike Noel, wrote personal checks to help defray Lyman's legal costs, attempted to use $100,000 in taxpayer funds to do so, and even made a T-shirt that likened Lyman to Martin Luther King, Rosa Parks, and Mahatma Gandhi. Ryan Bundy, meanwhile, instead of being grateful to Lyman for taking the fall in his place, went on the attack. On his Facebook page he wrote: "Phil Lyman, a traitor to the cause of freedom. Would not stand for constitutional correct principles. Instead allows himself to be used as a precedent to strengthen the federal overreach position. He had a grand opportunity to make a big difference but chose to cower to his fears. So sad, so sad." He went on to say that if *he* had been charged, "we would have made a strong stand based upon the constitution. It's simple, the land belongs to the people of this state not the Feds."

In response, perhaps Lyman should have followed Thoreau's lead. Thoreau was thrown behind bars for an indefinite period of time, only to be bailed out by his buddies, much to his chagrin, after one night. When Ralph Waldo Emerson asked,

"Henry, what are you doing in there?" Thoreau replied: "Waldo, the question is, what are you doing out there?"

CHAPTER SIXTEEN

THE RIVER

Most of us are poor now, like I am. Many of them blame John Collier, who made us reduce our flocks and herds because there was not enough grass for all. But I think the true reason is a change in the climate. When I was a young man this whole country was covered with tall grass. We had rains enough in summer to keep it alive and growing. Now the rains do not come and the grass dies. There are fewer sheep and horses now than when our family claimed this valley, yet all you can see is sand. The grass is gone. All we need to be rich again is rain.

—Navajo elder Hoskannini-Begay, who lived on Navajo Mountain near the confluence of the San Juan and Colorado Rivers, to Charles Kelly in 1945

"WE'RE GENIUSES!" BELLOWED GABE, AS WE embarked on a rafting tour of the San Juan River in March 2013. The mercury was pushing eighty under a cloudless sky, only a slight breeze blew upriver, and the water was unusually clear. The ranger had just told us we'd have the place pretty much to ourselves: several other parties had cancelled due to low water and a storm forecast for the middle of the week. We, however, knew better. Weather forecasts more than twenty-four hours out are almost always wrong, and the stream gauge was probably broken. There would be plenty of current to carry us along on a seven-day tour of sandy beach camps and Edenesque side canyons. Geniuses, indeed.

That was Saturday. By Monday, our confidence in our cleverness had waned and serious questions concerning our collective intelligence and mental health—most notably from Gabe's six-year-old son, Jack—were gaining strength among the mini-flotilla as it was battered by dust storms, snow, bitter cold, low water, and a *Lord of the Flies*-like ratio of seven children to four adults.

THE SAN JUAN RIVER IS TEMPESTUOUS, SILTY, SHALLOW, POLluted, and teeming with weird fish. It's also a lovely body of water. The Diné call it Sa Bitooh (Old Age River), Tooh Bika'i, (Male Water), Bits'iis Nineezi (One with Long Body), Bits'iis Nteeli (One with Wide Body), and Nooda i Bito (Utes' River). The Utes, who followed the seasonal rounds throughout the San Juan watershed, call it, among other things, River Flowing from the Sunrise, since it runs east to west for most of its length. Spanish explorers called it Rio de Nabajoo before rechristening it after Jesus's favorite disciple. It is the carotid artery of the Four Corners country, draining a good portion of the San Juan Mountains and the South San Juans, and is therefore an indicator of the region's health. Its tributaries include the Navajo, Blanco, Los Pinos, Animas, La Plata, Mancos, and Chaco Rivers, along with hundreds of intermittent streams, each of which become raging rivers after a thunderburst. If the snowpack is scant in the mountains, then the San Juan's flows will be weak, and vice versa. If mines are blowing out or draining heavy metals and acidic soup into mountain streams, then those pollutants will eventually wind up in the San Juan. The river is a shapeshifter, shallow and languid and warm at one moment, raging and violent the next. After one particularly big winter and the ensuing spring runoff, Albert R. Lyman wrote, "the old river seemed bent on retaking every acre of its ancient dominion."

In the 1880s, the "Bluff Excitement" erupted when someone

decided that the tiny gold flakes that had been carried down from the high mountains and deposited in the silt on the San Juan River bed could be extracted and marketed. Thousands of men, and a few women, too, descended on the river and Bluff, bringing their greed, whiskey, and Gentile ways with them. Like most gold rushes, this one was spurred on by hyperbolic newspaper reports, which in turn were fueled by those who stood to benefit from a mass movement of people, namely the railroads, merchants, and stage lines.

Fortunately for the day's Bluffites, most of these morally bankrupt souls wouldn't linger. The prospectors found what they were looking for, sure, but it was primarily in the form of "flour gold," tiny particles mixed with thick silt. While the metals could be recovered, the process was costly and time-consuming. Promises of easy money were blown. By mid-January 1893, the same newspapers that had fed the boom were declaring the whole thing a fraud, a "Fractured Boom," and "The San Juan Fake."

The handful of hangers-on who remained continued hauling themselves from Bluff and even Farmington to their downstream prospects via boat. Bert Loper, who would later become known as a whitewater river-running pioneer on the Colorado River, got his boating start looking for San Juan gold.

The gold-diggers would come and go. The river, however, wasn't going anywhere, and it would prove to be a far greater obstacle to the Mormon settlers. The San Juan near Bluff certainly looks friendly, particularly on a hot early summer's day before the monsoon arrives: the current is slow, the water warm and silty and shallow enough that it can be crossed on foot in places. It—and the warm climate and sandy soils along its banks—seem tailor-made for irrigated farmland. And so, shortly after they arrived, the Hole-in-the-Rock folks started building canals, ditches, and diversion dams to tame and harness and put the river to good use. But all it took was one good rain way up in the mountains to bring water levels up and wreck all the fruits of their hard work. A really big rain or a bountiful snowmelt would push the river out of its banks, washing fields and the occasional house away. The river's anger culminated in 1911, when eight inches of rain fell on the high San Juans and elsewhere in the region, causing the San Juan River to swell up to 150,000 cubic feet per second—which is more than ten times the typical volume of the Colorado River in the Grand Canyon—as it literally ran through the streets and houses of Bluff. The raging river inundated and ate away a good portion of the tiny city and ripped out the brand-new bridge at Mexican Hat, which, when it was built, stood thirty-nine feet above the river.

Water scarcity was just as likely as overabundance, and in the 1890s a region-wide drought so reduced the flow of the San Juan that, according to Lyman, "small pools were writhing with dying fish, and hunting them out of the larger ponds became a winning sport. Navajos offered them for sale by the sackful. In fact they learned, contrary to their old traditions, that fish are good to eat."

By the 1930s the population at Bluff had dwindled so that a traveler called it a "ghost city." The arduous and sometimes terrible journey across the desert may not have diminished the Hole-in-the-Rockers, but Old Man River sure as hell did.

When Gabe, Hilary, Jess, and I, along with four kids under the age of six and three teenagers, got on the river, and when we deemed ourselves geniuses, the San Juan was running at just 550 cubic feet per second, about one-fourth the median flow for that time of year. It was hard to imagine such a meagre stream wreaking havoc, perhaps because the river has been greatly diminished since those more tempestuous days.

As populations upstream along the San Juan and its tributaries grew, more demands were put on the water in those tributaries. Irrigators inundated fields with no thought for efficiency. Towns sucked up water for drinking and flushing and lawn watering. Mills and smelters used creek and river water for processing the metals. In 1962 the federal Bureau of Reclamation dedicated Navajo Dam about 120 miles upstream from Bluff, which backed up the San Juan and Los Pinos Rivers, inundating the heart of Dinétah as well as the towns of Arboles and Rosa and clearing the way for the Navajo Agricultural Products Industry, or NAPI, a vast expanse of fields on the edge of the Navajo Nation irrigated with San Juan River water. The Four Corners Power Plant and San Juan Generating Station were built in the early 1960s and 1970s, respectively, on opposite sides of the San Juan, together pulling billions of gallons of water from the river for use in steam generation, cooling, and cleaning. In 1976 the San Juan-Chama Project began diverting as many as thirty-five billion gallons of water per year from the Navajo River, a San Juan tributary, to the Chama River for use by Albuquerque and others along the Rio Grande. And in 2009 the Animas-La Plata Project was completed, drawing water from the Animas River to put in Lake Nighthorse near Durango.

Combine all that with prolonged drought—most scientists prefer the term aridification, since it appears to be permanent—and anthropogenic global warming, and you have all the ingredients for an ailing stream. Records from the US Geological Survey river gauge for the San Juan at Bluff only go back to 1916, unfortunately; the stats for flows during the 1911 flood are extrapolated from eyewitness accounts, from flows measured upstream, and from a 2001 USGS study of flood debris. But the data that do exist show a clear decline in flows over the last century. From 1916 to 1950 the annual peak flow exceeded twenty thousand cfs fifteen times, or during 44 percent of the years. In the seventy years since, the river has peaked out at that level just four times, or during about 6 percent of the years. In other words, the river is flooding less frequently and with less severity, meaning that if the Hole-in-the-Rock settlers just would have held on for a few more decades they may have been able to make a go of it in Bluff, after all. Maybe. But then, they may have run into the opposite problem, as well. The median flows for the month of April show an even more dramatic shift. The following are the number of years during the time period when April median flows were below one thousand cfs:

1914-1958 = 0
1959-1970 = 5
1971-2000 = 6
2001-2020 = 10

The numbers show a clear trend: the San Juan River is shrinking.

FOR ME, THE LOW WATER THAT YEAR WAS A DOUBLE-EDGED sword. On the one hand, it would mean that our rafts would move more slowly down the river, which would make our somewhat ambitious goal more difficult to achieve: doing both the upper and lower sections of the San Juan in a week's time. On the other hand, big water scares me, and 550 cfs is not big water.

It's not that I don't like water, it's just that I find its power intimidating and I tend to simply sink when I try to swim. I've long tried to justify and explain away my issues with water: I'm a desert guy, a Colorado guy, and a Virgo, which, they tell me, is an earth sign. The problem with these theories is that Gabe shares these same traits, yet he relishes in the power of water, throwing himself and his little plastic kayak into man-eating rapids on a fairly regular basis.

Maybe I'm just weak. In any event, for this reason, combined with my phobia for gear, I came to river rafting a little later than many of my Durango peers, and a good number of the rafting trips I've gone on have been instigated by Gabe. I had rafted and tubed and even "logged" down the Animas River a number of times, but never went on a real rafting trip until I was in college in Santa Fe, and some friends of ours told us they were running Westwater, on the Colorado River, and we should join them. My car was out of commission so we decided to take Gabe's tiny 1975 Fiat. Since we were planning on putting some miles on the rig, we figured it needed an oil change, so Gabe did that while I packed up. We headed out of town far too late and had made it about to Pojoaque, twenty minutes out of town, when smoke started pouring out of the hood of the car so thickly that we couldn't see. Shouting a string of obscenities, Gabe maneuvered through traffic onto the shoulder and popped the hood. Shiny, clean oil covered everything inside the engine compartment, and the oil cap sat casually on the engine block. By the time we finished blasting it all off at the car wash we were hungry, so, naturally, we went to Sonic in Española, where, not so naturally, we ordered green-chile hickory burgers which set off a chain of what I can only describe as painful, inverted chest burps that occurred intermittently for the next several hours.

We picked up a raft in Durango and lashed it to the top of the car and picked up a girlfriend of mine, C—, or maybe she was an ex by then and she didn't yet hate me enough to prevent her from getting corralled into driving up to Cisco, Utah, stopping only at the state liquor store in Moab to get a jug of Ernest & Julio Gallo Burgundy, to float a river. We were supposed to meet up with friends, but nobody even knew what a cell phone was back then and a "mobile" phone was something that only TV millionaires had in the back seat of their limos, so we just parked between the road and the railroad tracks near the put-in and cooked up some spaghetti and drank the Burgundy and waited until they showed up and nearly jumped out of our skins when the Amtrak shot by doing eighty, a streak of lights and bored faces pondering the darkness outside. Somehow we recognized our friends' truck and waved them down, and we went to their camp near the river under towering cottonwoods and drank far too much and C—

made love to me in the middle of a dusty two-track and I woke up in a bed of desiccated cow crap with a pounding headache and a mud-drool crust on my chin. We loaded up Gabe's old raft with no fewer than twelve people and set off on a harrowing trip. I think it was after we embarked, the weighted-down craft riding alarmingly low on the smooth, glassy water, that Gabe told me about Skull Rapid and the Room of Doom and how people sometimes needed to be airlifted out of the latter, assuming it didn't kill you. Then we realized we didn't have a bail bucket.

A few years later, after I had graduated from college and was drifting aimlessly, my friend Chris rousted me from my job at the seed factory and my solitary Santa Fe life and talked me into going on a weeks-long rock climbing trip across the Western United States. I'm not much of a rock climber, but I guess Chris couldn't get anyone else to go with him, so there we were, driving toward the Wyoming outback in his battered, blue Subaru. Before we left, Gabe, who was living in Salida at the time, called and told me he had something important to tell me and it had to be done in person. I figured he and his girlfriend were getting married, or maybe were having a kid, or Gabe had decided to abandon his Marxist ways and become a hedge fund manager. He met us at Turkey Rock, a climbing area on Colorado's Front Range, and dropped the bomb: "We've got a permit for the Grand and have a couple of extra slots. We want you to come."

I know, I know, that doesn't sound all that important to the uninitiated, but really, it's a pretty damned big deal. Getting invited on a private Grand trip is like getting a table at Balthazar, or whatever that place is, or getting your fiction piece in the *New Yorker*. Seriously. They were giving me the opportunity to spend three weeks with twenty other handpicked people in one of the most spectacular places in the world. I was unemployed, single, and, when not vagabonding across the West with sore arms, chalky fingers, and scabbed knuckles, I lived out of my 1973 Toyota Corolla under a giant ponderosa tree in Chris and Margery's front yard. That may sound a bit glamorous these days, when everyone's living the Instagram-ready #vanlife. Let's just say it's best that digital cameras didn't yet exist.

Still, I didn't immediately say yes because, well, I was scared.

"We have to know now," Gabe said.

"Umm, well, sure. I guess so. Yeah."

A couple months later I showed up at Gabe's place in Salida equipped as if going on a week-long backpacking trip only to find everyone else loading up guitars, volleyball nets, horseshoes, Halloween costumes, and a crapload of food and booze. It was only then that I learned that a raft is like an inflatable pickup truck, only one that can carry a lot more stuff. My sparse gear—literally everything I took fit into one leaky dry bag—was a source of constant ridicule, as was my abundance of fear.

I will refrain from going into detail about the trip, lest I destroy the reputation of otherwise perfectly respectable human beings who are now business owners, mayors, land-use planners, and teachers. Suffice it to say that it was an unforgettable experience and that the Grand Canyon is a natural wonder beyond compare. And, yes, I was scared. Not always. That's the thing about the Colorado River, it has long stretches of flat water between the rapids, stretches where you can just lie back on the dry bags and drift lazily downstream while pondering the magnificent cliffs and sky far above. The fear comes on slowly, a tingly feeling in the gut when you first catch a whisper of the sound of the rapids. The whisper rises to the sound of a jet plane flying far overhead, and then to a low roar. Your heart rate speeds up, maybe even flutters wildly—I should probably get that checked out—your bowels loosen and threaten to evacuate themselves, and you and Sarah, your boat-woman, start singing Neil Diamond songs at the top of your lungs in hopes of drowning out the growing anxiety of what's to come: Crystal, Lava Falls, Grapevine, Hermit, the ginormous rapids that can suck in a much bigger raft than ours, chew it up, and spit it out, broken and in disarray.

In some ways, the Grand Canyon can do the same thing to one's psyche. After three weeks we emerged and unrigged the boats and loaded them up and headed back towards home. As we drove up the long dirt road to the interstate, I was overcome by anxiety, just as when we approached a rapid, only this time it wasn't balanced out by even an inkling of sweet anticipation, and no matter how many stupid jokes I might make or how loudly I might sing cheesy seventies songs, I couldn't drown out the building roar of angst at the realization that the "real" world, the outside world, still existed and that I would have to return to it, and play some sort of role in it, and I had no job, no girl-friend, no money—I had to borrow cash for dinner because I had maxed out my credit card buying cases of Hamm's Ice for the trip—and no real prospects at all.

That sinking feeling didn't go away for quite a while, and the feeling that the "real world" is cruel and scary has never really left me. Still, if anyone invites you on a Grand trip, say yes, unequiv-ocally yes. If Gabe invites you on a San Juan trip in March during near-record-low flows and when a storm is approaching, you'd be forgiven for saying no.

When it comes to boating, the San Juan River in Utah has two main sections, the Upper and the Lower. Boaters doing the Upper put in at Sand Island, just below Bluff, and meander down past Comb Ridge and through the Raplee Anticline before tak-ing out at Mexican Hat. This section is archaeologically rich, with several dwellings and petroglyph panels along the way. With a permit from the Navajo Nation, the boaters can camp on the south side of the river and hike up Chinle Wash, retracing the steps of Juanico and others as they eluded Vizcarro and his goons back in 1823. Most of the twenty-seven-mile-long Upper section, which never gets too far from the highway or other roads, is fairly easily accessible by those without boats. With a good current or a strong rower, the Upper can be done in a day, most people take three days, and I once was on a quite leisurely five-day Upper trip.

The Lower section starts at Mexican Hat, where the Upper section ends. From there, boaters float under the iconic Mexican Hat Bridge before descending into the deep and curvy gorge of the Goosenecks on their way to Clay Hills Crossing, some fifty-seven miles downstream. Most boaters take four to five days to complete this stretch, which is accessible from off-river in only a few places, and those access points require big hikes and, in some cases, perilous climbs down sketchy cliffs. I know this because I've made those same climbs on more than one occasion to join up with already in-progress rafting parties.

So, even though the water was low, and we were trying to cover too many river miles in too short of a time span, I was pretty damned psyched to finally do the Lower from top to bottom and not have to hike across the desert to do so. I was legitimate at last, and by then had enough multiday raft trips under my belt not only to know how to pack for it, but also to be able to pilot a raft in a vaguely competent manner. I had a good job, a lovely wife, two wonderful kids, and plenty of room left on multiple credit cards. I felt as if, having finally reached middle age, I deserved to take it a bit easy for once and go camping in the desert without subjecting myself to all kinds of adversity. I even had a tent.

Not that the trip would be easy. Rafting trips never are. When you get to camp you have to de-rig, set up camp, cook dinner, wash dishes, and then in the morning you have to cook breakfast, wash dishes, break camp, rig the boats, and row for hours on end. Backpacking requires far less labor, it turns out. But then, there aren't Dutch oven enchiladas or an endless supply of cold beer when you're backpacking, either. So it all works out in the end. The first couple of days on our trip worked out well, too. The sun shone, the breeze was warm, the sky was blue. We checked out a Chacoan great house above what William Henry Jackson, when he came through the area in 1878, called Epsom Creek because its waters taste like Epsom salts. "For a distance of some 25 miles above its mouth the valley of this creek presents upon its eastern side a remarkable wall, some 400 feet in height, insurmountable throughout its whole length, with the exception of one place, where the Indians have made a way for themselves," he wrote, referring to Comb Ridge, the Spine of the World. From just beyond that point onward, wrote Jackson, the river "is then lost to all knowledge until it reappears mingling its waters with those of the still more turbid Colorado." It so happens that in 1916 surveyors suggested building a dam 264 feet high at this same spot, where the river goes into the Raplee Anticline, thereby inundating Chinle Wash, Comb Wash, and the town of Bluff.

We woke on day three, Monday morning, to a sepia-toned sky. It was beautiful and eerie and a little mysterious in that we couldn't really understand what kind of natural phenomenon we were witnessing. It vaguely resembled that orange-red cloud-glow that sometimes saturates the sky at morning, but only vaguely, since there didn't seem to be any clouds in the sky. As we ate breakfast, preparing ourselves for a big day, a breeze kicked up. It wasn't much, but by the time we broke camp it was strong enough to cause the nylon of the tents to flap loudly. Gabe seemed a little concerned as we rigged the boats. I didn't realize why until I cast off and started rowing—into a stiff headwind. A raft isn't exactly an aerodynamic craft, and rowing a heavy one against the wind is difficult. Rowing one against the wind when the current is virtually nonexistent can be Sisyphean, with any forward progress gained offset and then some when one pauses to take a breather.

We had three boats. Gabe and Hilary traded off at the oars of one, and their two young children were with them. Jess piloted another, a heavy beast of a craft that leaked air, with her two kids. And I rowed the third—a borrowed raft, meaning for the first time in my life I had perfectly adequate gear—with three passengers: my two teenaged daughters and one of their friends, who had just arrived from Germany for a three-month stay in Durango. It took us all morning to get just seven miles downstream, to a place where the river bends back into the base of Raplee Ridge before turning again for the final stretch before Mexican Hat. As we rounded the bend, the wind picked up even more, forming white caps on the otherwise smooth river's surface. Clouds moved in overhead, kids hunkered down between dry bags, even though it meant kneeling or lying on the damp boat floor. One of our chairs broke free of its strap and sailed, airborne, upstream. It might have been an aesthetically pleasing vision had it not meant that I would be sitting my middle-aged ass on the ground for the rest of the trip. I rowed frantically upstream to retrieve it, which turned out to be far easier than rowing back downstream to make up lost ground.

The final mile to the Mexican Hat put-in and takeout, where we had decided to stop for lunch, was the longest mile I had ever known. Our arrival there was not exactly reassuring, though. Normally at that time of year, spring break for Durango's schools, the put-in area would have been crowded with parties getting on and off the river. On that day it was empty, a sign as ominous as that morning's eerie sky. This time Gabe didn't crow about having the river to ourselves but instead walked around erratically in the way he tends to do when he's nervous or is trying to think. While the kids were secured at the shade structures, we adults did our best to prepare lunch, and as we were rooting around among our boats for the ingredients, the steady wind gusted, and Jess, who was standing somewhat precariously on her boat at the time, was lifted up into the air and slammed back down on the boat, her knee coming down hard and painfully.

As we ate our sandwiches, sand crunching in our teeth, Jess's knee swelling, we actually considered throwing in the towel, hitching a ride back to our cars, and bailing altogether. I think if we were slightly smarter, slightly less stubborn, slightly less proud, we would have done just that and headed home like all the other people who had been lucky enough to get permits but had chosen not to use them. Instead we all looked at one another as if the idea of using common sense was the craziest thing we'd ever heard of. Besides, we only had fifty-seven miles to go.

THAT MORNING'S MYSTERY OF THE SEPIA SKY WASN'T A MYSTERY for long. The phenomenon was caused by the same thing that was grinding our teeth down as we ate our sandwiches: dust. All across the Colorado Plateau, strong easterly winds were picking up sand and dirt, lifting them high up into the air, and carrying them across the sky into Colorado, where the dust particles would mingle with snowflakes, or perhaps even serve as the particles around which the snowflakes formed, and fall back to the earth. In the San Juan Mountains, the dust that was blowing past and above us would end up as a reddish-orange film on top of the vast fields of snow, giving them a rose-colored hue.

Dust storm feels too dramatic a phrase to describe the phenomenon. The incidents in the Four Corners country usually don't involve a wall of airborne sand, thousands of feet tall, rushing across the desert and gobbling up everything in its path, as sometimes happens further south in the Phoenix area. *Dust event*, on the other hand, feels too clinical. I prefer *aeolian*—or windborne—*dust cloud*, since its root is the Ancient Greek god of wind, Aeolus. These episodes are not uncommon in these parts, happening several times a year, most often in late winter and early spring. "Our party experienced a violent windstorm when we were several miles above the mouth of Piute Creek," wrote Hugh D. Miser in a 1924 report on a trip down the San Juan River on sixteen-foot boats. "It blew in gusts and picked up sand and fine yellow dust, which were carried up into the air for hundreds if not thousands of feet."

The episode in which our little flotilla was involved, however, was a doozy among a series of dust doozies. The Silverton-based

Center for Snow and Avalanche Studies was recording and analyzing every dust event at its Senator Beck Basin study plot near the top of Red Mountain Pass. According to the center's data, our dust event was the, well, dustiest in at least four years. In Durango the dust was so thick that it fell with rain as a gritty red slime, coating cars and buildings and just about everything else; the *Durango Herald* ran a woe-filled article about a window washer whose work was destroyed by the storm, forcing him to start all over again. Another dust event a week later would whip up a nasty wildfire near Farmington and contribute to a fatal car crash.

Meanwhile, in the mountains, all that dust brings about subtle but significant changes by throwing the snowpack's albedo out of whack. To quote the National Snow and Ice Data Center: "Albedo is a non-dimensional, unitless quantity that indicates how well a surface reflects solar energy. Albedo varies between 0 and 1. Albedo commonly refers to the 'whiteness' of a surface, with 0 meaning black and 1 meaning white." If a surface's albedo is zero, or black, then it absorbs all of the solar energy. If it is one, or totally white, it absorbs none of the solar energy, or reflects all of it. When dark-colored dust (or ash, or carbon, or what have you) coats the snow, it reduces the albedo, causing the snow surface to absorb more solar energy, thereby melting the snow more quickly.

In 2003 a group of snow-focused scientists founded the Center for Snow and Avalanche Studies to study the dust-on-snow phenomenon in the San Juan Mountains and to better understand its long-term effects. The San Juan Mountain snowpack is considered to be a giant, natural reservoir that stores up vast amounts of water in the form of snow during the winter months, slowly releasing it to flow down to the arid, surrounding lands in the spring, much of it ending up in the San Juan River. Those who use the water, whether they are irrigators or river rafters or fish, want an abundant but slow-melting snowpack. Dust on snow speeds up the snowmelt, disrupting alpine flora phenology and pushing the spring runoff earlier into the year. Reduced albedo enhances evapotranspiration and snow sublimation,[42] thereby reducing the amount of water that goes into the streams and rivers. Aeolian dust on the snow, alone, has pushed the peak of spring runoff of the Colorado River watershed up by three weeks, when compared to the period prior to the 1850s, and it has also reduced the total runoff volume.

These aeolian dust events are natural and have probably been taking place every spring since the end of the Pleistocene era and the retreat, some twelve thousand years ago, of the glaciers that carved many of the region's valleys. Maybe the dust events occurred during the last ice age and contributed to the melting of the glaciers, which was mainly caused by global warming resulting from a buildup of carbon dioxide in the atmosphere. That, too, was natural. But just as human activity is again causing an increase in carbon and a warming climate, so, too, has human activity exacerbated the aeolian dust cloud phenomenon.

By examining the sediment that had built up over nearly six millennia at the bottom of alpine lakes in the San Juan Mountains, researchers in 2008 concluded[43] that most, if not all, of the dust deposited on the San Juan Mountain snows is from the Colorado Plateau, not Asia or other distant lands, as has been hypothesized in the past. And they found that dust events have been occurring for thousands of years but picked up significantly beginning about a century and a half ago, coinciding with the white settler-colonist influx of the mid-1800s and peaking in the early part of the twentieth century, when volumes of dust were five times higher than they were prior to colonization. The timing leaves little doubt regarding the cause of the uptick in dust: a combination of the newcomers' land-disturbing ways, which include mining, development, tilling for farming, logging, and, perhaps most dust-raising of all, cattle grazing, which probably did as much to alter the landscape of San Juan County as anything else wrought by humanity thus far.

The cattle and sheep ate the native grasses and trampled the fragile soil, making way for non-native grasses to invade and preclude the return of the native vegetation, while also encouraging gulley-forming erosion. Butler Wash, which runs parallel to and just east of Comb Ridge, provides a dramatic example of this phenomenon. Where once ran a braided, intermittent stream along a wide, flat, sandy bed, now there is a channel so deep in places that reaching the water is almost impossible for cows or humans, and even then the streambed is choked with cheatgrass and other invasive species. These gullied arroyos are so common in the West—the Rio Puerco in northern New Mexico offers one of the most striking examples—that many observers assume that it is the "natural" state, and that they've always looked that way.

Cattle hooves will also wreck the fragile cryptobiotic crust that is critical to the desert ecosystem, and which, as renowned cryptobiotic crust researcher Jayne Belnap put it, holds "the place in place." Cryptobiotic crust, sometimes known as cryptogamic soil, is ubiquitous, or once was, in most of southeastern Utah. At first glance it looks just like, well, dirt, only with a dark-brown hue that resembles desert varnish. Bend down and look more closely, however, and you'll see a miniature, living world—a symbiotic mingling of cyanobacteria, lichen, and mosses—which is particularly noticeable when the crust is wet. The cyanobacteria are made up of filaments wrapped in sheaths. Writes[44] Belnap: "This sheath material sticks to surfaces such as rock or soil particles, forming an intricate webbing of fibers in the soil. In this way, loose soil particles are joined together, and otherwise unstable and highly erosion-prone surfaces become resistant to both wind and water erosion." And when the crust is destroyed, it leaves those same soils vulnerable to erosion and to the types of winds that were blowing our rafts upstream.

And the damage is, indeed, irreparable. Once wrecked, cryptobiotic crust may take decades, even centuries, to fully recover. In 2005 Belnap published a paper[45] on the impacts of decades of grazing on soils in southeastern Utah. She and her co-researcher ventured into the Needles District of Canyonlands National Park and compared an area that had been grazed from the 1880s until 1974 with Virginia Park, an area where an impassible cliff kept cattle at bay, and which is now a "relict area" shut off to people entirely, save for researchers with a light touch. Belnap's findings are disturbing. Even thirty years after the cattle had been removed from the historically grazed site, the land had not recovered. The cyanobacteria were distributed spottily, the lichen and moss were only beginning to come back, nutrients and organic material were more sparse than in the ungrazed area, and the soil remains far less stable, which means it more easily can get picked up by the wind and carried to the snow in the San Juan Mountains. Also troubling is the difficulty the researchers had in finding plots of land that had never seen grazing at all, even in a national park. Somehow the cowboys of yore were able to squeeze the cows and their attendant effects into just about every corner of the region.

Back in 1965, James Rodney Hastings and Raymond M. Turner compared historic photographs of a section of Sonoran Desert with modern ones and determined that cattle grazing in the late nineteenth century had caused a "shift in the regional vegetation of an order so striking that it might be better associated with the oscillations of Pleistocene time than with the 'stable' present."[46] If we are currently living in the Anthropocene, then an appropriate subset might be the Bovineiferous period or, more appropriate still, the Beefocene.

Clearly cattle are not the only culprit. ATVs, mountain bikes, cars, and bulldozers can wreck cryptobiotic crust and mobilize dust. Chaining huge swaths of juniper forest to make way for forage or even sagebrush is hugely destructive and dusty. Before each of the hundreds of oil and gas wells were drilled in San Juan County, more than an acre of land was scraped clean of all vegetation, top soil, cacti, sagebrush, and even centuries-old juniper trees. Every new house or hotel built on Moab's fringe stirs up dust. Springtime tilling of corn, bean, sunflower, and alfalfa fields kick up huge amounts of dust. Even a single human backpacker trodding through the P-J forest in hiking boots can crush and break up the living soil. All of these activities contribute. But cattle are special due to sheer numbers—some two million cattle graze on BLM lands each year—and their proclivity for finding every blade of edible grass in every nook and cranny, and their insatiable appetites.

As we sat and ate our sand sandwiches, we were right in the thick of this big cycle of soil disturbance, aeolian dust events, reduced albedo, faster-melting snow, diminished river flows. We were literally eating the dust at the same time as we grappled with its ultimate effect, a low river and a current that couldn't compete with the wind. It was a strange sensation and somewhat revelatory in that we were experiencing the interconnectedness of the region, the intimate link between desert and mountains, in real time.

We also viscerally were feeling the fallout of the public land wars and the successes of the Sagebrush Rebels and their industry enablers. Ever since the late nineteenth century conservationists and preservationists and residents have endeavored to get a handle on the impacts of grazing and development on public lands. More recently environmental groups like Great Old Broads, SUWA, and the Grand Canyon Trust have fought tooth and nail to reduce cattle numbers on sensitive public lands, to stop chaining, and to get ATVs out of the backcountry. But the politically powerful cattle industry, the motorized access crowd, and the anti-regulation ideologues—often with the complicity of the federal land agencies—always lash back, wielding money and the romanticized myth of the small-time rancher fighting against the likes of Rose Chilcoat to preserve his "way of life" and "customs and cultures." Hordes of cattle continue to graze San Juan County: according to the most recent agricultural census, the county is still home to almost fifteen thousand head of cattle, most or all of them spending a good portion of the year on public lands. And the winds still lift up tons of disturbed ground each spring, carrying the reddish-brown cloud across the Great Sage Plain and depositing it on the brilliant snow of the San Juan Mountains.

WE DIDN'T DECIDE TO CONTINUE DOWNRIVER. BUT WE ALSO didn't decide to bail and go home, so the default position was to get back on our rafts and continue onward into the wind and into the deep and kinky gorge known as the Goosenecks, thus following in the wake of E. L. Goodridge, who in 1882 piloted a wooden boat from Durango all the way to Lee's Ferry on the Colorado River in search of gold, oil, or other mineral wealth. In spite of the difficulty it felt good to be back at the oars where one has to think about one thing and one thing only: pulling oneself, the raft, and everything on it downstream as expediently and efficiently as possible. We drifted below the village of Mexican Hat then under the iconic bridge that spans the river. I spun the boat around so that I was facing upstream, both to get more power out of the oars and to enjoy the view as we floated past the point of no return.

Just then the wind kicked up. In reaction, I pulled hard on the oars, once, twice, managing to keep the forward momentum going, but also veering sharply to river right even as the river curved to the left. When I hit the cliff I felt it first as a light bump against the raft and then as a crunching yank of the oar out of my hand as it got squeezed between boat and bank. As I tried to comprehend what was happening I stopped rowing and the wind gusted, carrying me at least fifty yards upstream in a matter of seconds. My daughter was so hunkered down that she didn't even notice.

Just as I regained my composure and looked back to see the other boats way ahead of me, the ice started falling from the sky. Not ice, really, but miniature snowballs called graupel, which aren't quite as vicious as hail, but still sort of sting when they hit bare skin. The graupel soon transformed into schneeregen, another German term that literally means snow-rain, because it's not quite snow and it's not quite rain. The flakes were huge, cold, and soaked me through immediately. I couldn't stop paddling to put on any rain gear, lest I lose the precious progress I had made.

Relief came over me when I saw that the other boats had pulled over and the passengers were huddled in an overhang, sheltered from the menace thrown at us by the weather gods. Gabe had already lit a fire by the time I stuffed myself into the overhang. It helped thaw my hands, which were numb with the cold. I remembered then a time when I was about the age of Gabe's son, and my mom and dad and brother and I were camping at the mouth of Mule Canyon in Comb Wash. It was March, spring break, and I awoke one morning with a terrible sore throat.

I suppose some parents might have packed up, headed home, and taken me to a doctor at that point, but not mine. To be fair, I had sore throats, colds, and other minor respiratory sicknesses quite often, and they never turned out to be serious, so it probably did seem like overkill to end the whole camping trip just because of that. But to be fair to me, the root cause of my ailments may very well have been the incessant inhalation of the secondhand smoke that emanated from my parents at nearly every waking moment.

So we set out on a hike on that March day long ago, and a couple hours in the sky grew heavy and thick, wet flakes started to fall. I imagine I started to cry at the same time. My dad guided us to an overhang, not unlike the one that our rafting party had taken shelter under, and built a little fire. He took an empty generic orange pop can and poured water into it and tossed a bunch of Mormon tea branches in there and then set it on the fire. It tasted like hell, but the warm tea soothed my throat and made my eyeballs buzz a little bit, and we eventually made it back to camp without dying.

I started to tell the story to my overhang companions, but they clearly weren't up for one of my stupid stories, so I stopped. The mood under the overhang felt somber. It would have been one thing had we been out on a day hike and gotten caught in a storm and just had to wait it out before running home, but this was different.

"Uh, how far did you say we had to go still?" I asked, trying to make conversation.

Gabe looked at me and muttered, along with a sigh, "Fifty-seven miles."

At that, everyone fell silent, the only sound that of incessant dripping all around, and me doing some emotional-support snacking on a bag of peanut M&Ms that I wasn't supposed to be eating in front of the kids.

I turned to offer one to Gabe's son, only to find him gazing out into the falling snow, as if the truth were written on the cruel and angry sky. Then he spoke that which he had discerned: "You are *not* a genius, Dad."

WE WAITED A LONG TIME IN THAT OVERHANG, AND WHEN THE snow finally let up somewhat, we reluctantly boarded our boats and continued downstream. The wind was just the front part of the storm, it turns out, so it relented, making progress easier if not warmer. Not that our troubles were over. That night when we arrived to the planned camp, a nice sandy beach with willows that offered shelter and shade, it had been destroyed by what I can only describe as a mini-glacial event. Apparently the river had frozen upstream a month or so earlier, creating a sort of ice dam, which then broke free and crept downriver bulldozing everything along the banks, including campsites, leaving big piles of debris and precious few tent sites for rafters. I sent my kids to go set up a tent on the flattest spot they could find, and then I hit the box-wine a little too hard.

That night as we shivered around the little fire, I told a couple of my favorite ghost stories. There's the one about the 1911 flood and how it washed away an orphanage and all of its inhabitants upstream, and now the victims, water babies, lurk in the murky eddies of the San Juan, waiting to grab misbehaving kids and pull them under. And I told the one about ol' Chuck Steen and his uranium fortune and his golden arm. They're good stories, tailored to the place in which they are told. Sure, they scare the kids. Sure, some of the victims, er, kids, that get the privilege of hearing the stories all the way through end up with some pretty deep neuroses and may, eventually, need a lot of therapy. But someday they'll thank me. I think.

After that, the going got easier, even if the other parents weren't too happy with me and my tales. On day six on the river, the winds died and the air warmed enough to pacify the children and avert a mutiny. The snow that had fallen in the hills to the north and east melted. The river returned to its usual gray-brown hue and the water rose just enough to get us over most of the silt bars that have developed on the last runnable stretch of the river before Lake Powell. Back before 1963, the year Glen Canyon Dam was finished and the reservoir began to fill, the thousands of tons of silt carried by the San Juan's waters continued on to the Colorado River before settling out in Lake Mead.

But once the water started backing up, the silt did the same—at a rate of more than one hundred million tons per year—so that in 2011, a bed of silt twenty-seven meters deep had piled up in the San Juan River delta since the dam was built, according to

USGS data. As the silt collects, it reduces the storage capacity of the reservoir, even as bigger demands combined with multiyear droughts draw the water level down. Also of concern is what's in the silt, which includes everything from arsenic and beryllium to thorium and cesium and other remnants from the Nuclear Age of the West.

During the uranium days, more than a dozen mills sat on the banks of the Colorado River and its tributaries, all upstream from Glen Canyon Dam. Every single one of them dumped their tailings out in the open, uncovered and without any sort of stabilization, leaving them to the mercy of wind and water. Every single one of them allowed the liquid waste to pour either into ponds that leaked or broke or directly into the river. The material was laced not only with the highly toxic chemicals used to leach uranium from the ore and iron-aluminum sludge (a milling byproduct), but also radium-tainted ore solids. Of course, what goes into the river at Shiprock or Moab or Durango or Silverton doesn't stay there. It slowly makes its way downstream, carried along by the current until the current dies in the slack water backed up behind a giant concrete plug.

In the early 1950s, researchers from the US Public Health Service sampled western rivers and found that "the dissolved radium content of river water below uranium mills was increased considerably by waste discharges from the milling operations" and that "radiological content of river muds below the uranium mills was one thousand to two thousand times natural background concentrations." A later study by the same agency determined that Lake Mead was the "final resting place for the radium contaminated sediments of the Basin." With the construction of Glen Canyon Dam the sediments would pile up under Lake Powell.

I pulled the oars and pushed the heavy craft through the still waters while the silt rested beneath me, a billion-ton archive containing the sedimental records, the landscape-memory, of all that was dumped into the rivers upstream over the centuries, including the dust that was kicked up by the wind out here, carried to the San Juan Mountains, and deposited on the snowpack to eventually make its way back down from the mountains into the desert and home.

THE WATER WAS CALM AND SLOW, THE WINDS NONEXISTENT. Finally, I could rest my weary shoulders, lay back, look up at rock and sky and listen to the water lapping against the boat and geese honking in the distance. I thought about an old roadmap, from the forties or maybe early fifties, that I was looking at as part of some research on the area. At first glance it looked like a page out of a current road atlas. But as I looked closer I saw subtle, and not so subtle, differences: Highway 95 from Blanding to Natural Bridges National Monument followed a much different route than it does today, and it was gravel. The road to Halls Crossing Marina didn't show up at all, because the marina, and Lake Powell, for that matter, didn't yet exist. The stretch of highway from Bluff to Mexican Hat, traversed now in less than a half hour, was labeled in red: "CARRY WATER." Most heart-rending for me, however, was a little piece of text that appeared far from any road, right along the squiggly line representing the lower San Juan River. It was just ten words long, yet read like a poignant eulogy to something that is no longer possible: 191 MILE SCENIC BOAT TRIP MEXICAN HAT TO LEES FERRY. Oh, the things we have lost, I thought, as I watched a raven ride a thermal inches away from a sandstone cliff, hundreds of feet above. Oh the things we have lost.

Chapter Seventeen

Bears Ears: Beginnings

A THICK BLANKET OF CLOUDS KEPT DAWN'S LIGHT AT bay on a rainy morning when I awoke in my little tent on the edge of a canyon on the Great Sage Plain in mid-October 2015 and hastily broke camp. As I drove the hour or so to Bluff and watched the Bears Ears slowly emerge from the dark horizon before me while dodging potholes that looked deeper than the Silver Bullet was tall, I was overcome with gratitude, for this place, for the beauty, and for the fact that this was my job. It was only seven in the morning when I pulled up in the parking lot of the Twin Rocks Café under clouds of cobalt blue, but Mark Maryboy was already there waiting.

Maryboy—long a community organizer, activist, and leader among the Utah Navajos here in San Juan County—is tall and lean with broad shoulders, a light handshake, and dark, thick hair salted with white. Just days earlier, five tribal nations, including the Navajo Nation, had formally asked President Obama to designate a 1.9-million-acre swath of the canyon-crinkled land nearby as the Bears Ears National Monument under the 1906 Antiquities Act. Maryboy has worked side by side with environmental groups to fight for protections for the area for decades, sometimes succeeding, sometimes not. This was the most ambitious attempt of all and, having garnered the support of

two-dozen tribal governments, as well as the endorsement of the
National Congress of American Indians, it appeared to be the
most likely to succeed. Obama—surely wanting a grand gesture
to cement his environmental legacy—had little reason to bow
down to the predicted, and predictable, opposition from Utah
Republicans and the Sagebrush Rebels of San Juan County.

MARYBOY WAS BORN AT THE ST. CHRISTOPHER'S MISSION, JUST
upstream from Bluff, in 1955. He grew up in a hogan and, after
running away from boarding school, attended local public
schools. His dad, like so many Navajo men of his generation, was
a uranium miner who died of the sicknesses his avocation had
inflicted on his body. Inspired by Robert Kennedy's 1968 campaign visit to the Navajo Nation, Maryboy began advocating for
Cedar Mesa's protection as a teenager, back when the uranium
industry was buzzing and pothunting was an accepted Sunday
hobby and the public lands were still a free-for-all. He attended
the University of Utah then returned home and embarked on a
life of community organizing and politics. After a federal court
ordered the county to redraw its voting districts to allow for
more equitable representation of the Navajo populace, Maryboy
was elected in 1986 to the board of San Juan County commissioners, becoming the first Indigenous commissioner in Utah's
history. He butted heads regularly with his colleague Cal Black,
fought hard for improvements to roads and services on the
Navajo Nation portion of the county, and he also worked with
environmentalist groups to get stronger protections for the cultural and natural resources on the county's public lands. Later
his brother, Kenneth, would fill his seat on the commission, and
Mark would serve on the Navajo Nation Tribal Council.

    In 2010, the "secret" Obama administration list of places
under consideration for national monument designation sur-
faced and then-senator Bob Bennett stepped in to try to make

peace. Kenneth Maryboy was a county commissioner at the time, and he invited his brother, Mark, to participate in the process. He and others informally created Utah Diné Bikéyah, or UDB, to come up with a proposal. When Bennett lost the primary that year the process went dormant. But UDB continued working for protection, getting the endorsement of the Navajo Nation and all seven Utah Navajo chapters, publishing a book about Navajo ties to the land, and formally incorporating as a nonprofit. When Rep. Rob Bishop, R-Utah, picked up where Bennett left off and launched the Public Lands Initiative, or PLI, in 2013, UDB was ready.

The county formed a citizens' lands council to negotiate a proposal for the initiative, chaired by Lyman, the county commissioner, with Mark Maryboy representing UDB. Josh Ewing of Friends of Cedar Mesa went to bat for the rest of the local conservation community. Flying the Sagebrush Rebel banner was the San Juan Alliance, which hoped to transfer all federal land—including national parks—over to the county and the state.

Members of Utah Diné Bikéyah soon grew disillusioned with the process. Their efforts to bring in the perspectives of Hopi and Zuni people, whose ancestors had created and lived in most of the archaeological sites in question, were rebuffed by others in the group and even Utah congressmen because they didn't fit their definition of locals. And even if the lands council did come up with an agreeable proposal—which would be difficult given the fact that it was stacked with members who were hostile to any sort of environmental protection—it would then be sent to a notoriously dysfunctional Congress, where chances were slim that it would even get a reading. Rather than an attempt to achieve a grand bargain, the PLI process began to look like a tactic to ward off monument designation. The feeling grew darker in May 2014 when Lyman—the lands council chairman—led the protest ride down Recapture Canyon. Mark's brother Kenneth was still a county commissioner at the time, but Rebecca Benally, also Navajo, beat Kenneth Maryboy in the Democratic primary in 2014 and became the first woman to serve as San Juan county commissioner in November.

Utah Diné Bikéyah kept tabs on the PLI process while also striking out on its own. The Ute Mountain Utes, based in Colorado but with reservation land in San Juan County, threw their weight behind the project. And in July 2015, the tribal coalition, with representatives from the Ute Mountain Ute and Uintah-Ouray Ute Tribes, the Navajo Nation, Hopi, and Zuni, was officially formed. That in itself was noteworthy, given that historically there had been animosity between the Utes and the Navajos and the Navajos and the Hopis. Utah Diné Bikéyah handed off the effort to the larger group and all agreed that they'd name their effort after the Bears Ears buttes. They'd use the English name so as not to favor one tribal language over another. In October 2015 representatives from the five tribes formally announced their Bears Ears National Monument proposal at the National Press Club in Washington.

The proposal was notable for the amount of land it included (all under federal management), which was almost identical to that covered by the Grand Staircase-Escalante National Monument created by President Bill Clinton in 1996 in southcentral Utah. The proposed management structure was even more groundbreaking: a monument manager would be overseen by a commission made up of one representative from each of the five tribes and one from each of the three applicable federal agencies, the USFS, BLM, and National Park Service. Not only would that give tribes an unprecedented amount of control over a national monument, but it would also give nonfederal bureaucrats, all or some of them local (depending on your definition of the term), more control over the land than they have now. "It's a big healing process for Native Americans," Maryboy told me that autumn morning in Bluff beneath the Twin Rocks—a symbol of the Navajo monster-slaying brothers. "The colonization has been ugly. Protection of this land begins a healing process."

Before the healing could begin, however, new wounds would be opened.

THE ANTI-MONUMENT CAMP WAS QUICKLY POPULATED WITH those of the Sagebrush Rebel creed, as would be expected, along with Utah's Republican governor, congressional delegation, and a hefty chunk of the state legislature. Environmental groups migrated to the pro-monument side, though some went hesitantly, since national monument designation provides far less protection than a huge wilderness area would and also has the potential to cause visitation—and the impacts thereof—to increase. But wilderness designations require an act of Congress, which is getting harder and harder to secure, so a national monument was the most realistic path to some level of preservation.

Another anti-monument coterie emerged from the scuffle. Maybe you'd call them the anti-green green party, or the Sagebrush Rebel preservationists. They weren't monolithic—no camp ever is—and inhabited a spectrum of beliefs. At the risk of generalizing, I'd say a majority of them were middle-aged to older white men who adhered to the tenets of Edward Abbey and were environmentally minded but generally not fond of environmental groups, particularly those that receive funding from billionaires. A national monument designation would do little to preserve the land, they argued, land that is already protected by an alphabet soup of federal laws, from NEPA to NAGPRA to FLPMA and so on. Furthermore, by drawing a line around it and giving it a name you risked turning it into a commodity that more easily could be marketed to the masses. Soon, millions would be trodding all over the place, which would require more infrastructure, which would draw more visitors, which would lead to industrial tourism and "wreckreation." That, they say, will ultimately transform the area that author David Lavender once called "a million and a quarter acres of staggering desolation" into a playground for the privileged and convert Blanding and Monticello into the next Moab, overrun by tourists, housing crunches, crappy-paying service jobs, and Saturday afternoon traffic jams.

Also joining the opposition soon after the coalition had presented their proposal in Washington was a group of Navajo and Ute Mountain Ute locals led by San Juan County commissioner Rebecca Benally—once Maryboy's ally in facing down exploitative oil companies—who had allied themselves with the likes of Lyman and the third county commissioner, Bruce Adams. By the time I met with Maryboy, the Aneth Chapter had officially joined the anti-monument cause, passing a resolution in opposition, a big blow to pro-monument efforts.

Benally soon showed that she could out-Sagebrush-Rebel just about anyone. She and her allies grew increasingly strident in their attacks, not only on the monument, but also on its supporters. They went so far as to allege that tribal proponents were mere pawns, manipulated by "deep-pocketed" out-of-state environmental groups, and to question whether tribes like the Hopi and Zuni—ancestral ties be damned—have a right to participate in the process. "I am not sure where the Bears Ears proposal was created," wrote Bill Boyle, editor of the *San Juan Record*, "but I know it was not in San Juan County."

In response, Inter-Tribal Coalition cochair Regina Lopez-Whiteskunk, a Ute Mountain Ute tribal council member, urged a broader view of the situation. "It wasn't the Native Americans who drew the [state] line," she said. "We want to try something a little different, not for the sake of selfishness, but for the sake of healing all people. We all have to come together and…reach beyond the state boundaries and reservation lines."

Her plea fell mostly on deaf ears, and the local (meaning Utahns and San Juan County residents) vs nonlocal sentiment prevailed at a Utah Commission for the Stewardship of Public

Lands meeting held a few months after the proposal was made. Most of the state legislators were downright hostile toward monument supporters. They cut off Lopez-Whiteskunk in mid-speech. Benally said she supported protection of the land—even wilderness designation for the Bears Ears, themselves—but not a monument, which would be "devastation." "My people do not want a national monument," she said. "They want continued access…for medicinal plant gathering and wood gathering."

Benally and other proponents were pushing instead for the "ground-up" Public Lands Initiative proposal, which would have included protections on 945,389 acres, half of what the proposed monument covered, in the form of a handful of small wilderness areas, most of which are currently wilderness study areas, and two national conservation areas—one on Cedar Mesa and one in Indian Creek, a popular climbing area adjacent to the Needles District of Canyonlands. The Cedar Mesa NCA would be managed collaboratively by federal agencies, the state, the county, and the Navajo and Ute Mountain Ute Tribes.

The compromise was a no-go for most monument supporters, though. The management structure of the conservation areas reduced the tribal role and cut out the Hopi and Zuni Tribes altogether. It also left out of the proposed conservation areas significant places like Butler and Cottonwood Washes and the multitude of archaeological sites, Chacoan "roads," and spectacular rock art panels there. White Canyon and some of its tributaries, designated as a "special tar sands area" by the BLM during the George W. Bush years, would not only get cut out of the conservation areas, but would be included in the proposal's "energy zone," meaning development would be expedited.

The Sutherland Institute, a conservative Salt Lake City think tank with clear religious leanings (its board chairman runs the GFC—God, Family, Country—Foundation), with funding from the likes of the Koch brothers, exploited the resistance among local Navajo people. It produced a couple of slick videos, starring mostly Navajo people, claiming that a monument would rob locals of "lives and livelihoods." One featured a gaggle of cute schoolkids and implied that somehow their dreams for the future would be shattered by the designation, presumably because the extra protections afforded by a monument would kill the uranium mining or fossil fuel industries. The monument as proposed would withdraw the public land from new oil and gas leases and mining claims, yes, but existing claims and leases would remain in place, and there was simply no way that a monument would directly result in any job losses in the aforementioned industries. Still, Sutherland's efforts helped anti-monument crusaders disseminate the false notion that all local Indigenous people were opposed to the monument. In fact, only one of seven Utah Navajo chapters—Aneth—had withdrawn its earlier support; the other six remained firmly behind the monument effort.

IN JULY 2016, NINE MONTHS AFTER MY MORNING MEETING WITH Maryboy, I was once again in Twin Rocks Café, tucking into a plate of "Eggs Manuelito" and sipping coffee. Normally, canyon country in July feels a bit like Babel, overrun by hordes of European tourists enamored of red rock, sage, and big skies, but the depressed euro had thinned the herds significantly.

Bluff, population four hundred, was anything but quiet, however. Cars, including a silver Chevy with #RuralLivesMatter soaped on the window, haphazardly lined the dirt streets around the town's little community center. Alongside a dusty, weed-choked ballpark was a row of shiny black SUVs with government plates. On the other side, hand-drawn signs jutted from a chain-link fence like corn from a dryland field: "National Monument, Dooda, Dooda," read a yellow one, repeating the Navajo word for "no." "PROTECT," proclaimed another, above a drawing of a bear's head.

Over the next few hours, more than one thousand folks trickled into the center's grounds to give Interior Secretary Sally Jewell a piece of their minds regarding the Bears Ears proposal. As participants arrived, they were offered color-coded T-shirts: baby blue for monument supporters, brown for opponents. It was a visual cue of the polarization that had formed around the debate, but also demonstrated how wrong the old "Indigenous folks and environmentalists vs white Mormon land-use militants" can be. Some Ute and Navajo locals wore brown shirts, and many of them were also devout members of the Church of Jesus Christ of Latter-day Saints.

In the hours before the hearing started, folks congregated in whatever shade they could find and conversed, sometimes spiritedly. I mingled as inconspicuously as I could, practicing my own brand of introvert's journalism, also known as quietly observing and feverishly writing it all down in my little notebook. A brown-shirted young Navajo woman with a baby on her hip confronted a group of baffled teenaged blue-shirts and outlined the reasons traditional, on-reservation Navajos weren't fit to manage any more land. One Navajo man said that a monument was the best way to keep the oil companies from ravaging the mesas and canyons that the tribe holds sacred; another warned that a monument would lock Navajos out of those same areas.

"This is my home," Brooke Lyman, Phil's daughter, told Jewell. "We aren't vacationing here. San Juan County is America to me. For you to come in and make a monument and take our freedoms, it's like taking America from me." And when Navajo Nation president Russell Begaye, wearing a suit in spite of the heat, told Jewell that his people relate to the Bears Ears like an Anglo does to a family member, monument opponents, led by Benally, responded with boos and chanted, "Go home!" It was sickening to hear, since if anyone could call the canyons and plateaus of southeastern Utah home it was Begaye, whose ancestors had sought refuge near the Bears Ears from Euro-American

invasions of the past. And if the Hole-in-the-Rock ordeal entitled the descendants of the people who suffered through it some
say over this place, then the Long Walk should give all citizens of
the Navajo Nation the loudest voice of all.

But the intensity of the rhetoric wasn't surprising. Similar
vitriol had infused the debate for months. Flyers announcing
"open season" on Colorado backpackers were posted in public
places. Facebook posts about the monument became infested
with extremist rhetoric about the "BLM and FBI SS troops," calling Obama a "despot" and comparing the use of the Antiquities
Act to Hitler's atrocities.

Notah Tahy, wearing a wide-brimmed straw cowboy hat
and a formidable turquoise bolo tie, told me a monument would
make life harder for the already beleaguered Navajos living on
the reservation. "A lot of our medicine men get their herbs from
there. And others pick piñon nuts," he said. "Some pick enough
to make a little bit of a living." Turn it into a monument and next
thing you know, he said, they're charging everyone thirty bucks
to get in, "like the Grand Canyon."

Tahy's concerns were valid—show me a national monument
designation from the early twentieth century and I'll show you
theft of Indigenous land—but also a bit overblown. I dropped
my introversion for a moment and pressed him a little, pointing out that it would be nearly impossible to restrict entry into
the monument, let alone charge an astronomical entry fee, and
tribal comanagers would never allow a ban on foraging or ceremonial uses in the monument.

None of that swayed Tahy, though. He was firm in his beliefs,
probably in part because those beliefs are rooted in ideology as
much as in practical concerns. The Sagebrush Rebels and their
predecessors of yore were driven by self-interest and economics.
When J. A. Scorup pushed up against the proposed Escalante
National Monument, he was less concerned about federal overreach or local control than he was about his cattle having room

to roam and graze freely. And even Cal Black yearned for San Juan County to become home to a nuclear waste dump not so that he could "own" the rock-licking backpackers, but because it would bring a lot of jobs, cash, and customers to his hometown and his businesses.

But the practical reasons for fearing a Bears Ears monument designation mostly crumple upon scrutiny. In 1996, President Bill Clinton designated the sprawling Grand Staircase-Escalante National Monument in the counties east of San Juan County. It didn't kill any extractive industry jobs,[47] access is still relatively unrestricted and free of charge, and grazing has continued at the same levels[48] as before designation, as provided for in the proclamation establishing the monument. The monument has also helped make way for a budding tourist industry, which has brought more people and some fabulous cuisine to the communities next to the monument. Still, neither Escalante nor Boulder nor Kanab resemble Moab. Four years later, Clinton created the Canyons of the Ancients National Monument just west of the San Juan County line. Again, grazing, carbon dioxide extraction, and oil and gas development have not been significantly hampered. For better or worse, a national monument designation is not the draconian land grab Sagebrush Rebels make it out to be—and for the most part they know that. A national monument designation is little more than a name change. Whether it goes any further than that depends on the proclamation establishing it and on the management plan that follows. Nevertheless the local-control advocates continued to fight against Bears Ears, and in favor of getting the monument designation killed after it was in place, because it offended some deeply held ideology, the tenets of which aren't entirely clear.

After I spoke with Tahy, his wife, Maryleen Tahy, wearing mirrored aviator sunglasses, a velveteen blouse, and a stunning turquoise necklace, told me that nearly one-third of the local Navajos are Mormons, including her and her husband, and that most of the Mormon Navajos are opposed to the monument. Many of them are married to descendants of the Hole-in-the-Rock pioneers, and the local-control creed is embedded in their psyches. It jives with something Mark Maryboy had told me, that the Navajo monument opponents were mostly "holy rollers." There's nothing in the Book of Mormon saying that Saints should oppose national monuments, and Joseph Smith and Brigham Young both advocated for stewardship of the land, but it makes sense that devout churchgoers would align with their fellow congregants, most of whom are anti-monument, rather than with the tribal government.

Intra-chapter fights also can't be discounted. When I spoke to Maryboy in 2015, he regaled me with documents and anecdotes about the politics of the Aneth Chapter in order to elucidate how those politics spilled into the monument debate. Maryboy and his brother Kenneth are two of the most visible members of the chapter, and they have had their share of run-ins with fellow members over the years. In one instance, detractors of Maryboy were so hostile that two of them were escorted out of the chapter meeting by the police. Much of the tension in the chapter relates to royalties from oil development. About two-thirds of the revenue from the Aneth field goes to the Navajo Nation, with the rest divvied up between the Utah Navajo chapters; Anethians would rather the money stayed within their chapter, whence most of it originates. Meanwhile, neither chapter nor tribe gets royalties from oil or gas produced from McCracken Mesa, which the Navajo Nation obtained from the federal government in a 1958 land swap—another source of unease. It's likely that the bad blood, while unrelated to the efforts to get protection for the public lands on the western side of the county, spilled over into the Bears Ears debate.

Tellingly, two related provisions were slipped into the Public Lands Initiative bill sponsored by the Utah congressmen: one would have shifted the royalty split to favor the Aneth Chapter, and another would have transferred the McCracken Mesa mineral rights from the federal government to the Utah Navajos. Neither provision was likely to make it through Congress since neither would have passed muster with the Navajo Nation government, but they provided another reason for Anethians to support the PLI—and oppose the national monument.

"WE PREFER TO HAVE THINGS DONE WITH US, NOT TO US," ONE commenter said at Bluff. It sounded like a neat summation of the belief that any sort of federally imposed environmental protection represents an usurping of local self-determination and that the potential national monument designation would be yet another top-down decision thrust upon the unwilling residents of San Juan County—a reprise of the Clinton designation of Grand Staircase-Escalante National Monument, done with virtually no public input.

That wasn't, in fact, the case and raises an important question: To whom does *we* and *us* refer? After all, members of Utah Diné Bikéyah, a local, grassroots group, first planted the national monument seeds, and five tribes with deep roots in the Bears Ears region nurtured them and took the proposal to Washington. Then the bureaucrats from Washington came to Utah to get input from locals—white and Indigenous alike.

Secretary of the Interior Sally Jewell spent days in Utah, listening to local leaders, even ones who called her a despot, and exploring the proposed monument. She sat through hours of public comments at the Bluff meeting, listening intently. And Obama administration officials met with representatives of Energy Fuels, the uranium company that owns the Daneros Mine as well as the White Mesa Mill just outside of Blanding, to hear their concerns and suggestions for boundary adjustments. For months Jewell and other Obama administration officials were in constant contact with stakeholders, doing their best to come up with a compromise that would not be a "unilateral" or "top-down" decision imposed upon locals.

Yet among all these skirmishes, name-calling, and negotiations, some of the core ideas and entities behind the proposal were lost or intentionally obscured. The true locals were the tribes at the leading edge of the monument push. And the proposed monument designation would give those locals a little more say over land that by all rights belonged to them and that really should be given back to its original inhabitants, an admittedly complex and messy proposition, given the number of contemporary tribal nations that have roots there. Perhaps a monument designation, with those same tribes getting a voice in how it is managed, is the next best thing: an act of justice as much as preservation. It could give the people a space in which to tell their own stories of that landscape in their own ways. "The world is full of multiple knowledges, and Bears Ears is another opportunity to celebrate that," Jim Enote, the Zuni scholar, farmer, and organizer, told me. "We should have a national monument, not just because it's the ethical thing, but because it makes sense."

CHAPTER EIGHTEEN

A NEW MONUMENT, A NEW BATTLE

R *ISING FROM THE CENTER OF THE SOUTHEASTERN UTAH landscape and visible from every direction are twin buttes so distinctive that in each of the native languages of the region their name is the same: Hoon'Naqvut, Shash Jáa, Kwiyagatu Nukavachi, Ansh An Lashokdiwe, or "Bears Ears." For hundreds of generations, native peoples lived in the surrounding deep sandstone canyons, desert mesas, and meadow mountaintops, which constitute one of the densest and most significant cultural landscapes in the United States.*

So begins the proclamation, issued by President Barack Obama on December 28, 2016, establishing the 1.35-million-acre Bears Ears National Monument. From there the document only gets more poetic, eloquently describing the landscape and its history and laying out all of the reasons this wondrous place deserves protection. It didn't quite live up to the Inter-Tribal Coalition's proposal. The US Forest Service and the Bureau of Land Management would jointly manage the new monument, with "guidance and recommendations" from a commission made up of elected officers from the Hopi Nation, Zuni Tribe, Navajo Nation, Ute Mountain Ute Tribe and the Ute Indian Tribe of the Uintah Ouray. This arrangement put the tribes into an advisory role, rather than the comanagement position for which they'd hoped. Meanwhile, more than a half-million acres in the proposal were left out of the final boundaries.

The tribal coalition hailed the designation and its emphasis on Indigenous culture and knowledge, nonetheless. The proclamation states, "The traditional ecological knowledge amassed by the Native Americans whose ancestors inhabited this region…is, itself, a resource to be protected and used in understanding and managing this landscape sustainably for generations to come." University of Colorado Boulder law professor Charles Wilkinson, who worked behind the scenes with the tribal coalition on the proposal, told me that the strong Indigenous component promised to make the new monument "one of the most distinctive and uplifting landscapes in America's public land systems."

Bruce Babbitt, a former governor of Arizona and the interior secretary under President Bill Clinton when both the Grand Staircase-Escalante and Canyons of the Ancients National Monuments were established, echoed Wilkinson. "Canyons of the Ancients was perhaps the first to explicitly recognize that ruins do not tell the entire story—that ancients lived in, hunted, gathered and raised crops, and developed water and religious sites throughout the larger landscape," said Babbitt. "Bears Ears brings this concept to fruition in an even larger landscape."

The proclamation itself withdrew all federal lands within the boundaries from future mineral leasing, mining claims, and other forms of "disposal." Other than that, however, a national monument designation has little immediate on-the-ground effect, and the Bears Ears designation in particular was chock-full of concessions to those who were concerned about how it might hamper their ability to utilize the land therein. Traditional Indigenous access to firewood, herbs, and piñon nuts would continue. Existing mining claims, mineral leases, and grazing leases would remain in place, and the BLM and Forest Service were to continue to manage grazing under the pre-monument regimen, meaning modern-day J. A. Scorups such as Zeb Dalton and Zane Odell had no reason to be concerned about their ability to continue the tradition of running cattle on public lands. The proclamation opened the door to the purchase or exchange of state lands within the boundaries so that the state parcels would not be "landlocked." A similar provision in the Grand Staircase-Escalante National Monument designation had netted the state hundreds of millions of dollars more in revenue than the parcels otherwise would have generated.

The amount of land included was closer to the Public Lands Initiative proposal than the Inter-Tribal Coalition proposal. Among the lands left out were the lower portion of Recapture Canyon and Harts Draw, both of which have oil and gas development potential. Raplee Anticline and Lime Ridge, sites of early oil drilling and limestone quarries, were left out, as was a huge swath of uranium-rich lands west of Grand Gulch, despite the ecological and paleontological bounties found there. The Daneros uranium mine, which is under an active permit on standby mode, and is a candidate for expansion onto surrounding BLM lands, was cut out of the monument as well, indicating that the lobbying by Energy Fuels, the mine's owner, was successful.

Yet any hope that all of these sacrifices would appease the Sagebrush Rebels and thereby mitigate the backlash that Winston Hurst had feared was quickly dashed. The Utah legislature's public lands committee denounced the designation as "unilateral tyranny," and Utah Republican senator Orrin Hatch called it an "attack on an entire way of life." That's despite the fact that the only existing economic activity likely to be hindered by the monument is the pilfering and black-market sale of antiquities. "Some of the Utah delegation don't care about the actual proclamation," said John Freemuth, executive director of the Cecil D. Andrus Center for Public Policy at Boise State University. "They only care about confrontational politics and clichéd symbolism."

In fact, the biggest backlash of all had already manifested itself a couple of months before Obama's designation, namely the election to the presidency of Donald J. Trump, a reality television show star and failed real-estate developer. During the early phases of the 2016 presidential race, Utah and members of the Mormon Church in general were no fans of the demagogue from New York. He regularly violated their religious code of ethics, had no connection to nor knowledge of the rural West or public lands, his bigoted anti-immigrant stance stood in opposition to that held by most Mormons, and his overall lack of human decency offended them. In Utah's Republican caucus, Trump received just 14 percent of the vote compared to Sen. Ted Cruz's 69 percent, and after Trump's nomination a conservative Mormon and never-Trumper, Evan McMullin, jumped into the race as an independent. Pollyannaish Democrats let themselves believe that McMullin would siphon enough Republican votes away from Trump to give Utah to Hillary Clinton. Even Trump expressed concern about his chances in the state. It appears that Obama delayed the national monument designation until after the election in order to up Clinton's chances.

If that was the reason for the delay, it was a massive mistake. When Election Day rolled around, Utah voters cast aside any distaste they may have had for Trump and overwhelmingly voted for the Republican candidate—or, more likely, they voted *against* Clinton—regardless of McMullin's presence on the ticket. Sagebrush-Rebel-dominated counties tended to lean especially far in the red direction, and Phil Lyman, the San Juan County commissioner who had become increasingly radicalized, was a full-throated supporter of Trump before many of his Mormon brethren. Trump carried San Juan County, too, but with a smaller margin due to the large Indigenous population there. And all of that happened prior to the national monument designation.

By waiting until just a month before his tenure ended to

designate the monument, Obama put the creation of a management plan into the hands of a Trump administration. A monument designation is merely the overarching framework. The management plan is where the actual details are hammered out, such as where grazing is and isn't allowed, what kinds of recreation can take place and where, what kind of infrastructure might be built, and what areas are closed to all uses. The delay also made the monument more vulnerable to potential attacks from the new president, whose primary policy aim was to wreck or unravel every one of Obama's accomplishments in office. Within hours of Obama's designation, Utah lawmakers had pledged to urge the president-elect to overturn the designation, and Hatch toyed with the idea of ditching the Antiquities Act altogether.

Initially members of the pro-monument camp didn't express much worry about what Trump might or might not do with the monument. Even if he did bother himself with butting into a fight unfolding in a remote corner of Utah—which seemed unlikely— the law and courts would stand in his way. "Existing law tells us that Trump has little or no ability to alter this monument," said Wilkinson, a couple of weeks before Trump's inauguration. Even if challenged, "there is an overwhelming likelihood that courts will hew to existing law that the Antiquities Act allows presidents to create monuments but not to overturn them."

Meanwhile, environmentalists, archaeologists, and tribal nations hailed what they had accomplished. The public land wars surely would continue to rage, but the Bears Ears phase of it seemed to have come to an end. "Mormon history, the Constitution and laws, and white man's history are written on paper," said Octavius Seowtewa of Zuni. "Our history—the Native history— is written in stone on canyon walls. We celebrate, knowing our history at Bears Ears will be protected for future generations, forever."

The battle wasn't over, however. It was only just beginning.

CHAPTER NINETEEN

THE DISASTER KNOWN AS TRUMP

L IKE MOST OTHER AMERICANS WHO VALUE INTELLI-
gence, empathy, and decency in their public officials, I was
devastated when Trump was elected president. His blatant
bigotry and misogyny, his bombastic bile, his unearned wealth,
his anti-intellectualism, and his utter lack of humanity made me
sick. I worried about the people who were coming to America to
escape brutality or violence or crippling poverty. I worried about
the Americans who would be trampled by Trump's stampede to
enrich himself and his corporate friends.

Yet in the beginning I was not especially concerned about
him running roughshod over public lands. Why would he? Ronald Reagan had at least played a cowboy and rancher on TV, so
it didn't seem utterly insane for him to count himself as a Sagebrush Rebel. Trump, on the other hand, lived in a Manhattan
high-rise with a gold-plated toilet and had probably never once
stepped foot on land managed by the BLM. How could he even
pretend to sympathize with the plight of a public lands rancher?
And why would he even try? It's not like Trump had to win over
Utah's voters in order to get reelected. They had just demonstrated their unfaltering fealty to the Republican candidate, no
matter who it is or how sharply his values contrasted from theirs.

As for Bears Ears, I just couldn't imagine Trump concerning himself with something that, in the end, was relatively inconsequential.

I was deeply mistaken.

SHORTLY AFTER TRUMP'S 2017 INAUGURATION, HIS CHIEF ADVISOR Steve Bannon told a gathering of conservatives that the administration's goal was the "deconstruction of the administrative state." Anyone who thought that Bannon was espousing run-of-the-mill libertarian philosophy to shrink bloated government in order to make way for personal liberties was sorely mistaken. It would shortly become clear that Trump had no interest in anyone's personal liberties but his own, and that his "deconstruction" consisted of taking a wrecking ball to an array of norms and rules, thereby freeing both government and corporations—and, eventually, COVID-19—to run rampant over life, liberty, and land, all in the name of profit and power.

Nowhere was this scorched-earth approach more complete than when it came to the Earth, i.e. the environment and public lands. During his single term, Trump eviscerated rules limiting carbon and mercury emissions from power plants and methane emissions from oil and gas facilities. He weakened the Clean Water Act, Endangered Species Act, and the National Environmental Policy Act. He reopened loopholes allowing oil, gas, and coal companies to skirt paying royalties for extracting minerals from public lands, offered up millions of acres of public lands to oil and gas companies, and opened the Arctic National Wildlife Refuge to drilling. He rammed through the approval of the Dakota Access Pipeline,[49] despite the fact that it endangers water that the Standing Rock Sioux Tribe relies upon. He allowed companies to kill migratory birds with impunity. And his administration approved several BLM resource management plans that open the door to increased oil and gas drilling on public lands across the West. All in all, the administration rolled back or weakened more than eighty rules or regulations protecting the land, water, air, or human health.

Ryan Zinke, Trump's first interior secretary, surprisingly was not plucked straight from the ranks of the extractive industries, but he did receive hundreds of thousands of dollars in campaign contributions from oil, gas, and coal companies and served on the board of something called Save the World Air, which develops equipment for oil pipelines. He came to Washington from Montana, where he had served as a state legislator and then as a US congressman. An outdoorsman who liked to compare himself to Teddy Roosevelt, Zinke provided an early glimmer of hope to conservationists otherwise anxious of what Trump might do regarding public lands. That hope was soon dashed, however, as Zinke prostrated himself to industry and came to resemble Roosevelt far less than Albert B. Fall, the interior secretary under President Warren G. Harding.

Like Fall, Zinke wanted to open up public lands to drilling and mining, and, like Fall, Zinke opened himself up to favors and gifts from the industry. Zinke led the first phase of the Trump administration's systematic eviscerations of environmental protections, including its rollbacks of department actions that allegedly "burden domestic energy." Zinke struck all mentions of climate from his department's four-year strategic plan, and he set about to abolish, delay, or weaken various rules and land-use guidance policies. He axed the methane waste prevention rule, formulated under Obama, which attempts to rein in the loss of natural gas in the oil and gas fields and reduce emissions of methane—a potent greenhouse gas. He got rid of master leasing plans, which increased public input and brought a more holistic approach to "sight unseen" oil and gas leasing. And he set about to do away with provisions that mitigated the damage from development on public lands.

Zinke's most high-profile action was his 2017 review of every national monument established since 1996, the year that Clinton designated Grand Staircase-Escalante, starting with Bears Ears. The review was done at the behest of avowed Sagebrush Rebel Sen. Orrin Hatch. As the longest-serving Republican senator in history, and the chair of the Senate Finance Committee, the senator from Utah was critical for Trump to carry out his agenda. Hatch spearheaded the 2017 tax cut for the wealthy and attacks on the Affordable Care Act. Trump returned the favor by going after national monuments.

While Reagan's election had dimmed the Sagebrush Rebellion's zeal, at least in the short-term, Trump's ascendancy only emboldened the rebels and their kind. They celebrated the new era by ratcheting up their rhetoric attacking environmentalists and liberals and by urging administration officials to shrink the national monuments as much as possible. In San Juan County, the rebels acted with newfound audacity in relation to Gategate, or the case of Rose Chilcoat and Mark Franklin, barely bothering to hide the fact that their prosecution was, at least in part, politically motivated. Not only did Lyman, the county commissioner, produce and post a video in which he laid out what he called evidence of the alleged crime and in which he accused Chilcoat of perpetuating those crimes, but it later came to light that the county commission—Lyman included—held a closed meeting with the sheriff regarding the incident. All of this transpired just days prior to the launch of Trump's monument review.

That summer, the results of Zinke's review were made public: the Trump administration would shrink Bears Ears National Monument by 85 percent—from 1.6 million acres down to just over 200,000 acres—leaving some of the most culturally and ecologically rich areas unprotected. It would be divided into two units, Indian Creek and Shásh Jaa', Navajo for Bears Ears. Even the name was an insult to the Inter-Tribal Coalition, which had settled on "Bears Ears" because it didn't favor one tribe over another. Grand Staircase-Escalante National Monument would be chopped roughly in half, reopening huge coal deposits on the Kaiparowits Plateau, along with a paleontological treasure trove, to the prospect of mining.

Trump traveled to the Utah State Capitol building in Salt Lake City to commemorate the cuts. Lyman was there, wearing a MAGA hat, as was his fellow commissioner Bruce Adams, who had notoriously claimed that his white, Mormon ancestors were the first people to settle in San Juan County. At the capitol Adams wore a cowboy hat with "Make San Juan County Great Again" scribbled on it in Sharpie. Sagebrush Rebel Mike Noel, then the Utah state representative for southeastern Utah who once blamed pothunting on badgers, glad-handed his compatriots, his face flushed with the excitement of victory. Sen. Mike Lee, the extreme right-wing Utah Republican who would one day claim that "rank democracy can thwart" human flourishing, was also in attendance. All of them looked gleeful while outside thousands gathered in protest and mourning.

"Some people think that the natural resources of Utah should be controlled by a small handful of very distant bureaucrats located in Washington," Trump said, parroting the Sagebrush Rebels' main talking points. "And guess what? They're wrong." He implied that cutting the monuments would somehow usher in a new era of "wonder and wealth." He did not explain how that was supposed to occur.

ZINKE DIDN'T STICK AROUND LONG. LESS THAN TWO YEARS after his appointment he skedaddled out of Washington under a cloud of scandal regarding taxpayer-funded vacations and mingling a little too closely with executives from companies his department was supposed to be regulating.

He was soon replaced by David Bernhardt, who had served as a lobbyist for Halliburton and mining companies and who continued to run the department as if it were a subsidiary of

Exxon rather than a governmental agency assigned to protect millions of acres of the American taxpayer's land.

Both Zinke and Bernhardt stocked Interior with industry sympathizers and insiders, all of whom have insidiously infected the public land agencies with the "rape, ruin, and run" ideology that Cecil Andrus had promised to eliminate so many years ago. That included wise-use attorney Karen Budd-Falen as deputy interior solicitor for wildlife and parks, an obscure but powerful position. In addition to crafting the Catron County anti-federal land management ordinances of the 1990s, Budd-Falen has wielded trusty ol' RS-2477 to defend the bulldozing of a road through a wilderness study area in Colorado's San Juan Mountains. In 2007, Budd-Falen told *High Country News'* Ray Ring that her most important case was *Wilkie v. Robbins*, in which she used RICO, an anti-racketeering law, to intimidate BLM agents who had cited her client for violating grazing regulations.

The list of Interior appointees and hires with questionable backgrounds goes on, from Acting Solicitor Daniel Jordani, who had worked for the Koch brothers, to Special Assistant to the Secretary Kathy Benedetto, who founded the Women's Mining Coalition, to William Perry Pendley, who served unlawfully as Trump's acting director of the Bureau of Land Management for over a year.

BACK IN 1938 PRESIDENT FRANKLIN ROOSEVELT PONDERED abolishing the Castle Pinckney National Monument, created by Woodrow Wilson to commemorate a deteriorating structure that had been used for little else aside from imprisoning Union soldiers during the Civil War. Roosevelt's attorney general said it couldn't be done. "The grant of power to execute a trust," he wrote, "by no means implies the further power to undo it when it has been completed." Trump, true to form, didn't bother asking the same question prior to shrinking Bears Ears nearly to the point of abolishing it. Not that he'd let the unlawfulness of the action stand in his way if he had.

Legal experts agree that the Antiquities Act gives a president the power to create a national monument but does not give them the power to diminish or demolish it. And in the 1970s, as it put together the Federal Land Policy and Management Act, Congress confirmed the fact that the executive branch cannot reverse Antiquities Act actions. On that basis, the five tribal nations in the Bears Ears coalition sued the Trump administration to overturn the shrinkage.

The administration has argued that it slashed the monument because local leaders wanted it gone, and because the Obama boundaries encompassed land that didn't warrant protection. But closer scrutiny of the Trump boundaries reveal that darker forces were at play. The new boundaries at Bears Ears confounded most observers. Left out were places that even the local county commissioners had suggested remain in the monument. Meanwhile, other areas, like Arch Canyon, which is a favorite for local jeepers and ATVers, remained inside the new boundaries, thus making it more likely to be closed to motorized vehicles at some time in the future.

Hatch had argued that the monument took needed cash from Utah schoolchildren because it "captured" over one hundred thousand acres of Utah School and Institutional Trust Lands (SITLA), which are leased out or sold to help fund schools. But SITLA itself never outright opposed the monument designation, because with designation came the promise of a lucrative land exchange with the feds. Nearly two decades earlier, after the designation of Grand Staircase-Escalante National Monument, a similar swap proved quite profitable, according to an email included in a trove of review-related documents made public in response to a Freedom of Information Act request from the *New York Times*. SITLA associate director John Andrews wrote that the exchange netted SITLA $135.2 million in mineral leases alone, plus $50 million in cash from the feds as part of the deal. Adding in investment earnings and other lease revenues, Andrews concluded that a total haul of $500 million from the exchange would be a "conservative guesstimate."

After designation, SITLA officials asked Obama "to promptly address the issue by making Utah's school children whole through an exchange of comparable lands." The state hoped to give up the land within the proposed monument, most of which had only marginal potential for development, and receive oil- and gas-rich federal land, much of it in other counties, in exchange. When Trump shrunk the monument so drastically, he effectively killed the potential for a bonanza and left SITLA holding on to more than eighty thousand acres of isolated parcels that are unlikely to generate much revenue.

It became clear that Zinke had drawn the boundaries not to appease locals upset about monument designation, nor even to get the schoolkids a better deal, but to open up uranium, oil and gas, and potash to potential exploration, both at the request of industry and by his own accord.

The owner of the White Mesa Mill and Daneros Mine, Energy Fuels, sent lobbyists, including former US representative Mary Bono, R-Calif., to meet with Trump administration officials in July 2017 to get them to shrink or eliminate the monument. The company's official comment on the monument review stated: "There are also many other known uranium and vanadium deposits located within the newly created [Bears Ears National Monument] that could provide valuable energy and mineral resources in the future....EFR respectfully requests that DOI reduce the size of the [Bears Ears National Monument] to only those specific resource areas or sites, if any, deemed to need additional protection beyond what is already available to Federal land management agencies." Trump's shrinkage removed the entire White Canyon uranium district and other known deposits from the monument.

More than any of that, however, Trump and his lackeys were intent upon thumbing their noses at not only Obama, but also the monument proponents, including the environmental groups and tribal nations that had worked so hard to get it established. And they weren't finished yet.

THE DIRECTOR OF THE BUREAU OF LAND MANAGEMENT typically has been a behind-the-scenes career bureaucrat, someone who leaves the limelight—and the political posturing—to others. Yet instead of formally nominating someone from the ranks to take the agency's helm, in July 2019 Bernhardt named as acting director William Perry Pendley, a spotlight-hogging firebrand who has spent most of his career waging ideological and legal war against the very same agency that he was now being asked to lead.

After leaving the Reagan administration in the early 1980s, Pendley signed on with Watt's Mountain States Legal Foundation. Pendley served as president of MSLF for thirty years, during which the organization fought against environmentalists, Indigenous peoples, and any federal land management agency that stood in their way, particularly the BLM. They tried to overturn a ban on uranium mining near the Grand Canyon, attempted to block tribal nations from protecting sacred sites and from administering the Clean Air Act on tribal land, and fought to overthrow protections for endangered species, including the Canada lynx in Colorado's San Juan Mountains. The MSLF sued to block the respective designations of Grand Staircase-Escalante and Bears Ears National Monuments, and continues to defend Trump's shrinkage of the same. Pendley and the organization have represented San Juan County or fought side by side with them in a number of legal battles.

While Pendley and his ilk portray themselves as warriors fighting to get the oppressive federal government off the back of the small-time rancher or the working-class miner, they more often are working in the service of corporate extractive interests. The MSLF has represented or fought alongside dozens of big companies, as well as receiving hundreds of thousands of dollars in donations from the likes of Joseph Coors, Exxon, the Charles Koch Foundation, Yates Petroleum, Phelps Dodge, and other mining or oil and gas companies. In other words, the very same parties that Pendley was now tasked with keeping tabs on have been paying him to try to tear down the very agency he was chosen to lead. "I've said it before and I'll say it again," Pendley—Twitter handle @Sagebrush_Rebel—tweeted just weeks prior to taking the BLM helm, "fracking is an energy, economic, AND environmental miracle!"

Shortly after taking over at the helm of the BLM, Pendley said that wild horses were the biggest threat to public lands. It was clearly a message of allegiance sent to public lands ranchers, who don't want to share "their" forage with the feral beasts, but also to the oil and gas industry. By demonizing horses Pendley was downplaying the damaging effects of drilling and, more notably still, of climate change.

He oversaw major initiatives at the agency, including the move of its headquarters from Washington, DC, to Grand Junction, Colorado. Ostensibly the move was to get the DC bureaucrats closer to the land they managed, thereby alleviating accusations that rural westerners were being colonized by East Coast elites. Initially the plan called for moving about three hundred staffers to the mid-sized city, which could have gone a long way toward Grand Junction's economic and cultural transition from an oil and gas town and former uranium milling town to a recreational and retirement haven. It soon became clear, however, that the move was just another way to dismantle the administrative state and weaken the agency. In the end just a couple dozen employees moved to the new headquarters, which shares an office building with Chevron, the Colorado Oil and

Gas Association, and Laramie Energy. Others were scattered across the West, while still more left the agency altogether. It was an expedient way to clean house of senior staffers—particularly people of color who chose not to move to small, predominantly white western Colorado—and their expertise.

Pendley was in charge when the new management plan of the shrunken Bears Ears National Monument was completed. That a plan was pushed through even as the shrinkage was still making its way through the legal system was insulting to the Inter-Tribal Coalition. The plan itself, meanwhile, offered very little in the way of added protection for the smidgeon of land remaining within the national monument. Grazing and off-road motorized travel would continue as before and visitation would not be restricted or limited to additional sites, regardless of how fragile they might be. Even more distasteful to monument pro-ponents was the Monument Advisory Committee, which was stocked mostly with people who had been opposed to a mon-ument in the first place rather than with representatives of the tribal nations with roots in the area. Members included: Zeb Dalton, one of the livestock operators involved in the Gategate incident and a vociferous opponent of monument designation; Bruce Adams, the county commissioner who has been hostile toward federal land management agencies; Gail Johnson, a pub-lic lands rancher; and Jami Bayles, another vocal opponent of monument designation. There were no representatives from the tribal coalition that pushed for the monument in the first place. Instead, tribal representatives included Alfred Ben, vice presi-dent of the Aneth Chapter, and Ryan Benally, the son of Rebecca Benally, who was voted out of office in 2018. Both Ben and Benally were ardent opponents of the monument designation.

The administration likely rushed the management plan in order to solidify the shrinkage and possibly make it less vulnera-ble to legal challenges or reversal by a future administration. Yet it turns out that the management plan is on shaky legal ground, itself, because it was finalized under Pendley's leadership. In September 2020 Chief District Judge Brian Morris ruled that by putting Pendley in charge of the BLM without Senate confirmation, the Trump administration had violated the Federal Vacancies Reform Act of 1998, meaning Pendley was serving unlawfully as acting director. Morris went on to order "that any 'function or duty' of the BLM Director that had been performed by Pendley would have no force and effect and must be set aside as arbitrary and capricious." That included decisions that Pendley delegated to others, such as responding to protests on the Bears Ears management plan.

Meanwhile, in the weeks leading up to the 2020 election, Pendley continued to insist that he was still in charge of the BLM, judge's ruling be damned. The court order, he told the press, "had no impact." His refusal to face reality would turn out to be a precursor of what was to come, when Pendley's boss refused to concede the election even after it was clear he had lost by millions of votes.

Chapter Twenty

Sagebrush Site

A S THE FIRST LIGHT OF SUN SATURATES THE GREAT Sage Plain in southeastern Utah, I run along a swath cut through the brush, the Bears Ears clearly visible on the horizon to the left of me. Under here a pipeline carries carbon dioxide from the McElmo Dome to the east of here, where it's extracted, to the Aneth oil field, where the CO_2 is pumped back into the earth in order to stimulate hydrocarbon production—a bizarre, climate-altering ritual akin to chasing our own tail and bloodily biting it off. An owl alights from tree to tree ahead of me, and the air—still relatively humid from last night's early August rain—is redolent with the smell of sagebrush. An overgrown old two-track veers off from the right of way, and I veer, too, following it south across a high mesa, stretching out my legs on the slight downhill.

I stagger to a stop when I spot a cluster of rectangular sandstone blocks, rubble that once stood as a wall, on the red earth. Potsherds—a rim of a bowl, a handle of a mug, polished by calloused hands or smooth stones some eight hundred years ago—are scattered abundantly. It is one of thousands of archaeological sites spread out across southwestern Colorado and southeastern Utah, sometimes called the northern San Juan or the Mesa Verde region, which includes Bears Ears, Hovenweep, and Canyons of the Ancients National Monuments.

Yet this particular site—we'll call it the Sagebrush Site—is like hundreds of others in the region, in that it is not part of a national monument, or park, or other special protected area. Instead, it's on a Bureau of Land Management parcel that has been grazed, crisscrossed with de facto roads and pipelines, and even drilled for oil and gas. It lies a few dozen miles east of the outer edge of Bears Ears National Monument, yet it illustrates how Trump's shrinkage of the monument, while purportedly still protecting the "significant" cultural resources, is outdated, myopic, and leaves important sites unprotected. The Sagebrush Site shows what really is at stake with a national monument designation.

In 1923, President Warren G. Harding wielded the Antiquities Act to establish Hovenweep National Monument in reaction to wholesale looting of the pueblos perched on the edges of canyons in the southeastern corner of Utah. "Few of the mounds have escaped the hands of the destroyer," noted T. Mitchell Pruden in 1903. "Cattlemen, ranchmen, rural picnickers, and professional collectors have turned the ground well over and have taken out much pottery, breaking more, and strewing the ground with many crumbling bones."

At the time, only the well-preserved, large structures were deemed worthy of protection, so even today Hovenweep is a mere 785 acres, divided up into six discrete units that include the spectacular towers and not much else. Similarly, in 1907 President Theodore Roosevelt designated the Chaco Canyon National Monument, thus protecting several great houses, including Pueblo Bonito, that were built between the ninth and twelfth centuries and were being ravaged by unscrupulous archaeologists.

Roosevelt and his advisors didn't know it, but his monument only included a small piece of a vast Chacoan world that extended all the way into Colorado and what is now known as the Bears Ears region of southeastern Utah. It was made up of dozens of Chacoan outliers, along with thousands of smaller sites, shrines, "roads," and other architectural features with unknown function. Today that world endures, a cultural tapestry woven together with the natural landscape.

The Sagebrush Site, along with dozens of other such sites in the area, has connections to the towers of Hovenweep, yet was left out of the national monument, just like most of the Chacoan landscape lies outside of the Chaco Culture National Historical Park. Because these features are not in the national monument or inside a wilderness area but are on federal land, they are open to oil and gas leasing, to mining claims, and to other development.

IN LATE SUMMER 2019, THE BLM PUT DRILLING RIGHTS ON thirty-two thousand acres in eastern San Juan County on the block. Included were thousands of acres near the Sagebrush Site as well as three contiguous parcels along a section of lower Recapture Canyon. The Bears Ears Inter-Tribal Coalition had included that portion of Recapture in their original proposal, but the Obama boundaries left it out of the Bears Ears National Monument, thereby leaving it open to leasing. One Chaco-era village sits atop a steep-sided mesita in the middle of Recapture Canyon, like the Parthenon on the Acropolis in Athens, just a stone's throw from the lease's western boundary.

That September, representatives from oil and gas companies Kirkwood Oil and Gas[50] logged on to something called Energy-Net—a sort of eBay for exploiting public lands—and bid about three dollars per acre for the right to drill the three Recapture parcels. Theirs was the highest bid, which opened the door for them to get permits to drill and proceed to scrape the land of its cryptobiotic soil, sagebrush, and other vegetation; build roads

and pipelines; and drill deep into the earth, hydraulically fracture the well, and suck hydrocarbons out of the ground.

These auctions—EnergyNet aspect aside—aren't new.
They've taken place every three months for a century. When
Congress passed the General Mineral Leasing Act of 1920 it was
a major step up from the status quo. Both the Homestead Act
and the Mining Law of 1872 were literal land and mineral giveaways, with the feds getting virtually nothing in return. By contrast, the 1920 act gave companies the exclusive right to extract
federal oil and gas without transferring ownership. In exchange,
the companies paid rent on the land and royalties on the value
of the minerals extracted.

Most importantly—and the primary reason leasing differs
from transferring land to states or private entities—the Mineral
Leasing Act keeps the land in question under federal control,
meaning that the companies operating there are subject to federal regulations and oversight, and public access to the land is
retained. Since the land remains in public hands, the American
public still has a say over what happens there—theoretically, at
least. But it often does not play out like that on the ground. In
fact, once land is leased, the power of public oversight—which
puts the "public" in public lands—is greatly diminished. And in
that sense, the leasing process is a de facto version of the land
transfers that state supremacists, Sagebrush Rebels, and privatization advocates have long pushed for.

MANY WELL-INTENTIONED FOLKS—AND SOME WITH MORE
cynical aims—argued that a national monument designation
for Bears Ears was unnecessary, and the subsequent shrinkage
meaningless, because even if the land was leased it would still
be protected by multiple levels of federal rules and regulations,
from the Archaeological Resources Protection Act to the many
provisions of the National Environmental Protection Act and,

most relevant to oil and gas development, Section 106 of the National Historic Preservation Act. Section 106 requires developers of any sort of project to conduct a cultural inventory of the affected area. If any "significant" sites are found, the pipeline, road, or well pad must be rerouted accordingly.

The practice is known as "identify and avoid," and it has generally worked to keep the bulldozers from scraping major sites, Paul Reed, a longtime Chaco scholar, told me, but it hasn't done the same for surrounding features. Today, roads bisect villages, pipelines cut through ancient corn fields, and well pads have obliterated many "other super subtle things going on that are part of understanding that landscape," said Reed. "That's how ancient landscapes get fragmented."

"Even though agencies try to mitigate the impact, it isn't enough because you've literally destroyed the context in which those things exist," said Theresa Pasqual, former director of Acoma Pueblo's Historic Preservation Office and a descendant of the Pueblo people who occupied the Four Corners region for thousands of years. "Most of our pueblos are still transmitting their migration history through oral means. So when you have development that begins to impact many of these sites they are literally destroying the pages of the history book of the Pueblo people."

A national monument, on the other hand, can draw a line around not just the individual structures, but also the context that surrounds them, putting it off-limits to mining or drilling or new road building. It's a far more holistic approach, intended to protect every piece of the cultural landscape, not just the major sites. The difference between lands within Chaco park and those outside is a stark one, and it's startling to imagine what would have become of Pueblo Bonito and its surroundings had Roosevelt never acted.

As the understanding of the Pueblo people's connection to the landscape evolved, so did the way the Antiquities Act was implemented. In 2000, when President Bill Clinton designated Canyons of the Ancients National Monument (just over the Colorado line from Hovenweep) the proclamation blanketed a relatively large swath of landscape instead of just targeting individual sites. This ethos was extended to a much larger landscape when President Barack Obama designated the Bears Ears National Monument sixteen years later.

When President Donald J. Trump then eviscerated the national monument, he not only reduced the size of the monument by 85 percent, or about one million acres, but the new boundaries were redrawn in a haphazard way, rendering the notion of landscape-scale protection almost meaningless. It was akin to slicing up Yellowstone National Park into small units, one for Old Faithful, one for Yellowstone Falls, and so forth. Responding to the shrinkage, the Bears Ears Inter-Tribal Coalition put out a statement that said, "The Bears Ears region is not a series of isolated objects, but the object itself, a connected, living landscape, where the place, not a collection of items, must be protected. You cannot reduce the size without harming the whole."

Thousands of places resembling the Sagebrush Site were left without protection in the Bears Ears shrinkage. The site is subtle, the relatively small pile of rubble indicating that it was not a full-blown pueblo or year-round dwelling, but rather a smaller version of the nearby Hovenweep towers. Every potsherd I see is decorated with elaborate corrugation or black-on-white paint, suggesting that these weren't just functional vessels, that this was more than a shelter where someone could take a break from working in the fields. Perhaps it was a ceremonial shrine.

Someone carefully considered this precise spot, perhaps because it falls on the line stretching from the eastern Bears Ears butte to the peak of Ute Mountain, or because of some larger meaning. Maybe they were following their internal grid. Someone took the time to hew the stones, to mix the adobe, to carefully place one upon the other. People visited here, perhaps made offerings, for a century or more. This structure had meaning. It still does. And the law recognizes that by making it a crime to vandalize the site or even to take a single potsherd.

But someone could dig up the Sagebrush Site in broad daylight and cart away backpacks full of artifacts, possibly with impunity, since BLM rangers, stretched so thin out here, probably never venture down this little, old road. On the rare occasion that the feds are able to find pothunters and try to bring the perpetrators to justice, they face huge obstacles in getting a conviction, along with stiff resistance, as was the case during the Blanding raids of 1986 and 2009. Someday this spot is likely to be leased out to an oil or gas company or maybe even to build a solar or wind farm.

The leasing process starts when either an oil and gas company or the Bureau of Land Management nominates parcels. The applicable BLM field office then reviews the leases and the public is given at least forty-five days to comment or file a formal protest on any or all parcels. Protests have occasionally worked to get parcels removed or the lease sale deferred, but by and large the protests have fallen on deaf ears. BLM data show that over the last twenty years, the number of parcels protested has no bearing on how many were removed from bidding, regardless of who is running the Interior Department. It seems to be getting worse. I sorted through hundreds of protests that were lodged against nearly all of the 1.4 million acres offered by the BLM for lease in six western states in 2017—which at the time was the most recent year for which all of the data were available. Virtually every protest was dismissed or denied or "resolved" in a way that did not include removing the parcels from sale. Friends of Cedar Mesa and other groups protested the aforementioned Recapture parcels, as well, laying out in meticulous detail all of the reasons that turning over the land to oil and gas companies was not prudent. Their protests, too, were dismissed.

From 1988 to 2016, an average of 3.43 million acres of federal land was leased out to oil and gas companies each year for as little as two dollars per acre, vesting those companies with certain property rights. Those rights are retained for the term of the lease—ten years or more without development, and indefinitely after production begins—even if the land is then declared a national monument or gains some other protected status. By the end of the 2018 fiscal year, private interests controlled more than twenty-five million acres of federal lands, or about the same amount of acreage held in the National Landscape Conservation System. The Trump administration was so gung-ho to up that number that the BLM offered three times more land for lease than it received bids on in 2017, even at giveaway prices.

Many of the protests against leases are based on the fact that the BLM failed to adequately analyze the impacts of development under the National Environmental Policy Act, or NEPA. The agency's go-to response is that it will do the review during the drilling permitting process. While this may seem logical, it is problematic, because once land is leased, BLM officials have very little power to deny a permit to drill that land, as to do so would be considered a denial of the applicant's property rights. The public usually does not get a chance to comment on the permit. However, public oversight—and therefore ownership—is retained to the degree that permitting must be done within the federal regulatory framework.

The Trump administration's take-no-prisoners quest for "American energy dominance" was an attempt to blow up that framework. Zinke and Bernhardt axed Obama-era rules that regulated hydraulic fracturing, limited methane waste and emissions, brought more oversight to the leasing process, and tightened up royalty collections. They took aim at older rules, too, like stipulations on drilling permits and land-use designations intended to protect wild and cultural resources from development. That gave local land managers little choice but to let industry run rampant over public land, as if they owned it, while also shackling those same managers from acting on behalf of the public and protecting that land.

National monument status doesn't guarantee greater protection on the level of, say, a wilderness designation. Yet even in cases like Canyons of the Ancients, where energy development and grazing continue, monument designation has shifted the BLM's top priority from accommodating multiple uses to protecting the resources. This gives them more leverage to push development away from entire swaths of culturally valuable land and to close trails or roads if necessary.

Approximately 250 oil and gas wells have been drilled within the Obama-drawn boundaries of the monument over the last century and some, only a handful of which have yielded significant quantities of oil or gas, and drillers have in recent decades focused their efforts in other places. Nevertheless, between 2014 and the end of 2016, industry had nominated 63,657 acres within the monument-to-be for oil and gas leases, none of which were ultimately put up for lease. And Trump's shrinkage reopened every part of the monument that had even marginal potential for oil and gas, uranium, or potash development.

For now, the oil and gas onslaught that has ravaged the Greater Chaco landscape for decades is not being replicated in the former Bears Ears, and the uranium companies, after pressing for the shrinkage of the monument, haven't rushed in to file new claims. It's not that the resources aren't there, it's just that no one has figured out how to extract them profitably. That hasn't stopped people from trying, or from doing damage while doing so. Hundreds of wells were drilled over the decades, including dozens on Cedar Mesa and in Valley of the Gods and one that blew in and caught fire near the foot of the Bears Ears buttes. The wounds still haven't healed, fifty, seventy, one hundred years later. Several years ago an oil company scraped a road and well pad and put up a drill rig on Cedar Mesa's Cyclone Flats, just outside the Fish Creek Wilderness Study Area. The well apparently came up dry, but that doesn't negate the damage done finding that out. Nor does it mean the next one will be. The history of extraction in the West, after all, is one of commodity prices and innovation turning yesterday's dry wells into today's bonanzas.

Two decades ago oil companies weren't even attempting to go after oil and gas in the Mancos Shale formation in New Mexico, Colorado, and Wyoming, because it cost more to extract the hydrocarbons than they could get on the market. Then high oil prices spurred the development of new techniques and technology, leading to one of the largest drilling booms in US history, often referred to as the shale revolution. In 1955 President Dwight Eisenhower banned mining on Oak Flat in Arizona's copper country. The mining companies didn't protest very loudly because to them, the land offered nothing. But now a multinational corporation, having wrested the land from federal control, plans to use robots to go after the giant copper deposit buried more than seven thousand feet deep under the sacred Apache ground. It would be financial folly to go after the tar sands that underlie the spectacular White Canyon on the eastern edge of the pre-shrinkage Bears Ears National Monument today. But give it twenty or thirty years, and $200 per barrel oil, and that might change.

Besides, a monument does far more than keep looters or drillers at bay. It gives federal land managers more leverage to limit visitation, to steer people away from the most sensitive sites, to ban or strictly regulate motorized and nonmotorized recreation, to forbid mountain bike races and other competitive events, to keep BASE jumpers from launching themselves into Arch Canyon, and to stop "adventure guides" from leading dozens of paying clients through your favorite, no-longer-so-secret slot canyon.

So monuments do have tangible meaning, they do add another layer of on-the-ground protection against a variety of threats. But they are also symbolic. And Obama's designation of Bears Ears National Monument went a long way in this respect, acknowledging that tribal nations do have some say over their ancestral homelands, and that they, too, should be involved in not only managing, but interpreting those landscapes.

I leave the Sagebrush Site and continue south, jogging slowly now so as not to miss any other artifacts. Out to the west, a single pumpjack sits stoically against the sky like the skeleton of a T. rex, or perhaps a giant grasshopper, poised to leap. The detritus of humankind is scattered across this lonely landscape, but I could keep running for another five, ten, maybe twenty miles and see no one save a lizard or two, a laughing raven, a feral horse. It's a good feeling.

CHAPTER TWENTY-ONE

THE TOURISM QUANDARY

I NDUSTRIAL-SCALE TOURISM IS, LIKE PORNOGRAPHY, DIF-
ficult to define. But, like pornography, you know it when
you see it: visit Arches National Park on any day in May and
you'll understand. Wait in a line of traffic, breathing the exhaust
of the idling vehicles of the other seven thousand visitors that
day, drive along the asphalt ribbon that undulates through the
stone and dirt, fight the hordes for a place to park in the view-
ing turnouts then give up and snap a picture from the comfort
of your moving, air-conditioned car, jostle with crowds along
the wide, obstacle-free trails. Head back to Moab and pay five
bucks for a coffee and a front-row seat to view the amusement
park atmosphere on the main drag—a steady stream of gawking
window-shoppers, spandex, and side-by-side ATVs, consumers
of experiences, petroleum products, and combustion engines—
and ponder what you've witnessed. Gone is the solitude and illusion of discovery that earlier visitors must have felt. Gone the
freedom to wander off the beaten path and meander aimlessly
across the ocean of sandstone.

Draw a boundary around a landscape, give it a national
monument or park designation along with all the rules that
implies and slap a name on it and you've reduced something
indescribable and wondrous to a brand, a slogan, a commodity

to be marketed to the masses. Before you know it, the place will look a lot like it did during the uranium boom, only instead of Geiger counters, the hordes this time around will be hoisting GoPros.

Moab has become the poster child for the effects, both good and bad, of industrial-scale tourism, known cheekily by its detractors as "wreckreation." It's a funny phenomenon, rhetorically, because pretty much all factions involved in the modern public lands fights hold up industrial-scale tourism as a negative consequence of doing whatever it is they oppose. Opponents of national monument designation argue that the designation, itself, opens the door to industrial tourism and recreation and the attendant impacts. National monument designation proponents point out that a monument is the only way to mitigate the impacts of an inevitable wave of tourists. And the tourism and outdoor recreation industries, of the nonmotorized kind, tend to support conservation efforts, so long as they don't equate to loss of access to recreationists, because a ravaged landscape is less enjoyable to play in.

It's easy and tempting to attribute the Moab phenomenon to its proximity to Arches and Canyonlands National Parks and then to assume that the designation of Bears Ears National Monument would result in a repeat in San Juan County. Yet Moab's evolution from uranium town to tourist town shows that it's not so clear-cut.

DURING THE 1930S SCUFFLE OVER THE PROPOSED ESCALANTE National Monument, tourism was often held up by proponents as a way to replace the potential mining, drilling, and grazing that would be displaced by a monument. They weren't actually promoting tourism, but rather merely acknowledged that their efforts would affect the economies of the communities near the monuments, and that there were other ways of making a living off the land aside from blowing it up, poking it with drill bits, or covering it in cow shit.

In some cases they were proven correct: Zion National Park visitation in 1936 averaged a few hundred people per day, enough to inject a big dose of economic vibrancy into the gateway towns of Springdale and Rockville and forever alter the community complexion. Yet only about four hundred people *per year* visited Arches National Park or Natural Bridges National Monument during that time, far too scant a number even to support a single T-shirt shop or burger joint. It's no wonder then that the people of San Juan County were somewhat skeptical of the promise of the tourism industry. Visitation to Arches would gradually climb over the coming years, but did not even reach the one-hundred-thousand-per-year mark until the 1960s, when Moab was still in the throes of a uranium boom.

Even then, Moabites were intent on building up a tourism economy to supplement the extractive one. And they'd do it not by luring more sightseers to the natural wonders of Arches, but by attracting outdoor recreationists of the motorized kind. "I'm of the opinion that as Aspen has become the world-famous skiing Mecca," wrote Dick Wilson in the Moab *Times-Independent* in 1969, "so Moab can become the Jeep Capitol of America." Wilson, a reporter for the paper for years, was one of the biggest boosters in this regard. He helped push the BLM to establish the now world-famous Slickrock Trail on public land next to the town dump. The trail opened in spring of 1969, not for mountain bikes, which didn't yet exist, but for motorcycles (and, for a brief period in the late seventies, skateboards). Wilson wrote that BLM officials were concerned about motorbike riders venturing off the "nearly 100 percent indestructible" sandstone and damaging "the unique zoological and biological gardens" scattered amid the rocks, but the officials didn't do much—such as close the trail, for example—to keep that from happening. Those who disparage the Moab phenomenon often portray it as an invasion from outside, a thing done *to* Moab rather than *with* it. In fact, it originated from within.

At the same time, environmental groups were pushing quieter types of tourism, like backcountry recreation, as a sort of political tool: get enough folks to come visit the "secret" places in southeastern Utah and you'll create a constituency that will fight, and donate money, to protect them.

Thousands of born-again environmentalists strapped on their backpacks and ventured into brand-new wilderness areas and national parks (Congress passed the Wilderness Act in 1964, the same year that Canyonlands National Park was established), their Sierra Club cups dangling, clanking in rhythm with their stride. Tucked into just about every one of those Gerry, Kelty, and Wilderness Experience packs, alongside the freeze-dried beef stroganoff, was a copy of *Desert Solitaire* or, for the less radical backpacker, *A Sand County Almanac*. Many of the backpackers took Abbey's and Leopold's words to heart and stood up for the land that they loved, thereby earning the scorn of the Cal Blacks of the world, who considered "backpacker" to be synonymous with "environmentalist" and equally worthy of disdain.[51]

Even worse, the backpackers couldn't replace miners or roughnecks in terms of local economic input. Someone spending a week in Grand Gulch might buy some gas and a snack on their way through Monticello and a Navajo taco in Mexican Hat on the way out, but they were unlikely to stay in hotels or spend any substantial amount of money in those towns—unless they got stranded in a blizzard out on the Hole-in-the-Rock Trail, that is. Backpacking, back then, was a minimalist, anti-consumerism activity, appealing in part for its low cost as well as its low impact.[52] As the uranium industry faded, the denizens of Moab turned more and more to recreation and tourism in order to survive. In the early eighties Robin and Bill Groff lost their mining-related jobs and decided to open a bike shop called Rim Cyclery. At the time, a bunch of Marin County and Crested Butte longhairs had been converting old cruiser bikes into trail-riding machines for years and the mountain bikes were finally being mass-produced. The Groffs started selling the new bikes, which then started showing up out on the Slickrock Trail, and a new Moab industry was born. Cycling, at the time, like backpacking, rock climbing, kayaking, and backcountry skiing, was the province of the counterculture, practiced mostly by scruffy types with a penchant for duct tape, mung beans, and herbal tea.

Capitalism, however, wouldn't allow it to stay that way. Dirt-bag forms of recreation were gentrified. To go backpacking today one needs—or is conditioned to think they need—hundreds or even thousands of dollars worth of gear, from $300 sleeping bags and tents, to $100 carbon-fiber trekking poles and cushy sleeping pads, to $50 water filters, to $500 satellite doodads whose function I am unable to discern. It makes my twenty-year-old self want to pull a Whitfield and terrorize some yuppie solitude-seekers or throw a few backcountry trail markers off a cliff. It makes my achy-boned fifty-year-old self a bit envious.

Just because a bunch of money is flowing through these gateway communities doesn't mean any of it stays there. Those towns have to come up with ways to capture that cash, whether that is stores that sell gear and fix bikes, or coffee shops and brewpubs and decent restaurants. Next come the hotels and the vacation rentals; as the outdoors-people become more well-heeled, they begin to eschew camping for more comfortable accommodations. Town, county, and state governments levy sales and lodging taxes to catch some of the money flowing through and to fund the increased services that the incoming hordes demand. Leftover revenue is spent on quality-of-life amenities, such as bike paths and parks and libraries and community centers, as well as on marketing campaigns to lure even more tourists.

Utah's Mighty 5 campaign, for example, spotlighted the national parks in the southern part of the state—Zion, Arches, Canyonlands, Bryce Canyon, and Capitol Reef. The parks were receiving hundreds of thousands of visitors per year, but growth in visitation had stalled in the early 2000s and that wasn't acceptable to the business-oriented folks. The multimillion-dollar campaign, launched in 2013, had a global reach: I was baffled to see a colorful rendering of Delicate Arch riding by on one of London's trademark taxicabs during a visit a few years back. And it was effective. Zion had 2.6 million visitors in 2006; a decade later, 4.5 million visited, an average of more than 12,000 per day. Similar surges occurred at Arches and Bryce Canyon, with slightly smaller bumps at Capitol Reef and Canyonlands.

These same trends played out on the non-national-park public lands nearby. With more people came more impacts, from increasing air pollution and climate-warming carbon emissions from the stream of cars carrying the people to and from the trailheads, to trail traffic jams, to disturbance of wildlife, to trampled cryptobiotic soils, to a scourge of human waste and toilet paper scattered across the slickrock at popular dispersed camping areas. The influx of decent eating establishments and watering holes in gateway towns like Moab, along with the addition of amenities funded by the tourism industry and the freedom afforded by telecommuting, drew more people to live there, which drove up rents and real-estate values. Wages simply couldn't keep up, so the working class, the people who keep the local economy's gears grinding away, ended up spending a larger and larger portion of their paychecks on housing, putting them into financial distress. The already abysmal gap between the rich and poor continues to get wider and deeper.

It's no wonder, then, that some folks get nostalgic for the mining days, when tourists were few, housing costs were low, and the wages were good. And it's no surprise that they find it maddening when they're told not to worry about losing those traditional industries because tourism can be lucrative, communities next to public lands are more wealthy than others, and the masses spend billions each year on outdoor recreation. But it's misguided for them to blame their plight on land-use designations or environmentalists, in general.

It's true that burgeoning visitation to Arches National Park has fed the industrial-scale tourism of the region. But consider the alternative. If Arches had not been named a national monument back in 1929 and instead remained relatively unprotected federal land like most of the landscape around Moab, would the spectacular stone formations have gone unnoticed and remained undiscovered except by a handful of intrepid adventurers willing to wander into the non-national-park wilderness? I think not.

Instead, Arches would have become just another part of the area's recreationist amusement park, where adrenalin junkies would be swinging from Delicate Arch, slacklining from fin to fin in Devil's Garden, and mountain biking and ATVing a web of trails through and maybe even across some of the arches. Moab is not an industrial-scale recreational hub because of nearby national parks, but despite those land-use designations. Moab is *Moab* because it is surrounded by spectacular, relatively unrestricted public lands that lie *outside* of the national parks, where for years extractive industries and then motorcyclists, jeepers, rock-crawlers, mountain bikers, climbers, jumpers, runners, and hikers were allowed and even encouraged to dig and drill and drive and play unfettered.

Environmental groups and Edward Abbey, for that matter, deserve some of the blame and credit for the metastasis of the phenomenon in southern Utah. They shone a spotlight on a region that for decades was considered no more than a desolate wasteland valued primarily for its uranium and educated the public about the wonders therein. And in more recent years, as the toll of industrial-scale tourism has become more apparent, environmental groups have failed to speak out as forcefully as they should against industrial tourism and recreation on the public lands. That's in part because when the extractive

industries upon which a community was built suddenly abandon that community for economic reasons, the community
often has no choice but to turn to tourism and recreation as at
least one part of the economic puzzle. It's also because the Outdoor Industry Association has become a potent ally[53] in the fight
to preserve public lands.

A COUPLE OF YEARS AFTER OBAMA HAD DESIGNATED BEARS
Ears National Monument, I took a detour while driving home
from Flagstaff to go to Bluff and see whether the monument had
spawned an industrial tourism boom. But first I wanted to check
out Page, Arizona, home of Glen Canyon Dam and the now-de-
funct Navajo Generating Station, a place where industrial-scale
tourism and industrial-scale power generation long stood side
by side.

As I passed by the parking lot for Horseshoe Bend, the little
thermometer that hung from my rearview mirror to monitor the
interior atmosphere of my old car read 110 Fahrenheit. But even
the high temperatures couldn't deter the masses from seeing
the sights. Hundreds of people had disembarked from their air-
conditioned tour buses and rental cars and risked heat stroke
and dehydration in order to plod through the heat to see the
place where the sandstone gorge of the Colorado River bows
back on itself to create what has become an iconic image.

Page locals say they had the overlook mostly to themselves
for a long time. Then, beginning in the last decade or so, the
masses began converging. More than one million people made
the short, sandy hike to Horseshoe Bend in 2017, according to
National Park Service statistics, and the numbers held steady
until 2020, when COVID-19 put a damper on things. The slickrock pilgrims spoke French, German, Mandarin, Russian. They
got into car crashes, took photos of marriage proposals, suffered
from heat-related ailments, shot images of their feet dangling

over the abyss, one died, and dozens had to be rescued by local emergency officials.

This surge of visitation has nothing to do with land-use designation, however, or even official marketing campaigns. Horseshoe Bend has been a part of the Glen Canyon National Recreation Area for more than half a century, and the iconic image has appeared in magazines and marketing materials for nearly as long. It wasn't until after the first wave of Instagrammers arrived that things started getting out of hand. Images shot from the overlook—usually including someone either scantily clad, in a yoga pose, or both—began to proliferate on social media. That, in turn, brought more hopeful Instagrammers, selfie sticks and yoga pants in tow. The more #horseshoebend images show up on Twitter or Instagram, the more visitation increases.

I passed by Horseshoe Bend without stopping, just as I'd done a dozen or more times before, and rolled into downtown Page, which looks and feels like the strip-mall, big-box fringe of any other town. Page was established as a man-camp for the workers who constructed Glen Canyon Dam in the fifties and early sixties, then became the main residence and supply town for the people who built and worked in the massive coal power plant, which sits on Navajo land just outside of town. In the early days the man-camp atmosphere endured, and the power plant dominated both the economy and the skyline.

But Page is also the main gateway to Lake Powell and Glen Canyon National Recreation Area. More than four million people visit Lake Powell each year, with 80 percent or more of them coming through Page, and the town of eight thousand has managed to build up an industry to capitalize off of it. The National Park Service, together with the major concessionaires running the marinas at Lake Powell, employed nearly three times as many people as the power plant when it shut down at the end of 2019. Nearby Navajo communities have managed to reap some benefits from tourism, as well, by monetizing the most spectacular part of Antelope Canyon, which sits on Navajo land. Page proves that extractive industries and tourism do not displace one another. The houseboaters on Lake Powell and the Antelope canyoneers were not deterred by the layer of yellow-brown, sulfur-dioxide-tainted smog that lingered over them, nor did they rise up and demand that the utilities responsible for the cloud do anything about it.

When the Navajo Generating Station and its associated mine on Black Mesa shut down in 2019 because the owners were no longer making a profit off of it, hundreds of workers lost their high-wage jobs, and the Navajo Nation and Hopi Tribe saw royalty and lease revenues plummet. Some observers predicted that Page would dry up and blow away—local schools have lost students and funding, and municipal government has seen revenue fall. But thanks to its long embrace of tourism, Page will survive in a slightly different form. Once a power plant town with a growing tourism industry, it is now a full-on tourism town with a bit of amenity-migrant retiree action on the side.

I DROVE OUT OF PAGE, PAST THE COAL SILO FOR THE BLACK Mesa mines, alongside the ominous-looking volcanic plug known as Agathla Peak, and toward the red rock spires of Monument Valley. Rain had fallen there, without managing to cool off the air much. In the distance, I thought I saw a human, this time in the middle of the highway. An accident? I let off on the accelerator, prepared to stop and jump out and help. But no, just more people getting that iconic shot, the selfie with the ribbon of asphalt stretching off into the distance.

I continued on past the uranium tailings repository, the flat gray of the liner rock striking against the burnished red earth, across the San Juan River and then on to Bluff, the self-proclaimed gateway to Bears Ears National Monument.

The swarms were already there, however, and the monument

did little to augment them. There is currently no way to accurately count the number of people who visit either the original national monument or the shrunken one. The best we can do is use Natural Bridges National Monument, which sits right in the center of the Obama-drawn boundaries, as a proxy. Visitation there jumped by nearly 20 percent in 2016 and 2017, after the debate over the proposed monument spread to the national media,[54] then it dropped back down considerably in the following two years, never even getting close to 1990s numbers. The monument bump was a dud.

Bluff got a new high-end resort and spa in 2019, a far cry from the pink-walled, David Lynch film-esque rooms rented out by the Dairy Café on the opposite side of town that my wife and I once stayed in, but also not quite Moab. There are enough eating establishments in town that my friends and I wouldn't end up having to eat dinner at the C-store if we didn't want to. The few properties for sale in Bluff as I write this are listed at astronomically high prices. As unlikely as it may seem, gentrification of a sort has come to roost in Bluff. Surely the hype over the monument is a contributing factor, but only a minor one. The real reason Bluff is growing more popular and more expensive is because it is in a beautiful place, shaded by cottonwoods and willows, situated between sandstone cliffs and the San Juan River. Nor is it alone. Housing prices are shooting up across the West and nearly everywhere else, becoming further out of reach of the working folks.

Bluff's not Moab nor will it ever be. But it will continue to grow and get more expensive, and the tourists will continue to come. The people and businesses of Bluff, Blanding, and Monticello can either adjust to them and build businesses to capture some of their money, or they can reject them and watch them drive through town and maybe stop and fill up the tank or grab a snack before moving on. The public land agencies can either let them run roughshod over the slickrock and cryptobiotic crust and cultural sites, or they can try to manage the onslaught that arrived years ago by funneling visitors into already popular sites, keeping less well-known places out of the spotlight, and shutting down sensitive sites to visitation altogether. The agencies can do this with or without a monument, but a monument and a strong management plan and the extra funding that comes with it sure would help.

Back in Page, before heading out of town, I thought about stopping for lunch at some barbecue joint that got decent reviews, but when I saw the clientele lined up outside the door I thought better of it and went to the gas station convenience store, bought some chips and a pop, instead, and headed down to one of the Colorado River overlooks. This one offered a nice, straight-on view of Glen Canyon Dam, the 9.6 million tons of concrete wedged into the canyon. Behind it stood the stagnant, shrinking, silt-filled waters of Lake Powell, the murky green tomb to hundreds of miles of canyon and river bottom and willows and dwellings and villages and oasis-like alcoves. Seventy years earlier somebody thought it would be a good idea to drown the whole lot of it, bury it in silt and murky green water so that they could have a giant evaporation pond out in the desert, motorboats skimming across the glassy depths.

My heart ached as I pondered all that had been lost and that would never be recovered. Then, for whatever reason, something that Winston Hurst, the archaeologist, had once told me popped into my brain. He had said that national parks and monuments "feel like theme parks that have an artificial stasis imposed upon them. They feel dead. It's the death of Place...we're not saving anything. Imposing monument status is like taking a corpse, painting its face with rouge and lipstick, and taking its picture for money."

I chuckled, perhaps somewhat bitterly, at this. For what I

was witnessing was indeed the long-dead carcass of a wondrous Place once known as Glen Canyon. Humans had indeed imposed artificial stasis upon what was once a tumultuous, vibrant, and moody river. But of course the killer was not a national monument but a dam, the idea of progress, the myth that the waters of the Colorado River could be brought under the yoke of technology to make the desert bloom.

Things could have been different. The marvels of Glen Canyon might have been saved with a mere flourish of President Franklin D. Roosevelt's pen. Had he paid more heed to posterity and preservation than to shortsighted Utah politicians and used the Antiquities Act to establish the Escalante National Monument back in the thirties, he would have installed a huge barrier to the construction of Glen Canyon Dam. There's no guarantee that a national monument would have stopped the dam from being built. However, it would have given environmental advocates a more powerful weapon with which to oppose the dam. After all, the Sierra Club and its allies were able to bring a halt to the proposed Echo Park Dam on the Green River on the basis that it would flood Dinosaur National Monument. Surely the same argument could have been used to stop a dam that would flood the heart of an Escalante National Monument.

Maybe Hurst is right. Perhaps something ineffable was lost with the designation of Bears Ears National Monument, if only the ability to lose oneself in its nooks and crannies like Everett Ruess had in the place now under Lake Powell. Maybe the monument will expose previously obscure places to the masses and maybe more people will run and hike and ride their mountain bikes in the region now that they know it is there. But maybe it will also stop a future Glen Canyon Dam. It's a tradeoff, for sure. But it's well worth it, isn't it?

I get what Hurst was getting at, I really do. I'm no fan of national parks. I don't enjoy paying an entrance fee to cross some line that some president drew arbitrarily to signify the boundary of a national monument. I resent being corralled onto paved trails and getting canned interpretations of natural or cultural wonders. Trail markers across remote slickrock plains are—irrationally, I admit—nearly as odious to me as survey flags among the sagebrush, and I fully support the removal of both.

The highway across the arched steel bridge over the Colorado River gorge teemed with cars and a few pedestrians. A blanket of smoke and clouds lingered above, imbuing the sandstone with an eerie red hue, and I reflected upon a visit I had made to Zion National Park at the peak of canyon-country tourist season. I went into it with an open mind. Nevertheless, I spent the entire few hours in a state of misanthropic claustrophobia, horrified by the crush of humanity.

And yet, I also spent a lot of that time gawking, awestruck, at the surroundings, at the way the light lingered on the sheer cliff faces, at the way a spiderweb stretched between the delicate petals of a scarlet-red lobelia flower growing from a crack in the stone. That I was sharing that beauty with some seventeen thousand other people that day did not, in itself, diminish the beauty in any way. Sure, I would have preferred to be there alone or with just a few friends and would have preferred to be there before all the roads and parking lots and shuttle buses were there, but, with apologies for anthropomorphizing, I kind of doubt that the Place really gives a damn whether all those people are looking at it or not. The masses have an impact, of course, but to imply that they somehow suck the soul out of the place, to think that it is any less sublime because of the masses is to underestimate the power and strength of Beauty.

Even the dam in all its ugliness was sublime in its own way: glassy waters reflecting the blanket of smoke and clouds that lingered overhead. Emergency vehicles, sirens blaring, raced down to the water's edge, adding to the general surrealism of the scene. On the still waters of the lake a giant houseboat sat oddly close to the dam. Maybe, I mused with a vague glimmer of hope, it was filled with explosives, Hayduke at the wheel.

CHAPTER TWENTY-TWO

GATEGATEGATE

I N JULY OF 2018, MORE THAN A YEAR AFTER MARK FRANK-
lin had closed a gate on a corral and he and his wife were
charged with prison-worthy crimes, the prosecutors dropped
all charges against Rose Chilcoat due to lack of evidence. They
kept after Franklin, however, for almost another year. Finally,
in April 2019, just before the case was scheduled to go to trial,
Franklin entered a no-contest plea in abeyance to two misdemeanors: criminal mischief and trespassing. The attempted
destruction of livestock charge was dropped. As long as he paid
a $1,000 fine and stayed out of trouble for the following year, the
misdemeanors would also be dismissed.

"Who could have imagined that a day recreating in Utah
could turn into such a nightmare," Franklin wrote in a prepared
statement. "As I have learned, it was never about me. This case
was meant to punish my wife for her years of successful conservation advocacy and to intimidate and silence those who speak
out for protection of their public lands."

While the threat of prison time no longer hung over Franklin or Chilcoat's head, the stress of it all had taken its toll on their
finances, their health, and their marriage. "It's debilitating to be
under that threat every minute of every day," Chilcoat told me,
three years after the incident. And the saga had not yet ended:

following the resolution of Franklin's case, Chilcoat sued San Juan County, Zane Odell—the rancher who owned the corral—and San Juan County attorney Kendall G. Laws on the grounds that she was illegally detained by Odell without probable cause, that the charges against her were politically motivated, and that Laws had fabricated evidence to build his case against her. San Juan County was removed as a defendant, but after discovering that the county commissioners had held a closed meeting to discuss the case prior to charges being filed, Chilcoat asked the judge to reinstate the entity as a defendant. The case was still pending as of January 2021.

Laws has vigorously denied that the charges were politically motivated. Yet, after Franklin's plea, Laws told the *Durango Herald* that the whole case should serve as a lesson for visitors: "The people in San Juan County don't have a problem with people coming to our area. But if you come here and recreate…respect the way of life people have here, and I think you'd be surprised the respect will go the other direction just as quickly."

At first glance, this may seem like a harmless aside: you respect us, and we'll respect you. But given the context in which it was said it sounds a little bit like a threat, whether it was intended to or not. He's not just asking visitors to respect the residents of the county, but the *way of life* there. These are the chosen catchphrases of the Sagebrush Rebels: "way of life," "customs and culture," "tradition," "rural heritage." Sen. Orrin Hatch claimed that the Bears Ears National Monument designation was an attack on a "way of life." The wise-use ordinances that attempted to wrest control over federal land were intended to preserve the "customs and cultures" of the local populace. Urban elitists are invading the communities of southern Utah and wiping out the "rural heritage." And by deigning to ensure that public land managers and grazing allottees follow the laws regulating Americans' public lands, Rose Chilcoat is threatening San Juan County's "way of life."

These terms are fabricated. There is no homogenous, mono-lithic San Juan County way of life or, for that matter, rural or ranching culture, just as there is no single urban culture. San Juan County is a diverse place, with myriad ways of life and cus-toms. There is no rural-urban divide. Ranching is an occupation, not a culture, and the people who practice it come from an array of backgrounds. Some consider themselves cowboys, some not. Some read the *New Yorker*, some read the *Free Range Report*, and neither is more or less of a cowboy for it. Heidi Redd, who for fifty years ran the Dugout Ranch in J. A. Scorup's old Indian Creek stomping grounds, is every bit as much of an authentic local rancher as Zeb Dalton. The Nature Conservancy, which now owns the Dugout Ranch and grazes cattle on three hundred thousand acres of public land in San Juan County, is a ranching operation, as well, and no less so for being an environmental group.

The powerful create these myths, more often than not, to retain their power and to further enrich their corporate bene-factors.

WHILE THE 2016 PRESIDENTIAL ELECTION HAD OBVIOUS RAMI-fications for public lands westwide, another election two years later may have been even more consequential for public lands in southeastern Utah. A federal judge had ordered San Juan County to redraw its voting district lines once again in order to give the Indigenous population proportionate representation in county government. The redistricting dashed any chance of Phil Lyman getting reelected, so he threw his hat into the ring for state representative for all of southeastern Utah, a position then-held by a soon-to-retire Mike Noel. Lyman won that seat handily. Willie Grayeyes, a member of Utah Diné Bikéyah who has long been active in San Juan County politics, ran for Lyman's seat and won. And Kenneth Maryboy beat Rebecca Benally in the Democratic primary and won that seat as well. Bruce Adams held on to the third commissioner seat.

For the first time ever Indigenous people had a majority on the San Juan County Board of Commissioners and, perhaps just as significantly, it was the first time that the majority of the members were pro–public lands and pro–Bears Ears National Monument. The Sagebrush Rebel contingent panicked. Suddenly their entire local-control worldview had been thrown into disarray. The county commission had always been the flag-bearer of the ideology, the voice of the locals—the white, conservative ones, that is. The commissioners were the ones who took San Juan County's concerns about federal overreach to Salt Lake or Washington. They were even the ones who led protests up Arch Canyon or down Recapture Canyon.

As one might have expected, the white anti-monument crowd lashed back. On two separate occasions, once leading up to the election and again afterwards, Grayeyes's political opponents claimed that Grayeyes lived in Arizona, not in San Juan County, and so should be ineligible to run for or hold office. It was a charge that reeked of the racist "birther" campaign that the likes of Donald Trump had waged in regards to Obama's US citizenship. It also reminded me of an exchange I'd had with a Grand County resident regarding local opposition to Bears Ears National Monument. He claimed that all locals were opposed to the monument. When I challenged him, he conceded that plenty of San Juan County residents were in favor of the monument, but that since they were in favor of the monument, they weren't *really* local. Residency, then, is a condition of ideology, not where one actually resides.

The preelection charges were brought to County Clerk John David Nielson by Wendy Black after she lost the Republican primary, and the opportunity to go up against Grayeyes in the general election, to Kelly Laws. Nielson took the matter to County Attorney Kendall G. Laws, Kelly's son and one of the principal players in the Gategate saga, who then asked the sheriff's department, which was still led by Eldredge, to investigate. Deputy Colby Turk was dispatched to Piute Mesa in the Navajo Mountain Chapter, where Grayeyes was born, has a residence, and from where he had long voted. Turk claimed he found evidence that proved Black's claim, which essentially amounted to this: Grayeyes had spent a lot of time in Arizona. Nielson then removed Grayeyes from the ballot. Grayeyes sued the county and prevailed, his name was put back on the ballot, and he won the election.

The saga wasn't over, however. After the election, Kelly Laws repeated Black's claims and asked a state court to overturn the election results. Laws was represented in the case by Peter Stirba, the same attorney who had defended Lyman during his Recapture Canyon trial. Stirba was also the registered agent of the Rural Utah Alliance, a group formed in the wake of Lyman's trial. The Utah legislature granted the organization $250,000 in 2016 to carry out its mission to "defend and protect rural counties' interests by providing legal assistance for county officials when faced with land use and ownership legal issues." In late 2016 RUA sued Obama's Interior Department in hopes of overturning a coal-lease moratorium the administration had implemented. The case became moot when the Trump administration axed the moratorium on its own, and the RUA, after getting more money[55] from the taxpayers (they charged counties $5,000 annually for membership), appeared to go dormant after 2018.

When a judge ruled against Laws, thus confirming Grayeyes's victory again, the white minority took a different tack: county-level secession. They proposed slicing San Juan County into two, maybe even three separate counties in a way that would confine most of the Navajo residents into one county, while leaving another to the white residents. This effort ultimately fizzled as well.

Once all the obstructionism faded, pundits warned that the new commissioners would use their seats to go on an activist rampage to, as one writer[56] put it, expand "tribal sovereignty beyond the Navajo Reservation into Bears Ears country." In fact, during their first two years in office, they both engaged in far less activism than their predecessors Lyman and Benally, and certainly have been more ideologically subdued than prior commissioners such as Lynn Stevens and Cal Black. The new commissioners—who both resigned from Utah Diné Bikéyah prior to taking office—disentangled the county from some of their predecessors' activism by extracting the county from expensive litigation regarding Bears Ears National Monument and other public land issues and severing ties with the Mountain States Legal Foundation. After the election of Joe Biden to the presidency, they passed a resolution in support of the restoration of the Obama-era boundaries of the national monument. As expected, those initiatives passed on two-to-one votes, with Bruce Adams dissenting. More often than not, however, all three commissioners vote in concert. Sometimes Maryboy and Grayeyes vote in opposition to one another. Whereas the previous board spent hundreds of thousands of dollars litigating public lands fights, the current board is more interested in fiscal belt-tightening and pulling the county through the crisis brought by COVID-19.

The general tone of county commissioner meetings has changed, as well. In one December virtual meeting, the three commissioners bantered about predator control, joking about shooting coyotes and mountain lions. And Energy Fuels CEO Mark Chalmers gave a rambling monologue in which he informed the commissioners that his company and the White Mesa Mill were delving into the rare earths business; that Energy Fuels wanted to help clean up abandoned uranium mines and was doing one such cleanup for free near Grants, New Mexico; that he hoped to employ more Navajo people; and that his company had never been opposed to the Bears Ears National Monument designation and that he supported a "reasonable reevaluation" of the decision to shrink it.

Not that it's up to Chalmers or Energy Fuels. President Joe Biden will almost certainly restore the original boundaries of the monument and maybe even then some, regardless of what Chalmers supports. His pick for interior secretary, Rep. Deb Haaland, a member of Laguna Pueblo in New Mexico, has ancestral roots in the Bears Ears landscape. As a congresswoman, Haaland sponsored a bill that would have enlarged the monument to the 1.9 million acres originally proposed by the Inter-Tribal Coalition.

Yet, even as it became clear that President Biden would likely restore Bears Ears National Monument, there was nowhere near the same sort of backlash or outcry from Lyman or others as there was in the lead-up to the original designation. It almost seemed as if the residents of San Juan County, even the avowed Sagebrush Rebels, finally realized that a monument wasn't such a bad thing, after all.

In his book *The Sound of Mountain Water: The Changing American West*, Wallace Stegner wrote: "One cannot be pessimistic about the West. This is the native home of hope. When it fully learns that cooperation, not rugged individualism, is the quality that most characterizes and preserves it, then it will have achieved itself and outlived its origins. Then it has a chance to create a society to match its scenery." It's a tall order in San Juan County, one of the most scenic places on the planet, but progress is being made.

IN THE SPRING OF 2020 I SAT CROSS-LEGGED UPON A HIGH outcrop of sandstone in San Juan County and gazed out at the land and sky unfurled before me. I had stood in that or other high points nearby that afforded vistas of the Four Corners region many times in my life. With only a few notable occurrences, the view always had been blotted out by smog emanating from the smokestacks of a handful of coal-fired power plants scattered around the region. The resulting haze perpetually had reduced the mountains and formations on the horizon to soft-edged, deep blue silhouettes. The spires of Monument Valley were always so obscured that they looked like two-dimensional cardboard cutouts, even from just thirty miles away. I not only had grown accustomed to the omnipresent smog, but I had never known anything else, as the power plants were all constructed just before or after I was born and had been cranking out power and nastiness ever since.

Call it normalized degradation, the phenomenon that occurs when we become accustomed to the deterioration all around us. It's rampant in these parts. Nearly every inch of dirt or forest has been trampled or driven over or grazed down to the nubs or bulldozed or otherwise defiled. Poison pours from dead mines and taints the most pristine-looking streams. Radiation rises from a pile of yellow earth. It seems as if this state of decay and destruction is the status quo, the way things are meant to be. Society suffers from this ailment as well. Values and democracy and the concept of truth and the rule of law atrophy, displaced by fascism and demagoguery and disinformation.

But this time, something was different, so different that I thought my eyes might be playing tricks on me. I could see details in far-off features like never before. The air was so clean and the light so vivid that it felt as if I could almost reach out and touch Ute Mountain over in Colorado, and Dibé Ntsaa, the Navajo sacred peak of the north beyond that. A gray curtain of rain or maybe even snow hung from a cloud over the ominously dark Carrizo Mountains in Arizona, and I could even make out the low silhouette of Black Mesa, long plundered for its coal, rising up from the desert near Kayenta. I wondered if maybe I was imagining things, or even hallucinating. It was as if a fog that had been there for five decades had suddenly lifted.

That's because it had. A few months earlier the Navajo Generating Station had shut down after spewing smog-forming and climate-warming pollution from its three giant smokestacks for nearly fifty years. Prior to that, two other multi-decade-old power plants near the Four Corners were downsized and new pollution controls put on the remaining stacks. I was witnessing the result and, honestly, it was shocking and seemed abnormal, as if something was off-kilter when, in fact, it was finally back in kilter.

And you don't even notice it occurring until you're walking through the desert and stumble upon a little alcove that is too unremarkable for humans to seek out and too steep or small for cattle to wander into, and see the most intricate cryptobiotic structure and what seems to be a perfectly thought-out garden of cacti and ricegrass and yucca and penstemon. Or you wake up out on the Great Sage Plain on a March morning and look westward and can, for the first time in your life, really see the monuments of Monument Valley, the light and shadow and crevices and colors. And you think: this is what was, this is what could have been, this is what still could be, one day, perhaps.

Nighthawks boomed through the lilac sky of dusk and I looked back out across the newly clean air and wished my father was there to see it, and Whitfield, too. I thought back to that trip into Escalante River country that I took so many years ago with the two of them, and I thought about that final day out there and the way I steered them away from spending another three days in the canyons, and I don't regret much in my life but goddamnit do I regret that. If only I had understood why they wanted to remain out there and if only I had known such demons that haunted them both and the solace they found between those sandstone walls under the river of stars where the battle against the cold gives relief from the one against the psyche. Now I know.

I'll never get those three days back. Whitfield finally grew weary of the degradation of the soul and he took his own life one chilly night out on the edge of the Great Sage Plain. A couple of years later cancer came and killed my father. Whitfield died just a few months prior to the establishment of Grand Staircase-Escalante National Monument, which included the canyon we had backpacked down a decade earlier. So I never got his opinion on the matter, nor do I remember talking with my father about it. I regret that, too. I would give just about anything to sit down on the sandstone somewhere and hear what those two had to say about that, and Bears Ears, and all of these scuffles over the public lands. I imagine those two would stay up late, sitting cross-legged in the dirt, shiny Budweiser cans piling up in the moonlight, conversing spiritedly about it all, with Whitfield taking the anarchic approach and my dad a slightly more philosophical, but no less passionate, tone, arguing for the need to bring Indigenous knowledge to bear on the archaeology and ecology of the land.

"Why can't they just leave it the fuck alone?" Whitfield might say.

"It's too damned late, James. It's too damned late. Now it's time for the healing to begin."

ABOUT THE AUTHOR

JONATHAN P. THOMPSON's parents first took him camping in Comb Wash, which slices through the center of San Juan County, Utah, when he was just a toddler. That launched a lifelong fondness for the canyons, mesas, and cultures of the region and a deep interest in the politics, particularly those around public lands, which he began covering as a journalist two decades ago. He worked at and then owned the *Silverton Standard & the Miner* newspaper, then was hired on at *High Country News*, an independent magazine covering the issues of the American West, where he has served as associate editor, editor-in-chief, senior editor, and is now a contributing editor and writer. Thompson holds a BA in Philosophy and Mathematics from St. Johns College in Santa Fe, was a Ted Scripps Fellow at the Center for Environmental Journalism at University of Colorado, Boulder, and has worked as an artisan baker, bike mechanic, janitor, and seed-germination technician. He is the author of *River of Lost Souls: The Science, Politics, and Greed Behind the Gold King Mine Disaster* and *Behind the Slickrock Curtain*, a novel that takes place in southeastern Utah. Along with his wife, Wendy Thompson, and daughters, Lydia and Elena, he splits his time between Colorado and Bulgaria.

GLOSSARY OF TERMS

Public Lands — Land managed by the federal government for the American public. In southeastern Utah, most of this land is under the jurisdiction of the Bureau of Land Management, the US Forest Service, the National Park Service, and (albeit rarely) the US Fish and Wildlife Service.

Bureau of Land Management (BLM) — Federal land management agency that oversees 246 million acres of what was once termed "the public domain," and 700 million acres of subsurface mineral rights, mostly coal and oil and gas. The BLM is under the Department of the Interior.

Sagebrush Rebellion — Strictly speaking, this term refers to a movement that erupted in the rural West in the late 1970s in reaction to heightened regulations on extractive industries on public lands. In this book I liberally use the term to refer to similar uprisings throughout history that have gone by other names—such as "wise-use" in the 1990s and the Bundy-led insurgencies in the 2010s—or no names at all. The threads binding the various Sagebrush Rebellions are: a desire for local control over public lands; anti-environmental regulation; conservative ideologies that often extend beyond the realm of public lands into, say, gun rights and "constitutional sheriffs"; a disdain for federal land management agencies and their staffers; support of extractive industries; and belief in county and state supremacy. The term is imperfect. Many of the so-called Sagebrush Rebels are not at all fond of sagebrush, since its economic uses are limited, nor are they really rebels, as their so-called revolts are more likely to benefit those in power rather than to subvert the power structure. Nevertheless it's the most succinct name for the group of people from the rural western United States who take a utilitarian approach to the land, frown on regulations on public land, advocate for local control, particularly when it comes to public lands, and generally lean to the right, politically.

ENDNOTES

CHAPTER 1: GATEGATE
CHAPTER 2: STATE LINE
CHAPTER 3: POTSHERD PURLOINER
1. Elias, Scott A., Jim I. Mead, and Larry D. Agenbroad. "Late Quaternary Arthropods from the Colorado Plateau, Arizona and Utah." *The Great Basin Naturalist* 52, no. 1 (1992): 59-67. Accessed February 9, 2021. http://www.jstor.org/stable/41712696.

CHAPTER 4: BEARS EARS GENISIS
2. Witkind, Irving J. "Geology of the Abajo Mountains area, San Juan County, Utah." (US Geological Survey Professional paper 453). 1964.

CHAPTER 5: SHASH JÁA SANCTUARY
3. Jett, Stephen C., and John Thompson. "The Destruction of Navajo Orchards in 1864: Captain John Thompson's Report." Arizona and the West 16, no. 4 (1974): 365-78. Accessed February 9, 2021. http://www.jstor.org/stable/40168367.

CHAPTER 6: BLIZZARD AT MOON HOUSE
4. It's important to note that Young and Smith's communalism extended only to members of the LDS Church, not all of society.
5. And it gets far more complicated—and downright racist—if you factor in the Book of Mormon's take on America's Indigenous peoples and the blatant racism of church leaders in later decades, particularly the middle part of the twentieth century. That's material for another book.
6. Lyman, Platte D. "The only surviving day to day account of the Hole-in-the-Rock Journey, December 16, 1879-January 9, 1881." Hole in the Rock Foundation. Accessed February 9, 2021. -Lyman-D.asp

CHAPTER 7: SAGEBRUSH REBELLION ROOTS
7. A stake is a group of wards, or congregations, of the Church of Jesus Christ of Latter-day Saints, and is analogous to a parish. The San Juan

Stake was based in Bluff and included all of San Juan County and extended into New Mexico and southwest Colorado.

8. The Homestead Act allowed for claims of up to 160 acres, which was deemed insufficient for arid lands in the West, so in 1877 the Desert Land Act allowed for claims up to 640 acres, and in 1909 the Enlarged Homestead Act made provisions for 320-acre claims.

9. The Homestead Act did not apply in Utah until 1869 due to conflicts between the LDS Church and the federal government, so leaders set up their own land-claiming system, which continued to be used in San Juan County up until the early 1900s. Additionally, the individualistic urge behind homesteading didn't jive with the Mormons' early collectivism—Brigham Young taught that people could not own land. The church urged its members to instead settle in villages, organized on a grid and divided into large lots. For these reasons, the Hole-in-the-Rock party members and descendants did not patent any federal homestead claims in San Juan County until the early 1900s.

10. The Grazing Homestead Act of 1916 allowed for 640-acre claims for ranching purposes. Given that some 200 acres per cow is necessary for open range grazing in arid lands, that still wasn't big enough.

11. This is almost certainly an undercount. The giant Carlisle outfit reported driving thirty thousand head of San Juan County–fattened cattle to market in one year. And in 1892, when Congress was toying with making the county a reservation, witnesses said there were upwards of fifty thousand head in the county.

12. Roosevelt, Theodore R. "December 3, 1901: First Annual Message." University of Virginia, Miller Center, Presidential Speeches. Accessed February 9, 2021 https://millercenter.org/the-presidency/presidential-speeches/december-3-1901-first-annual-message.

13. As mentioned earlier, the settlers had made no official homestead claims and therefore were, technically, squatters for the time being. The exception was in the northern part of the county at La Sal, where a handful of homestead claims were patented in the late 1880s.

14. When land is "withdrawn" from the public domain, it simply means that it is no longer available for "disposal." That is, it can't be privatized via homesteads or mining claims.

15. In 1892 the Utah Territorial Legislature passed a law making it illegal to graze livestock in a watershed within seven miles of a city. Monticello was initially left out of this because it didn't meet the minimum requirements for being a city. That led to the city making the appeal to the Interior Department for relief.

16. The Mineral Leasing Act of 1920 had created a mechanism by which oil, gas, coal, and other companies could lease federal lands for drilling and pay a royalty in return. See the Aneth Oil chapter for more information.

17. There are a number of instances both pre- and post-Taylor Grazing Act of angry white ranchers killing hundreds of head of livestock owned by Navajo ranchers simply because they were grazing on the north side of the San Juan River. After the act was put in place, the killing continued, only this time with the help of the BLM. For example, in 1952, presumably at the request of the all-white grazing advisory board, 115 horses and 35 burros owned by Navajo residents were rounded up by BLM officials and taken to slaughter because they were purportedly encroaching on BLM grazing land leased by white ranchers. The Navajo residents sued and won a $100,000 judgment.

CHAPTER 8: J. A. SCORUP: PROTO-SAGEBRUSH REBEL

18. Lambert, Neal. "Al Scorup: Cattleman of the Canyons." Utah Historical Quarterly 32, no. 3 (1964): 301-20. Accessed February 9, 2021. http://www.jstor.org/stable/45058434.

19. The account of this meeting is drawn from the *Moab Times-Independent* and other newspapers in the region.

20. Freeman, H.D. "Pleads for Preservation of River Wilderness." *Moab Times-Independent*, June 11, 1936. Accessed February 9, 2021. https://newspapers.lib.utah.edu/ark:/87278/s6v42637/20231969.

21. Interestingly enough, the Utah delegation wanted the lands to stay public because "Utah stockmen cannot afford to own the land and carry the tax burden."

22. Devoto, Bernard."The West Against Itself." Harper's, January 1947. Accessed February 9, 2021. http://mdevotomusic.org/?p=94.

CHAPTER 9: YELLOW MONSTER

23. When I was a student at Durango High School in the 1980s, we were often treated to speakers brought in by the John Birch Society. One guy, whose name I cannot remember, stood on stage in front of a bunch of gullible teenagers and ate a chunk of uranium to demonstrate how nonharmful it was.

24. Quinn, D. Michael. "Ezra Taft Benson and Mormon Political Conflicts." *Dialogue: A Journal of Mormon Thought* 26, no. 2 (1993): 1-87. Accessed January 3, 2021. doi:10.2307/45228582.

25. Even townspeople in Monticello recognized one health danger from the nearby uranium mill. In 1945, residents sent a petition to the

Vanadium Corporation of America asking them to get a handle on sulfuric acid fume emissions from the mill, because "these deadly fumes destroy vegetables, shrubs, and trees … [and] also affect the health of some who are in their direct path." (San Juan Record, April 1945) https://newspapers.lib.utah.edu/ark:/87278/s6k36zn6/9788907

26. Malin, Stephanie A. and Petrzelka, Peggy (2010) 'Left in the Dust: Uranium's Legacy and Victims of Mill Tailings Exposure in Monticello, Utah', Society & Natural Resources, 23: 12, 1187 — 1200, First published on: 05 October 2010 (iFirst) http://dx.doi.org/10.1080/08941920903005795

27. The Victims of Mine Tailings Exposure committee has managed to get hundreds of thousands of dollars in federal funding over the years for screening and studies.

28. That said, I've never heard anything in all of the Sagebrush Rebel rhetoric mentioning the federal government's coverup of the health effects of uranium mining, of its deadly disdain for the people of Sagebrush Rebel country when it performed nuclear testing in Nevada, or of its failure to compensate people who lived near mills and mines for the harm the government had done.

CHAPTER 10: ANETH OIL

29. Sen. Reed Smoot of Utah was also involved. The two were from different sides of the conservation coins, and had different motives. Fall wanted the Leasing Act to facilitate development on public lands, while Smoot wanted to ensure that the public received something for the development of their lands. Smoot worried that oil and gas drilling might otherwise go the direction of hard rock mining, which is lightly regulated and which pays no federal royalties.

30. The public land battle was quite heated at one time, however, particularly on McCracken Mesa, which sits north of the town of Montezuma Creek. Prior to 1958, McCracken Mesa was BLM land and leased to white ranchers under the Taylor Grazing Act. Navajo sheepherders regularly brought their herds onto the mesa, as they'd done for centuries. The ranchers—and the BLM—claimed the Navajos were trespassing. In 1958, BLM land on McCracken Mesa was swapped for Navajo Nation land around Glen Canyon Dam in order to make way for the dam and the town of Page, Arizona. However, the mineral rights under the McCracken land were not transferred and are still owned by the federal government, meaning the royalties go to the feds, not the Navajo Nation.

CHAPTER 11: THE THREE RS AND THE FIRST SAGEBRUSH Rebellion

31. Andrus's conservationist approach wasn't so much new as it was a revival of the ethos of Stewart Udall, the interior secretary under President John F. Kennedy. It's worth noting that both Udall and Andrus were lifelong rural westerners. Udall was also a Mormon.

32. The mother of current Supreme Court Justice Neil Gorsuch.

33. In 2020 the fee remained at $1.35 per AUM, which is the lowest it is allowed by law to go. Meanwhile Utah charges five times that for a cow-calf pair to graze on state land, and private fees are much higher than that.

34. Earl Shumway was prosecuted and convicted under ARPA and sent to prison in 1995. He died of cancer in 2003, not long after being released.

35. The Native American Graves Protection and Repatriation Act of 1990 addresses this flaw by acknowledging that human remains and other cultural items removed from federal or tribal lands belong to the descendants or affiliated tribal nations. However, it does not extend to private land.

CHAPTER 12: F&^%$#LL CANYON
CHAPTER 13: WISE USE?

36. One passage from the article, written by NFLC staffer Jim Faulkner, eerily portended the aftermath of the 2020 presidential election: "What if the elitists in power also used their paid political hacks to manipulate the voting process? We do know that ANY electronic voting machine can be rigged to make sure that only the elitist chosen candidates will win. That's when it's time for an alert and vigilant militia to be on guard."

CHAPTER 14: BACKLASH

37. Gregory's report is fascinating—not just the geology, but the history and other information—and can also be slightly creepy. At one point he notes: "Like the rest of Utah in general, San Juan County has a remarkably virile population of almost pure Nordic stock." Coming as it did in 1938, this is downright chilling.

38. Lopey would later distance himself from Mack and the CSPOA, but continued to adhere to similar ideologies up to his retirement in 2020.

39. Chilcoat remained associate director after Egan's departure and

Shelley Silbert became executive director.
40. Lyman appears to be associating Chilcoat and Great Old Broads
with the 2009 pothunting raid. In fact, neither Chilcoat nor GOB were
in any way involved. Nor did they have anything to do with the prosecution of Brown and Felstead.

CHAPTER 15: RECAPTURE
41. Anderson would crop up again a couple of years later during the
occupation, led by Ammon and Ryan Bundy, of the Malheur National
Wildlife Refuge in Burns, Oregon. During the occupation Anderson
called himself Captain Moroni, presumably after the Angel Moroni, an
important figure in Mormon theology. Anderson told Oregon Public
Broadcasting's Amanda Peacher, "I didn't come here to shoot, I came
here to die." He would end up being one of the few occupiers to do jail
time.

CHAPTER 16: THE RIVER
42. Evapotranspiration: The evaporation of water after the snow melts.
Sublimation: When snow goes from a solid state straight to a gaseous/
vapor state without melting first.
43. Neff, J., Ballantyne, A., Farmer, G. *et al.* Increasing eolian dust
deposition in the western United States linked to human activity. *Nature Geosci* 1, 189–195 (2008). https://doi.org/10.1038/ngeo133.
44 Belnap, J. "Cryptobiotic Soils: Holding the Place in Place." US Geological Survey. https://geochange.er.usgs.gov/sw/impacts/biology/
crypto/.
45. Neff, J., Reynolds, R., Belnap, J., Lamothe, P. "Multi-Decadal Impacts of Grazing on Soil Physical an Biogeochemical Properties in
Southeast Utah. *Ecological Applications*, 15(1), 2005, pp. 87-95.
46. Hastings, J., Turner R., *The Changing Mile: An Ecological Study of
Vegetation Change with Time in the Lower Mile of an Arid and Semiarid
Region.* University of Arizona Press, 1965.

CHAPTER 17: BEARS EARS: BEGINNINGS
47. When the monument was designated, Andalex, a Swiss company,
was looking to mine a 23,800-acre swath of the Kaiparowits Plateau,
which contains one of the biggest coal deposits in the United States.
Clinton's monument designation didn't kill those plans, though it did
make access and transportation to the deposits more difficult, so the
feds used $19 million from the Land and Water Conservation Funds to
buy out Andalex's leases. When the Trump administration shrunk the

monument in 2017, it opened the land back up to potential development. Given the economics of coal, however, it is highly unlikely that it will ever be leased or mined.

48. A 2017 BLM staff report noted, of Grand Staircase-Escalante: "Although grazing use levels have varied considerably from year to year due to factors like drought, no reductions in permitted livestock grazing use have been made as a result of the Monument designation." In 1996, there were 77,400 active Animal Unit Months, or AUMs, on the monument, and in 2017 there were 76,957, a negligible decrease.

CHAPTER 18: A NEW MONUMENT, A NEW BATTLE

CHAPTER 19: THE DISASTER KNOWN AS TRUMP

49. The pipeline was built by Energy Transfer Partners. Energy Transfer's CEO Kelcy Warren contributed $250,000 to Trump's inauguration fund, and he and Energy Transfer gave $10 million to Trump's 2020 reelection campaign.

CHAPTER 20: SAGEBRUSH SITE

50. Kirkwood, the high-bidder on the Recapture leases, received royalty reductions on no fewer than fifty-four BLM leases, many of them in Utah. Casper, Wyoming-based Kirkwood is a member of the Petroleum Association of Wyoming, a client of Mountain States Legal Foundation. Robert Kirkwood, the company's co-owner, is also on the board of Energy Fuels, Inc., the operator of the White Mesa Uranium Mill, just about five miles away from one of the newly leased parcels. Energy Fuels successfully pushed the Obama administration to exclude uranium mining areas from the Bears Ears National Monument and then lobbied the Trump administration to drastically shrink the monument even further—as did MSLF. It just goes to show how incestuous this whole public lands thing can get when the administration stocks the agencies with extractive industry folks.

CHAPTER 21: THE TOURISM QUANDARY

51. Black was a proponent, however, of certain kinds of industrial-scale tourism. He did, after all, own Halls Crossing Marina on Lake Powell, which relied wholly on tourism to stay afloat, so to speak.

52. Relatively low impact, that is. Chicago Basin—an alpine valley in the Weminuche Wilderness of southwest Colorado—was smoggier than its namesake city on many a summer morn in the seventies, thanks to a multitude of backpacker campfires and a temperature inversion. More recently, areas on Cedar Mesa were so inundated that

the BLM had to set up a permit system and limit daily visits.

53. The recreationist-green alliances can be shaky, however. Some mountain bike user groups have pushed to allow the bikes into wilderness areas. And while the International Mountain Biking Association does not favor opening existing wilderness to bikes, they do push back on new wilderness designations that could affect popular mountain biking routes. In the 1990s, when the National Park Service asked climbers to voluntarily abstain from climbing at Devil's Tower National Monument because of the formation's significance to area Indigenous peoples, some climbers pushed back and sued. The climbers were represented by Mountain States Legal Foundation and William Perry Pendley.

54. The surge could be attributed to national monument-related media exposure, but it just as easily could be attributed to spillover from the Mighty 5 campaign.

CHAPTER 22: GATEGATEGATE

55. A number of similar groups operated on a similar business model: get the Utah legislature to give you money to do anti–public lands activism. The Foundation for Integrated Resource Management, or FIRM, received at least $400,000 from the Utah taxpayers in order to do battle with Obama's Interior Department. When Trump was elected they faded into the woodwork, but never returned the money.

56. Keshlear, B. "Meet the New Boss, Same as the Old Boss." *Canyon Country Zephyr*, February/March 2019.

INDEX

Torrey House Press

Voices for the Land

The economy is a wholly owned subsidiary of the environment, not the other way around.
> —Senator Gaylord Nelson, founder of Earth Day

Torrey House Press publishes books at the intersection of the literary arts and environmental advocacy. THP authors explore the diversity of human experiences with the environment and engage community in conversations about landscape, literature, and the future of our ever-changing planet, inspiring action toward a more just world. We believe that lively, contemporary literature is at the cutting edge of social change. We seek to inform, expand, and reshape the dialogue on environmental justice and stewardship for the human and more-than-human world by elevating literary excellence from diverse voices.

Visit www.torreyhouse.org for reading group discussion guides, author interviews, and more.

As a 501(c)(3) nonprofit publisher, our work is made possible by generous donations from readers like you.

Torrey House Press is supported by Back of Beyond Books, the King's English Bookshop, Maria's Bookshop, the Jeffrey S. and Helen H. Cardon Foundation, The Sam and Diane Stewart Family Foundation, the Barker Foundation, Diana Allison, Klaus Bielefeldt, Patrick de Freitas, Laurie Hilyer, Shelby Tisdale, Kirtly Parker Jones, Robert Aagard and Camille Bailey Aagard, Kif Augustine Adams and Stirling Adams, Rose Chilcoat and Mark Franklin, Jerome Cooney and Laura Storjohann, Linc Cornell and Lois Cornell, Susan Cushman and Charlie Quimby, Betsy Folland and David Folland, the Utah Division of Arts & Museums, Utah Humanities, the National Endowment for the Humanities, the National Endowment for the Arts, and Salt Lake County Zoo, Arts & Parks. Our thanks to individual donors, subscribers, and the Torrey House Press board of directors for their valued support.

Join the Torrey House Press family and give today at www.torreyhouse.org/give.